Play as Therapy

of related interest

DRAMATHERAPY AND FAMILY THERAPY IN EDUCATION
Essential Pieces of the Multi-Agency Jigsaw
Penny McFarlane and Jenny Harvey
ISBN 978 1 84905 216 0
eISBN 978 0 85700 451 2

CREATIVE COPING SKILLS FOR CHILDREN
Emotional Support through Arts and Crafts Activities
Bonnie Thomas
ISBN 978 1 84310 921 1
eISBN 978 1 84642 954 5

GROUP FILIAL THERAPY
The Complete Guide to Teaching Parents
to Play Therapeutically with their Children
Louise Guerney and Virginia Ryan
ISBN 978 1 84310 911 2
eISBN 978 0 85700 516 8

A MANUAL OF DYNAMIC PLAY THERAPY
Helping Things Fall Apart, the Paradox of Play
Dennis McCarthy
ISBN 978 1 84905 879 7
eISBN 978 0 85700 644 8

NARRATIVE APPROACHES IN PLAY WITH CHILDREN
Ann Cattanach
ISBN 978 1 84310 588 6
eISBN 978 1 84642 734 3

PLAY THERAPY WITH ABUSED CHILDREN
2nd Edition
Ann Cattanach
ISBN 978 1 84310 587 9
eISBN 978 1 84642 782 4

CHILDREN'S STORIES IN PLAY THERAPY
Ann Cattanach
ISBN 978 1 85302 362 0
eISBN 978 1 84642 782 4

SOCIAL SKILLS GAMES FOR CHILDREN
Deborah M. Plummer
ISBN 978 1 84310 617 3
eISBN 978 1 84642 836 4

Play as Therapy

Assessment and Therapeutic Interventions

*Edited by Karen Stagnitti
and Rodney Cooper*

Forewords by Professor Gail Whiteford
and Steve Harvey PhD

Jessica Kingsley *Publishers*
London and Philadelphia

First published in 2009
by Jessica Kingsley Publishers
73 Collier Street
London N1 9BE, UK
and
400 Market Street, Suite 400
Philadelphia, PA 19106, USA

www.jkp.com

Library of Congress Cataloging in Publication Data
Play as therapy : assessment and therapeutic interventions / edited by Karen
Stagnitti and Rodney Cooper ; forewords by Steve Harvey and Gail Whiteford
    p. ; cm.
   Includes bibliographical references and index.
   ISBN 978-1-84310-637-1 (alk. paper)
   1. Play therapy. I. Stagnitti, Karen. II. Cooper, Rodney, 1965-
   [DNLM: 1. Play Therapy--methods. 2. Child. WS 350.2 P72153 2009]
   RJ505.P6P522 2009
   618.92'891653--dc22

                                                2008039082

British Library Cataloguing in Publication Data
A CIP catalogue record for this book is available from the British Library

ISBN 978 1 84310 637 1
eISBN 978 1 84642 928 6

Dedication

This book is dedicated to our children: Jessica, Monique, Sam, Jacob, Josiah, Miriam and Esther. And to all children everywhere.

DISCLAIMER

Unless otherwise acknowledged, all case studies are fictitious.

Contents

LIST OF FIGURES

LIST OF TABLES

Foreword

Interestingly, the night I sat down to start reading *Play as Therapy* there was a programme on television which offered some serious prognostications: that, among other things, children these days were less school ready, more obese and more likely to suffer from mental illness than previously. Sobering stuff, as were the scenes of children lining up for toast and cornflakes being offered at primary school breakfast clubs to cater for seemingly increasing numbers of children who don't routinely get breakfast at home. Wondering what had happened in society to contribute to such concerning trends (the programme suggesting that whilst focusing on economic development we took our eye off the ball of social development) I looked at the manuscript in my lap and wondered if this book might hold some answers – or at least useful responses. The good news is: it does.

As well as representing a timely response to the concerning child related phenomena suggested above, the book has three important qualities. First, it is informative and useful. Second, it is engaging and third, it is deeply reassuring. Let me expand on these qualities.

I am not a play therapist, but my background as an occupational therapist gives me a broad conceptual base through which to understand play as the occupation of children and its central role in development across the lifespan. Despite not being involved as a specialist in this arena, I was able to gain an immediate sense of the value and utility of the many chapters of the book written by acknowledged leaders in the field. The beginning chapters that lay the conceptual foundations are clear and are of fundamental importance. Jennifer Sturgess reminds us, for example, that it is the ontological standpoint of the child that is most important in understanding play in context, whilst the inherently *transactional* nature of play is stressed by Rodney Cooper.

Similarly, Karen Stagnitti's chapter on children and pretend play is not just conceptually significant but is also, in a word, *riveting*. In the chapter she makes a compelling case about the centrality of pretend play to the development of not only literacy and numeracy skills but cognition and social learning. I hope that, as I did, you read her chapter and are able to reflect back on your own childhood. For me, it was with a sense of nostalgia but also with a new appreciation of the value of many hours spent in backyards and creek beds playing long complex games with dogs, doll, siblings, other children and basic props such as cardboard boxes, sticks, stones and rusted saucepans. In my opinion, this chapter should be required reading for educators, parents and health professionals alike.

In terms of conceptual foundations, the contribution of Athena Drewe's chapter on the need to understand play as a socioculturally situated phenomenon reminds us all that cultural values are explored, expressed and to some extent enshrined through play forms across age groups. Indeed, as she suggests, it is through play that societies express themselves: i.e. through music, poetry and art – hence the need for us to be mindful of the ways in which *playfulness* per se can be infused into the increasingly time pressured everyday worlds of adults. Indeed, balance and restoration spring to mind as the natural outcomes of playfulness as a daily meditation. As well as conceptual groundings though, the chapters on assessment provide a sound basis for the work of students and practitioners alike. They are epistemologically sound and cover everything from the fundamental elements of what constitutes the reliability and validity of assessments through to the need to consider play assessment in different settings. Tiina Lautamo's chapter on play in social settings and Judi Parson's chapter on play in hospitals are two clear examples.

As well as being informative and useful, this book is easy to read. Actually, it's more than easy to read, it's an *engaging* read. This is good news because there is nothing worse than being time pressured and trawling through a tome of leaden writing! What makes it particularly engaging are case stories and vignettes: they are rich, evocative, occasionally uplifting and sometimes disturbing. I couldn't help but find myself wondering about the unfolding narrative of some of the children described – would, for example, Kelly (described in Stagnitti's chapter on the *Learn to Play* programme) have an expanded psychoemotional repertoire as a result of having learnt to problem solve through play rather than relying on Batman® or Superman® to save every situation? Has Stagnitti provided her with not just the ability to be a 'player' with other children but also to ultimately become a more successful co-actor in life? Similarly, I found the case of Melanie described by Virginia

Ryan as deeply compelling but one reflecting bald realities. At the end of the chapter Ryan suggests, quite starkly: 'The case presented, while showing some signs of progress and hopeful outcomes, also demonstrates that 'life is a perilous journey" where other factors may influence outcomes more power-fully than any therapeutic intervention is able to achieve (p.202).'

So, the case stories are engaging yes, but as evidenced by this quote, they are also grounded in reality, a quality which only enhances their salience.

Finally, as I suggested at the outset, the book is *reassuring*. What do I mean by this? Well basically, the overall tenor of the book is grounded – the work of the contributors and editors is based on solid track records of expe-rience and research. It is not fad-ish. As importantly, the book is underscored by a post modern sensibility: it acknowledges identities as unique, distinct and context bound. The authors are respectful of the multiple cultural, his-toric and linguistic traditions that interact dynamically to shape and influ-ence play and play behaviour in children and families. Ultimately however, it is the overall orientation of the book towards complexity that really im-presses me. This is because we have arguably been in the grips of a neo liberal discursive era. This is an era in which there has been a concerning trend to-wards instrumentality and technical rationality expressed through the impo-sition of often simplistic regimes of measurement and accountability. Such a discursive pitfall has been steadfastly avoided in this work.

In closing, as the saying goes 'for every complex social problem there's a solution that's neat, simple and WRONG'. Play is complex and situated. Un-derstanding, assessing and intervening in and with play requires sophisti-cated knowledge and skill sets. This book delivers.

Professor Gail Whiteford, Pro-Vice Chancellor (Social inclusion)
Macquarie University Australia, November 2008.

Foreword

There is a contrast between players and those who study and write about it. This contrast is even more pronounced between the emotional and thinking states between these two groups. All too often the results of this difference lead to books that focus on a specific part of play or the players to better define and focus our thoughts and purpose of this quite special state. There are books about play in development, for uses in psychotherapy or assessments of various kinds, and in studies related to family or cultural life. By focusing on single and smaller parts of play much of the larger picture becomes lost from view. Fortunately players keep right on playing no matter how it is reduced for study, offering we observers more to see. Also fortunately we now have a book that presents several aspects and views of play in one single volume to challenge the reductionist tendencies necessary for a single study.

Karen Stagnitti and Rodney Cooper have put together a book that leads the reader though a highly understandable presentation of many aspects and influences of play and players. The editors have organized this view starting with a very important observation that play is a natural activity for children and that when play doesn't happen something has gone wrong for that child. In the chapters that follow, the authors present how ability to play and experience playfulness is impacted by experiences such as development, abuse, families, peers and the larger culture a child lives in. Each chapter is well documented and offers a full range of references for further review about the specific area presented.

There is a very good overview about how children's play can be observed and contribute to assessment and treatment planning for children. The book ends with a presentation of various ways the play experience can be crafted to assist children with change and ways to participate in the world more fully. Wisely, in keeping with the theme of complexity of play, this volume presents interventions that have quite different approaches, theoretical backgrounds and applications. This new work will help readers expand their thinking about the multiple and complex factors related to children's play.

Steve Harvey , PhD., Consultant Psychologist
November 2008

Preface

This book focuses on the therapeutic use of play. This means that play is used specifically and as a focused medium for children so that their health and well-being can be enhanced. Play is first and foremost a powerful medium for children. To the untrained eye, play appears simplistic and certainly doesn't have a lot of 'street cred'. Ironically, play is one of the most complex of human behaviours because it encompasses all abilities of the child: motor, sensory, cognitive, social, and emotional. Defining the essence of what is play has taken up volumes. When a child can't or doesn't play something has gone terribly wrong for that child.

Play not only reflects a child's development and inner world, but contributes to his or her development as an active, dynamic and open-ended process that continually challenges and facilitates growth, development and individual competence. How children play, where they play, and what they play largely reflects their culture and environment. This book is set against a contemporary background of social change, which is being spurred on by consumerism, rapid technological advances and globalisation. For many parents, their children's academic achievements or future job prospects are the priorities, so much so that play is not valued and children's time is increasingly structured, allowing little time to spontaneously initiate play. On the other hand, many parents struggle to survive in this competitive climate and being responsive to their children and encouraging play is not considered or understood. The lack of time to play is often compounded by a lack of space to play, with social play activity moving indoors and reorientating around 'virtual worlds', computer games and other technology 'toys'. Fear for children's safety in public spaces has also influenced parenting with parents becoming increasingly reluctant to allow children the freedom to explore their neighbourhoods. We believe that play should be taken seriously, as the self-initiation of play is central to the development, health and well-being of children.

Play continues to be utilised by child professionals in therapeutic, health and education settings. Therapists working with children with special needs or children with emotional and health crises often rely on play for assessment and/or treatment. While play may be viewed as a treatment tool of choice, especially for children under school age, the theoretical and practice underpinnings of play-based therapeutic approaches often remain unclear to individual practitioners. With paediatric interventions increasingly being questioned and individual practitioners being asked to provide evidence-based practice, the need for a more coherent understanding and discussion on children's play and utilisation of play for therapeutic purposes is needed, especially as societal expectations and lifestyles change.

This book sits between the early childhood literature on play and the specialist literature on play therapies. The early childhood literature largely discusses developmental play along with gender differences and social issues surrounding play while the more specialised play therapy literature concentrates on how play can be used therapeutically with different clinical populations. This book draws on both sources as it examines and discusses play as therapy, and presents several approaches to the use of play for assessment and therapy, while acknowledging environmental and social issues surrounding play.

Amongst the contributors to this book are well-known international authors. What this book also brings is a perspective on play from the Australasian region of the world. Play, however, presents recognisable issues that cross all geographical borders and cultural perspectives. This book is for paediatric professionals working in health, therapeutic or early intervention settings anywhere in the world. It is to be hoped that it will provide them with a knowledge base so that they can observe a child playing or not playing and know what to observe, why it is important, what play skills are missing and what to do about it. This book will also give paediatric professionals guidance on how to work with the challenging situations presented by children with impairment, emotional or health needs, which prevent them from engaging in normal activities such as play.

The book is divided into four sections. In section one, four different theoretical understandings of play are presented. These perspectives draw from and build on the views already in the literature. In section two, the fundamentals of play assessment are broadly overviewed and three new play assessments are introduced. These assessments measure preschool children's pretend play, self-reported play in middle childhood and play in social settings. This is followed by a section on play contexts. There are many aspects to consider when looking at the impact that the clinical environment, family and different cultures have on children's play. Section four introduces some therapeutic play interventions: developing children's pretend play skills; non-directive play therapy; enabling the child with a physical disability to play; and considering the range of different environments where using play therapeutically is a challenge. It is our hope that this book will provide a greater understanding of play as therapy to those health professionals who work with children.

Karen Stagnitti and Rodney Cooper

SECTION ONE

Theoretical Understandings of Play

CHAPTER 1

Play as Child-Chosen Activity

Jennifer Sturgess

CHAPTER OBJECTIVES

This chapter will explore the concept of play as an essentially child-chosen activity. A conceptualisation based on a metaphor of a sandcastle will be presented. This will be used to describe play as built on both the relevant skills a child has acquired and on the child's intention to play.

What is play?

A child knows when he or she is playing although it is not always obvious to an adult observer. For example, a child might have been sent by a parent to clean his teeth before going to bed. The parent notices that he is lying on the floor exactly where other household members wish to walk. From the parent's perspective he is being disobedient and thoughtless. In contrast, from the child's perspective he is enlivening a boring task of teeth cleaning by going to the bathroom while traversing a field of hidden 'mini-zappers', one of which has just disabled him for the count of 30! In this instance the child and parent view the same action from differing perspectives – neither incorrect. While play is essentially personal and intrinsic (Bundy 1997), it occurs in a human and nonhuman relational and environmental context. Thus two components can be seen as essential to an understanding of play: the perspective of the child doing the playing, and the context in which the play occurs.

Children and their parents have differing views of play because each person brings a different part of themselves to the play situation. However, only the child is totally involved in the play. Parents are limited to *thinking about* the play they are watching, and will process these thoughts via their own personal experience of play and knowledge about their child. This is naturally different to how the child will experience the play. Another more practical cause of different views relates to context. Children demonstrate different play skills, as well as a different quality of play skills, according to the contexts in which they are playing, whether at school, inside, outside, with a friend or alone (Dargan and Zeitlin 1998; Malone and Stoneman 1990; Power 2000). Parents are not present the whole time, and so for parents to evaluate their children's play skills means they have to guess and extrapolate from observing their children in a restricted range of contexts. Children, on the other hand, are present in every context in which they play.

HISTORICAL AND CULTURAL INFLUENCES ON PLAY

The type and extent of children's play can be seen to be moulded by innumerable factors, some of the most influential being amount of time for playing, contemporary socioeconomic factors, suitable space and play objects. Two hundred years ago, children were usually involved in work in the home or with their parent's occupation or, from as young as seven years, in their own job (Barnes 1998). There were few opportunities for these children to play within the existing restrictions of health, physical security, materials for play and time. However, there are many indications that a child's capacity for playfulness has always been able to transform non-play situations, such as work or learning, into play (Bazyk *et al.* 2003; Sanders and Graham 1995). Evidence indicates play and toys existed thousands of years ago and that the presence of, and responses to, toys varies culturally and temporally (Davis and Polatajko 2006).

The outward expression of play, the activity an observer sees, is also sensitive to cultural and temporal influences (Bazyk *et al.* 2003). Contemporary play is probably a more separate and condoned activity in the everyday life of children than it was in the early years of the twentieth century. Contemporary play is different in terms of objects and spaces used with many more commercially available toys, more play in private spaces, the proliferation of 'virtual play-scapes' and associated reduction in tactual play, and the influence of media and marketing on the play choices of children (Provenzo 1998). Children's play has also changed in overt features due to rapid changes in modern lifestyles. For instance, it has been reported that parents supervise children in play so that they avoid injury more than used to be the case (Cole-Hamilton, Harrop and Street 2002; Sturgess 2003). Increased parental supervision may diminish the child's ownership of play. In examining play in modern childhood, particular reference to the following influences is pertinent:

- parental confidence in the value of play and family priorities
- amount and type of play space and perceived risk elements
- computers, electronic games and the commercialisation of toys
- time available for play.

Play opportunities for children in Western society are currently affected by paradoxical influences. On the one hand, knowledge of developmental imperatives linked to adequate play opportunities have never been greater. There are more resources dedicated for play, including craft and construction materials, creative toys or props, board games, and skill-based play-tools than has ever been the case. On the other hand, there are clear trends which can be seen as contributing to decreased opportunities for children to play in a manner conducive to developing play skills (Cole-Hamilton and Gill 2002; Dargan and Zeitlin 1998; Rivkin 1998; Sturgess 2003). Decreasing play time and space as well as parental concerns about safety in what were once conventional play spaces (i.e. streets and parks) has largely forced play indoors. Increasing safety consciousness in playgrounds leading to a lack of challenge, decreasing opportunities for play in multi-age groups, and decreasing opportunity to play free from adult intrusion or supervision have also been noted by social commentators. While the influence of these contemporary factors on play is recognised, the objective of this chapter is to present a conceptualisation of play which will remain useable despite cultural changes.

A DEFINITION OF PLAY

Play can be conceptualised as activities that are chosen by the child, that are identified by the child as play and the child engages in them playfully. The view of play proposed will also focus on the playful or 'as-if' attitude and the child's intrinsic motivation to engage in the activity (Fein 1981). Therefore play is an episode of activity that is child chosen and viewed as play by the child. Each play episode has some or all of the following descriptive characteristics: spontaneous, non-literal, pleasurable, flexible, means-oriented, intrinsically motivated, meaningful, active and rule-governed (Barnett 1991; Rigby and Rodger 2006; Russ 2004; Stagnitti and Unsworth 2000). Take the example of a sudden game of 'tiggy' or 'tag' started by a group of children running across a school playground. This could be spontaneous but would not be symbolic. Positive affect such as giggling and cheering would probably be a feature. Flexibility to allow a child on crutches to 'tag' with crutch rather than hand could be agreed. However, it is a stereotyped rather than unstereotyped activity. Technically the aim is not to get 'tagged', however, it is played for fun, not to win, hence it can be interpreted as means oriented and is both active and rule-governed. Children play this game because they want to. Adults observe these definitional play features to which the children are oblivious.

Play occurs across the life-span and encompasses a range of types of play (e.g. symbolic, imaginative, pretend, exploratory, creative, constructional, or functional). Play occurs in different social situations (e.g. alone, in a group, in a dyad, in games with rules, in a multi-age group); different physical settings (e.g. at home, in a playground, at school, at a friend's place, inside, outside) and in a range of emotional or psychological circumstances (e.g. during a time of change or transition).

Play occurs at times that are predetermined, occasional and/or opportunistic. For example, a conversation travelling home from a child's football game may begin simply as recounting events and end up as a playful episode. The child might mimic another child's behaviour and then exaggerate it greatly, enjoying their ideas and to entertain companions, who might also be subtly invited to join in. This would be language-based playfulness incorporating humour, opportunistically occurring in a family and social and time-limited context (Bergen 1998).

Play occurs in different contexts and as a result of many different stimuli. Some examples include: being bored and doodling on paper and then turning this into playfully making a picture of an invention, or capitalising on finding a discarded plastic bottle while walking with friends and initiating a game of kicking the bottle with transitory rules developed from pre-existing knowledge of the rules of other games. All the definitional features previously listed can be linked to these two examples of play. The common link is the child's interpretation of the situation, and intention to play.

In these instances it is evident that the child needs to have both developmentally derived skills and some skills at making an event playful. It is possible to call the combination of these skills 'play skills', and see them as having primarily evolved through modelling and practice (Rodger and Ziviani 1999). Play skills provide the child with the capability of playing when the opportunity arises, and of viewing the same activity as playful or not according to whether they have *chosen* to frame the activity in terms of these play skills (King 1986). The child does not consciously determine 'I am going to play' but if asked would probably describe the episode by including some clue as to its 'as if' quality. Children become more sophisticated at being able to identify their level of choice in play. King (1986) found that five-year-olds say something is *work* when an adult requires the activity, whereas eight-year-olds judge the same activity, mandated by an adult, to be play as long as they find it intrinsically enjoyable or can add a playful element. Children asked to tidy up for example, might make the task into a playful competition to see who finishes first, or mimic the sound of a vacuum cleaner while gathering small pieces, thus entertaining themselves. Similarly, it is the child's interpretation of what is happening in play that is important rather than an adult's perspective (Dockett 1998). 'Play is what I do when everyone else has stopped telling me what to do' (Cole-Hamilton *et al.* 2002, p. 7).

A SANDCASTLE MODEL OF CHILD-INITIATED PLAY

The child-determined and skill-based activity of play proposed in this chapter could be conceptualised as building on a range of developmentally acquired skills and as being situated within contextual features such as available social and material resources, time, and a play-generating stimulus. This conceptual basis is consistent with the discussions of playfulness provided by Lieberman (1966) and by Barnett (1991). The author previously developed the 'sandcastle model' (Sturgess 2003) on the premise that typically developing children acquire a set of skills for use in play if they are reasonably healthy and have a supportive environment. When they have healthy play skills children recognise a situation *right* for a play episode, and can take this type of opportunity in a variety of contexts. This is congruent with a definition of play, which makes the child the decider of whether an activity is play or not.

Why a sandcastle?

Figure 1.1 illustrates an episode of joyful child-chosen play from the child's perspective. The metaphor of a sandcastle constructed on a beach was chosen to represent play because sandcastles, at least in the Western cultural tradition, are considered complex but temporary – essential characteristics of play. A sandcastle constructed on a beach (sound base) to an emerging rather than planned design will disappear (or alter) with the tide (over time). Additionally, the sandcastle metaphor symbolises the growing, adaptable, constructive, creative, imaginative, fragile and repairable nature of play skills – all terms used in seminal and recent literature (Elkind 2001; Erikson 1975; Heidemann and Hewitt 1992; Johnson 1998; Piaget 1962; Seja and Russ 1999).

Figure 1.1 A sandcastle model of child-initiated play

Conceptualisation of child-chosen play. Jennifer Sturgess with illustration by Rodney Cooper. This figure is a modified version of 'A sandcastle diagrammatic model of a child-initiated play episode', Jennifer Sturgess, *Australian Occupational Therapy Journal*, 2003, Blackwell Publishing. Reproduced with kind permission of Blackwell Publishing.

The development of play skills can be viewed as part of normal development. By combining knowledge of normal skill development and the sequences in which play matures (both in social play, symbolic play and other subcategories of play) with an understanding that developmental change in play is evidenced by additional play skills rather than the replacement of earlier ones, a logical understanding of play skill development occurs. Cooper (2000) developed a model of factors that impact on the development of play in children which combines the definitional features of play (e.g. freedom to suspend reality) with the individual and contextual elements (e.g. cognitive play skills in a particular environment). The sandcastle concept to some extent builds on this earlier model.

Individual elements of a sandcastle relate both symbolically to and accentuate the contextual features of play. Sandcastles can be built alone or in a group, spontaneously or at a planned gathering, or because the location inspired it. Furthermore, sandcastles evolve and change while being built and although they require some persistence, they generate pride and can be left behind or joyfully destroyed in an expression of physical and sensory play.

Components of a sandcastle

The components of a sandcastle are described and numbered in Figure 1.1. The 'drawbridge' (1) symbolises that almost intangible stimulus that children recognise in themselves and/or in the situation and environment which they choose to seize for play. This element is closely aligned to spontaneity (Lieberman 1966). The 'moat' (2) accentuates the set of circumstances that best supports a playful episode, and also that the play is actually or conceptually isolated or protected from intrusion. Conceptual isolation, recognised by the child or children involved, is known as 'framing' (Bundy 1997). Circumstances include the existence of a favourable setting and a set of physical resources and suitable timeframe (in the child's mind at least).

The support base of upturned buckets of sand, 'buttressing the castle proper' (3), indicate the need for a strong base of support skills for play. Adequate development of social, communication, cognitive, symbolic, physical, organisational, adaptive and self-concept skills are the 'towers' (4), which support play. The 'body of the sandcastle' (5) represents the specific play skills a child develops with time, experience, and nourishing environments. Examples of play skills are the abilities of the child to decide together with a friend what they want to play, how to use found objects to construct something for fun, or to make themselves feel better by playing something they find comforting. As each sandcastle is unique, so each child will have differing skills according to their age, gender, personality/temperament and life experiences.

As a decorative feature, the 'pinnacle' (6) represents the personal play style of the individual child, such as play or toy preferences, group, dyad or individual play choices, preference for imaginative or constructive or challenging play activities, and many other often subtle features. Play style is individual and derives from the particular interaction between genetic endowment, environment, contexts and experiences that a child has. Play style is linked to, and equally as important as, play development (Dockett 1998). Some children, due to restricted opportunity or negative experiences have little sense of playfulness and consequently a limited repertoire of play skills (Cooper 2000), and these factors influence their play style. This pinnacle also can be understood as symbolising the holistic nature of play (Ferland 1997), even though play can be deconstructed and shown to be made up of component skills.

The 'flag' (7), represents the child's ownership of the play. Children may also choose to take a playful approach to an activity introduced as work by an adult (King 1979; Sanders and Graham 1995). However, the child's view is the primary criterion for deciding if the episode is play or not (Ferland 1997). Adult observers can make mistakes in decisions about whether a child is or isn't playing. The flag therefore states play ownership, 'I played here'. In circumstances where skills existed, and many of the environmental opportunities were appropriate, the episode still may not be chosen by or enjoyed by the child, and therefore would not be play.

Taking this metaphor further, the sandcastle could vary according to individual circumstances. For example, the 'sandcastle' of a child with physical impairment will not have such a stable base. While a 'hurried child' (Elkind 2001) without much time for self-chosen play may have an approaching wave or tide which breaches the moat wall!

Two other components are included. The environment in which the child lives, interacts, responds to sensory stimuli and feels safe or threatened is signified by the 'sky' (8). The child's personality is signified by the 'ocean' (9) which flows into the moat. Environment and personality are conceptualised as equally important influences on the child's play skill development. A report in an Australian newspaper described how a school had removed play equipment and shortened play time to reduce potential litigation risk should children get injured playing on the equipment (Milligan 2002). An understanding of these factors would be necessary in order to fully explore the play environment of a child attending this school, and similar factors will exist in every child's environment.

The context in which children play, here represented as the 'beach' (10), is intimately connected to their play skills and this construct is supported by literature (Cox, Baker and Coombs 2005; Oden and Hall 1998; Sutton-Smith 1992). As proposed, a child may be more comfortable playing in one context than another but, in general, well-rounded development is characterised by adequate competence in most play contexts. A child aged five years may prefer solitary constructional-imaginative play (e.g. with Lego) but still be able to enjoy playing Lego with other children and active outside games. This would be considered age-appropriate, however, if a child played well with Lego but not with other children or outside, there might be cause for concern.

Barnett (1991) reviewed many studies which showed a child's play may vary according to whether they are at school or not, at home or away, in a familiar or an unfamiliar place, or in rooms which have different layouts. Environment is often understood in predominantly physical terms. The term context is used in this instance rather than environment, because physical environment is only one aspect of context. Other aspects include companions, safety, time pressure, supervision, expectations and props. Thus social, physical, cultural and temporal components of context are essential considerations. For example, a child may be playing alone in a fenced yard with a sand pit and other play props, while an adult inside may be completing household tasks, occasionally looking out to monitor the child and remaining available to supply extra props or engage the child. Here aspects of the context are supportive. Context cannot be fully described without attention to some expectations and attitudinal issues which may affect whether the child chooses to initiate play or not.

CONCLUSION

Based on a selective review of some historical and recent research and analysis about children's play, and on experience as a practitioner, a conceptualisation of child-initiated play has been proposed. The underlying concepts have been graphically linked to a metaphor of a sandcastle, the value of which is to reinforce the need to identify and align these with the child if their play is being examined, evaluated or used in an intervention situation. The sandcastle model (Sturgess 2003) provides a useful starting point for therapists and teachers considering the many factors in an individual child's world which may affect their play choices. Just as importantly, this conceptualisation has potential for use with parents in discussion of issues in the life of their family, which have an impact on the play of their children. It is engaging and also stimulates parents to remember the positive value of play.

REFERENCES

Barnes, D. R. (1998) 'Play in Historical Contexts.' In D. P. Fromberg and D. Bergen (eds) *Play from Birth to Twelve and Beyond.* New York: Garland Publishing.

Barnett, L. A. (1991) 'The playful child: Measurement of a disposition to play.' *Play & Culture* 4, 51–74.

Bazyk, S., Stalnaker, D., Llerena, M., Ekelman, B. and Bazyk, J. (2003) 'Play in Mayan children.' *American Journal of Occupational Therapy 57,* 273–283.

Bergen, D. (1998) 'Play as a Context for Humor Development.' In D. P. Fromberg and D. Bergen (eds) *Play from Birth to Twelve and Beyond.* New York: Garland Publishing.

Bundy, A. C. (1997) 'Play and Playfulness: What to Look for.' In L. D. Parham and L. S. Fazio (eds) *Play in Occupational Therapy for Children.* St Louis: C.V. Mosby.

Cole-Hamilton, I. and Gill, T. (2002) *Making the Case for Play – Building Policies and Strategies for School-Aged Children.* London: National Children's Bureau.

Cole-Hamilton, I., Harrop, A. and Street, C. (2002) *Making the Case for Play – Gathering the Evidence.* London: National Children's Bureau.

Cooper, R. J. (2000) 'The impact of child abuse on children's play: A conceptual model.' *Occupational Therapy International 7,* 259–276.

Cox, A., Baker, K. and Coombs, N. (2005) 'Schoolyard participation group.' *Skills for Kids: Paediatric Occupational Therapy Symposium, 7–8 October,* Melbourne: OT Australia – Victoria.

Dargan, A. and Zeitlin, S. (1998) 'City Play.' In D. P. Fromberg and D. Bergen (eds) *Play from Birth to Twelve and Beyond.* New York: Garland Publishers.

Davis, J. A. and Polatajko, H. J. (2006) 'The Occupational Development of Children.' In S. Rodger and J. Ziviani (eds) *Occupational Therapy With Children: Understanding Children's Occupations and Enabling Participation.* Oxford: Blackwell Science.

Dockett, S. (1998) 'Thinking about Play, Playing about Thinking.' In E. Dau and E. Jones (eds) *Child's Play – Revisiting Play in Early Childhood Settings.* Sydney: Maclennan & Petty.

Elkind, D. (2001) *The Hurried Child: Growing Up Too Fast Too Soon,* 3rd edn. Cambridge, MA: Da Capo Press.

Erikson, E. H. (1975) *Studies of Play.* New York: Arno.

Fein, G. G. (1981) 'Pretend play in childhood: An integrative review.' *Child Development 52,* 1095–1118.

Ferland, F. (1997) *Play, Children with Physical Difficulties, and Occupational Therapy: The Ludic Model,* trans. P. Aronoff and H. Scott. Ottawa, Canada: University of Ottawa Press.

Heidemann, S. and Hewitt, D. (1992) *Pathways to Play: Developing Play Skills in Young Children.* St Paul, MN: Redleaf Press.

Johnson, J. E. (1998) 'Play Development from Ages Four to Eight.' In D. P. Fromberg and D. Bergen (eds) *Play from Birth to Twelve and Beyond.* New York: Garland Publishing.

King, N. R. (1979) 'Play: The kindergartener's perspective.' *The Elementary School Journal 80,* 81–87.

King, N. (1986) 'Play and the Culture of Childhood.' In G. Fein and M. Rivkin (eds) *The Young Child At Play.* Washington, DC: National Association for the Education of Young Children.

Lieberman, J. N. (1966) 'Playfulness: Attempt to conceptualise a quality of play and of the
    player.' *Psychological Reports 19*, 178.
Malone, D. M. and Stoneman, Z. (1990) 'Cognitive play of mentally retarded preschoolers:
    Observations in the home and school.' *American Journal of Mental Retardation 94*, 475–487.
Milligan, L. (2002) 'Out of bounds playtime now a painful lesson.' *Weekend Australian*,
    September 17, p. 8.
Oden, S. and Hall, J. A. (1998) 'Peer and Sibling Influences on Play.' In D. P. Fromberg and D.
    Bergen (eds) *Play from Birth to Twelve and Beyond*. New York: Garland Publishing.
Piaget, J. (1962) *Play, Dreams and Imitation in Childhood*. London: Routledge & Kegan Paul.
Power, T. G. (2000) *Play and Exploration in Children and Animals*. Mahwah, NJ: Lawrence
    Erlbaum.
Provenzo, E. F. Jnr (1998) 'Electronically Mediated Playscapes.' In D. P. Fromberg and D.
    Bergen (eds) *Play from Birth to Twelve and Beyond*. New York: Garland Publishers.
Rigby, P. and Rodger, S. (2006) 'Developing as a player.' In S. Rodger and J. Ziviani (eds)
    *Occupational Therapy With Children: Understanding Children's Occupations and Enabling
    Participation*. Oxford: Blackwell Science.
Rivkin, M. S. (1998) 'Children's Outdoor Play: An Endangered Activity.' In D. P. Fromberg
    and D. Bergen (eds) *Play from Birth to Twelve and Beyond*. New York: Garland Publishers.
Rodger, S. and Ziviani, J. (1999) 'Play-based occupational therapy.' *International Journal of
    Disability, Development and Education 46*, 337–365.
Russ, S. W. (2004) *Play in Child Development and Psychotherapy*. Mahwah, NJ: Lawrence Erlbaum.
Sanders, S. and Graham, G. (1995) 'Kindergarten children's initial experiences in physical
    education: The relentless persistence for play clashes with the zone of acceptable
    responses.' *Journal of Teaching in Physical Education 14*, 372–383.
Seja, A. L. and Russ, S. W. (1999) 'Children's fantasy play and emotional understanding.'
    Journal of Clinical Child Psychology 28, 269–277.
Stagnitti, K. and Unsworth, C. (2000) 'The importance of pretend play in child development:
    An occupational therapy perspective'. *British Journal of Occupational Therapy 63*, 121–127.
Sturgess, J. (2003) 'Viewpoint: A model describing play as a child-chosen activity: is this still
    valid in contemporary Australia?' *Australian Occupational Therapy Journal 50*, 104–108.
Sutton-Smith, B. (1992) 'The role of toys in the instigation of playful creativity.' *Creativity
    Research Journal 5*, 3–11.

CHAPTER 2

Play as Transaction:
The Impact of Child Maltreatment

Rodney Cooper

CHAPTER OBJECTIVES

This chapter introduces play as a 'transaction' between the child and the environment influenced by family and culture. This conceptualisation is used first to examine typical play and then used to explore some of the circumstances for the play transaction not taking place. Finally, the impact of child maltreatment on the play transaction is examined with specific reference to the findings of a research study.

HOW DO WE RECOGNISE PLAY?

'Billy'

'Billy' (aged three) has discovered the waiting room Duplo box. He sits on the floor and carefully selects the wheeled Duplo blocks which he adds to his pile. He sings a little tune as he does this. He places a different animal on each wheeled Duplo block. He persists with balancing a cow that keeps falling off. He then carefully links the wheeled parts together and replaces each animal which has fallen off. When six Duplo blocks have been joined together he takes one end and drives it along the floor dodging around obstacles all the while making 'choo choo' noises and repeatedly saying 'all aboard'. Whenever he stops, he manually makes the animals get off and on the 'carriages'. When the line of 'carriages' overturns going around a chair leg he laughs uproariously, then carefully replaces all the animals and continues. The adults talking in the same room are ignored.

Is this play? 'Billy' appears to be totally absorbed in the activity and therefore intrinsically motivated. The activity is self-chosen, appears meaningful to the player, and is probably episodic in that it has a continuing theme. He uses representational toys in a symbolic or 'as if' manner, his singing may indicate pleasure, and his approach is playful, all of which are characteristics of play. 'Billy' certainly appears to have 'shut out' the external environment and the adults present have given him tacit permission to play. Furthermore, his developmental skills appear to be within his age range.

From our adult perspective, we recognise this behaviour as 'play'. While this vignette is made up, it is representative of a multitude of similar examples, which are readily observable. Play means many things to children and adults. In similar scenarios to this one I often ask the parent whether they noticed their child playing. A frequent response is 'no, but I could tell they were happy'. Interestingly, when I ask children, their answer is often 'just playing' or 'having fun'. According to Bateson's (1972) concept of 'framing', the activity is play when everybody, players and observers, are aware that what is occurring is play.

MAKING SENSE OF PLAY

While most child therapists agree on the value of play, there is less agreement on a definition. Play has been variously defined as pleasurable, intrinsically motivated, spontaneous, internally controlled, non-literal behaviour, which is free from externally imposed rules, and is an active process characterised by attention to the means rather than the ends (Dockett and Fleer 2002; Rubin, Fein and Vandenberg 1983). When play is viewed as a predisposition, the focus shifts from the outcome of what the child does to the process or what the child brings to the play situation. This also suggests that play is internally controlled by the child (Neumann 1971) and that the 'frame of play' is established by the players through communication cues (i.e. 'this is pretending') so that players and observers understand that this is play (Bateson 1972).

Within the play literature there have been three general definitional approaches. The first adopts the view that the best way of defining play is to focus on the individual child's predisposition to play (Rubin *et al.* 1983). The second has been to examine the play context and delineate environmental characteristics most likely to stimulate play behaviours (Tizard, Philps and

Plewis 1976), while the third has been to define play according to observable characteristics that conform to either specific definitions of play behaviour or a developmental taxonomy (Krasnor and Pepler 1980). All of these play approaches have arisen out of Western theoretical understandings of play. In a multicultural society it cannot be assumed that these views of play will automatically apply to all children, regardless of their ethnic background and cross cultural experience (Fleer 1998). Clearly, play needs to be considered in the social and cultural context in which children live if we are to avoid making judgments or generalisations, either consciously or unconsciously, about typical play forms (Dockett and Fleer 2002).

If we believe that play is a child's natural medium of self-expression, problem-solving and creativity and therefore essential to development and emotional wellbeing, it is important that we are able to clearly communicate why we believe this, especially to parents, therapists, early childhood workers and teachers as well as service managers. This is much harder than it sounds as everybody has a view of what play is, usually based on their own perceptions or experiences. The following is my view of play based on my experiences working with traumatised children and being a parent.

PLAY AS A TRANSACTION

I understand play as a special kind of 'transaction' between the child and his or her environment, which is characterised by internal control, freedom to suspend reality and intrinsic motivation, and is influenced by family, culture and ecological contexts (Bundy 1997; Cooper 2000). Play only occurs when there is a 'just right' fit between the child and the environment (Cooper 2000). The child's contribution and the environmental elements that constitute the play transaction are now examined in a way that can serve as a guide for looking at play within the child's socio-cultural contexts.

The child's contribution to the play transaction

The child brings his or her developmental play skills along with preferences and play disposition to the play transaction. Successful play engagement is largely reliant upon developmental maturation with play reflecting the child's developmental skills. Developmental play skills include cognitive, motor and social play skills. Cognitive play skills enable the child to use play opportunities and play materials in more adaptive and elaborate ways (Piaget 1962) whereas active play allows the child to build gross and fine motor coordination enabling them to gain more control over their bodies. Language and communication skills determine a child's ability to successfully coordinate his or her play within a social situation (Dockett and Freer 2002). Play with peers allows for practise of social knowledge of sharing, turn taking, group cooperation and exercising self-control, developing empathy and getting along with others without resorting to aggression.

Although developmental skills underpin children's play actions, it is the individuality of preferences and a sense of fun or playfulness that is most re-cognisable as play. Internal locus of control can be seen in the child who is totally absorbed with internal processes expressed in external play actions (Vygotsky 1976). By temporally suspending reality, the child is free of some of the constraints that the situation would normally impose allowing pre-tence in play. The ability to substitute objects, attribute properties and ac-tions to objects, or introduce time, space and other elements not present in the immediate play setting is evidence of symbolic representational thought (Stagnitti and Unsworth 2000). Play is also engaged in solely for its own sake with the source of intrinsic motivation determining the child's curiosity and absorption in play.

The play environment as part of the transaction

Every potential play setting has physical and social elements present, which either stimulate or restrict play opportunities. The physical play environment includes: available man-made or natural spaces, potential play materials, and whether the setting is inside or outside, familiar or unfamiliar. The presence of familiar or unfamiliar children, siblings, friends or different-aged children, adults or parents all affect how a child interacts with the human and nonhuman objects in the environment. Although playmates usually contribute to the play transaction in a mutually cooperative manner, conflict is just as likely to occur within the social play context (Dockett and Fleer 2002). Some everyday environments actively discourage play while other environments (i.e. playgrounds) are recognised as dedicated play areas.

The influence of the child's socio-cultural context and familial/care milieu

Each play transaction also reflects the cultural expectations and experiences of the child's world. For example, when children grow up in multicultural environments with adults and peers who possess differing traditions, their play is often a reflection of cultural pluralism or cultural borrowing (Fleer 1998). Ecological factors including family, socio-economic status, ethnic identity and gender roles either directly or indirectly shape the child's experience (Bronfenbrenner 1979). Different cultural beliefs and child rearing practices also influence children's play (see Chapter 11) and the cultural sanctions or cues that parents, extended family, friends and the broader community give to children convey a message about the importance of play (Grille 2008).

Parents have considerable influence on how their children play by the way they interact, control or fail to respond to their children's play. For example, within the first year of life, it is the quality of parent–child interactions which best promotes the development of a secure attachment (Morton and Browne 1998). Central to attachment theory is the notion that 'internal working models affect an individual's interpretation of information, evaluation of situations, and hence their emotional and behavioural reactions' (Moncher 1996, p. 345). Sensitive parental feedback and ability to adjust interactions to meet their child's developmental and play needs is an important determinant of the child's development of social identity (Pearce and Pezzot-Pearce 1994).

HOW DO WE RECOGNISE PLAY DYSFUNCTION?

'Bob'

'Bob' (aged four years) sits on the floor in the middle of the play area. He tips over toy containers to empty their contents around him and rakes his hands through the piles, occasionally selecting an object to look at closely before moving to another container or toy. This therapy play environment includes a range of construction, creative and pretend play materials such as action figurines, puppets, dress up clothes, blocks, animals and drawing materials. His attention shifts to the dress up clothes in the corner of the play room and he puts on a superhero cape. He then rolls across the floor scattering toys. Sitting up he selects a toy dinosaur then picks up an action figurine and brings the two toys together while making an 'Ooof' noise before dropping the figurine. He repeats this action eight times with different figurines and animals, each time making the same noise before dropping the toy. He then holds the dinosaur sideways and pushes it before him through the piles of toys in a 'ploughing' action while making a noise, 'Brmmmm Brmmmm', not unlike a bulldozer. He then lies across the toys, sits up and looks around without expression. He appears disinterested.

Is this play? Is this typical behaviour for a four-year-old? How do we distinguish between age appropriate play and play problems? These are valid questions when confronted by children who appear not to be able to negotiate the play transaction. While 'Bob' is fictitious, this description is broadly based on similar play observations made during my clinical work with children with play problems. Recognising play deficits is important for therapists. I will now identify how the play transaction has become a problem by considering the child's contribution, the play environment and the socio-cultural context.

The child's contribution?

Bob's play appears to be stimulus driven with no clear purpose or meaning. While he relates toys together and shows some understanding of their function (i.e. dress up cape) this is not developed past the obvious. He possibly uses object substitution (i.e. dinosaur for a machine?), but this is fleeting and may be unrelated to pretence. His use of the play space is largely physical – he sprawls on top of the play materials and manually spreads toys across the floor. It appears that he has low playfulness and he shows no expression of enjoyment. Given his age, his actions are suggestive of those of a much younger child and could indicate delayed developmental skills. It would appear that Bob has poor internal control, delayed cognitive play skills and decreased intrinsic motivation. Formal investigation of any underlying pathology and assessment of his developmental skills as well as play skills would provide further insight into his abilities.

The play environment

On the other hand, the indoor therapy play environment on which this scenario is based may not have had the right elements to support a play transaction. Children like 'Bob' often respond differently to the unfamiliar clinical play setting, especially if they perceive it as overstimulating (too much choice) or not safe. Likewise, the lack of other children or the presence of adults, common to the clinical setting, may further inhibit a child's engagement in play. Interviewing parents and early childhood teachers can provide further information about a child's play preferences and typical play behaviour in different play settings.

The child's socio-cultural context

Bob's socio-cultural context would be much harder to observe. Usually a referral, case history or carer interview provides some of this information. In my own clinical practice, I try to take every opportunity to spend some time observing a child in his or her home or school environment as this enables me to better understand the child's socio-cultural context. In the previous scenario, Bob's family or care milieu may be very relevant to why he wasn't able to initiate meaningful play in this particular setting. If his experience included child maltreatment, for example, this could impact on his ability to contribute to and respond to the play setting. In the next section the impact of child maltreatment on play will be examined.

CHILD MALTREATMENT

Child maltreatment can be viewed as the failure of the child's care environment (and socio-cultural context) to protect and nurture the child. It encompasses a wide range of deliberate acts, all of which involve some form of detrimental physical, sexual, psychological or emotional harm to a child or the failure of carers to protect a child from such harm. Maltreatment occurs across all socio-economic, religious and ethnic groups and is usually a result of a complex interplay of environmental, family relationship and parental risk factors, and child characteristics.

THE IMPACT OF CHILD MALTREATMENT ON THE PLAY TRANSACTION

Play is sensitive to environmental disruption with an abusive or neglectful family milieu likely to adversely affect a child's play development (Cooper and Sutton 1999). I will now use the conceptualisation of play as a transaction to frame a discussion of the impact of maltreatment on children's play. This will be illustrated with specific reference to a research study based on this conceptualisation and premise. It is postulated that children who experience a chronically maltreating care milieu will be less able to engage in competent play or contribute to new play situations, including the individual play setting used in most therapeutic approaches. A study conducted by the author (Cooper 2001) examined three aspects of the play transaction: (1) what impact maltreatment has on the child's contribution as represented by his or her developmental play skills and play behaviour choices; (2) how children respond to the individual, indoor play environment modelled on the clinical play setting and; (3) the influence on play of chronic intra-familial maltreatment as representative of a child's experience of dysfunctional parental care.

Maltreated preschool children's play: A research study

The aim of this exploratory study was to compare the play skills of maltreated and non-maltreated preschool children in order to understand how maltreatment effects the play transaction. It was hypothesised that the detrimental impact of chronic, intra-familial maltreatment would manifest in significantly delayed developmental play skills; difficulty initiating and sustaining adaptive, imaginative and positive play behaviours and more overtly aggressive play actions compared to non-maltreated children. Ethics approval was obtained.

Study sample

The subjects in this study were 110 preschool children aged 3–6 years (mean age 53 months) recruited in a major Australian city in the late 1990s. Subjects were predominantly Caucasian (85%) with non-Caucasian subjects including six Indigenous children. Fifty-five of the subjects (28 boys, 27 girls) were selected from clinical referrals to therapy programmes following documented intra-familial child maltreatment. Varied maltreatment experiences included physical abuse (67%), sexual abuse (58%), emotional abuse (93%) and neglect (66%), severe enough for 24% to be placed in foster care. Domestic violence was reported in nearly 67 per cent of cases. Maltreatment histories revealed that the majority had experienced multiple experiences of maltreatment, which in over half of the subjects (54%) lasted two or more years. Perpetrators included parents, step parents, relatives and carers with 18 per cent being maltreated by more than two perpetrators.

Fifty-five non-maltreated comparison children, individually matched for age, gender, ethnicity and socio-economic status with the maltreated subjects, were recruited from community preschools and child care centres in the same city. Matching was statistically comparable for age, gender and ethnicity but not socio-economic status.

Play sampling method

All subjects' individual free play was videotaped (45 minutes) in an indoor setting using a standard selection of toys with the primary carer present but out of camera range. Play materials were representative of preschool and therapy settings. The child was familiarised with the playroom and encouraged to play while the researcher interviewed the child's carer. Information about the child's developmental milestones, living situation and parental stress was also obtained.

Two independent raters, blind to subject grouping and age, used a battery of play scales to rate randomly assigned videotaped play samples. Prior inter-rater and intra-rater reliability was established for both raters. Six observational play measures were used to rate videotaped play samples including the *Preschool Play Scale* (Bledsoe and Shepherd 1982; Knox 1997) *Lunzer's Scale of Organisation of Play Behaviour* (Hulme and Lunzer 1966), *Singer's Emotional Affect, Imaginativeness, and Play Concentration scales* and composite *Play Aggression scale* (Singer 1973).

Study findings

Analysis revealed significant group differences ($p<.001$) for developmental play skills with maltreated children's play age equivalents as calculated on the *Preschool Play Scale*, generally lower (mean of 45.4 months) compared to their non-maltreated counterparts (mean of 52.1 months). Multivariate analysis of covariance revealed significant group behavioural differences ($p<.01$), with the maltreated children showing less play enjoyment, decreased play imagination, reduced play concentration (*Singer's scales*) and more cognitively disorganised play behaviour (*Lunzer's scale*) relative to the non-maltreated children after adjustment for covariates (socio-economic status, family type, preschool attendance, carer's education). Significant ($p<.001$) gender and group predictors of play aggression were identified in a logistic regression analysis of play aggression, with maltreated boys most likely to engage in aggressive play behaviour.

IMPLICATIONS OF FINDINGS

The child's compromised play contribution

The maltreated children performed significantly lower than non-maltreated children on all developmental and behavioural play variables confirming support for the hypotheses. The maltreatment group engaged in play that was more functional, exploratory and less complex in its cognitive integration with fewer observed instances of pretence, whereas the non-maltreated group introduced more make believe and object substitutions into their play.

Alessandri (1991) reported observations of maltreated preschoolers spending extended periods of time engaged in purposeless pounding, touching and repetitive handling of toys without apparent insight. It is even possible that some maltreated children have never learned how to play and therefore are more likely to engage in sensory-motor or exploratory play 'stuck' at developmentally younger levels (Howard 1986). Examination of the maltreated children's videotaped play samples revealed considerable tangential behaviour, desultory manipulation, increased expression of frustration or boredom and, in some cases, hypervigilance. On the other hand, the comparison children used play materials meaningfully, introduced more pretend elements and were engaged in more behaviour that could be confidently rated as play. Play disorganisation may also be indicative of the maltreated child's developmental immaturity, increased behavioural disturbance and inability to internally control his or her play actions and choices. Darwish *et al.* (2001) found that the ability to successfully initiate play interactions distinguished between maltreated and non-maltreated preschool children.

The maltreated children were also less positive in their expression of emotional affect during play whereas the comparison children showed more pleasure through laughter, smiling, singing, animated conversation and playful exchanges. Although individual children expressed pleasure, as a group the maltreated children appeared to be less playful.

Behavioural disturbance is likely to be apparent in social play interactions (Éthier, Lemelin and Lacharité 2004). Harper (1988, p.37) noted that 'the normal child is in control of the situation and is able to alter or terminate play without difficulty, whereas the disturbed child may become so involved that reality and fantasy merge and play seems almost out of control, on the verge of disintegration'. Fagot *et al.* (1989) reported both physically abused and neglected preschoolers' play as more aggressive than non-maltreated and sexually abused children's play. A disturbed sense of self can manifest in aggressive or destructive play behaviour, such as deliberately breaking toys or disrupting games (Caughey 1991). Harper's (1991) exploration of sand tray symbolic play themes found that physically abused children's play was more aggressive, while obsessive themes of sexuality dominated the play of sexually abused children.

Maltreated boys were significantly more likely to direct aggressive play behaviour at toys than comparison children or girls in the maltreatment group. Examination of the raters' transcripts revealed a range of aggressive play actions with the most common being, 'predictable aggressive' content (i.e. making action figurines fight). Others engaged in what can be described as 'ritualised aggression' – sporadic aggressive actions directed at toys accompanied by aggressive dialogue (i.e. adopting aggressive character roles). Out of the total sample, only four boys in the maltreatment group engaged in 'overtly aggressive' play which seemingly became 'stuck' and out of control. This sustained behaviour included a threatening aspect and tended to increase in emotional intensity and physical force with aggressive actions dominating the play sample. For example, one boy, while exclaiming 'you are a bad boy', repeatedly punched, karate kicked or hit an inflatable dinosaur with increasing ferocity.

Safe and unsafe play environments

Maltreated children may have a 'world view' in which a sense of potential threat is constantly present with this anxiety invariably extending into any new or unfamiliar play situation (Glaser 2000). It is likely that some of the children in the maltreatment group reacted to the play assessment environment negatively due to either the ambiguous and potentially unsafe nature of the setting or the child's slowness to adapt to the novel play environment. Post traumatic stress disorder symptoms can be reactivated by different environmental stimuli or even toys, resulting in a child exhibiting regressed or distressed behaviour in otherwise normal play settings (Davis 1999).

The selection of toys offered in this play environment, were chosen as representative of the play therapy setting. Toys included construction toys (Duplo blocks), symbolic toys (figurines, animals, doll's house), domestic play toys (stove, play dough, kitchen utensils, baby doll), creative materials (craft media and junk items) and role play props (dress ups, toy sword, inflatable dinosaur). Some of these toys probably stimulated stereotypical play transactions, although this varied between individuals. For example, the inflatable dinosaur was an obvious prop for aggressive play, yet it was also dressed up, 'fed', used as a pretend 'playmate', with one comparison subject even using it as a 'dinosaur car'. However, the sampled maltreated children appeared to be less able to utilise the selection of play materials or initiate and organise their play activity in this individual play environment compared to their non-maltreated peers.

The indoor play environment utilised in this study was limited by its lack of social opportunity, restricted space and time constraints. It seems likely that the more socially oriented children were sensitive to the artificial nature of this play assessment setting. Likewise, the passive presence of adults including parents, who in a small number of cases could have been party to maltreatment, may also have influenced some children's play transactions. It is possible, albeit speculative, that the heightened aggression observed in some of the maltreated boys was also due to social information-processing biases which caused increased emotional arousal when these boys interpreted the ambiguous play setting as potentially threatening (Scerbo and Kolko 1995).

The maltreating familial or care milieu

Growing up in an abusive or neglectful home environment can limit a child's development of competent skills needed to engage in positive play transactions. For example, physically abusing mothers have been observed to be more controlling of their children's play and less able to give positive play reinforcement (Bousha and Twentyman 1984; Kavanagh et al. 1988) whereas, neglecting parents ignored or were unresponsive to their children when they played (Gaudin et al. 1996). Many maltreating parents were themselves maltreated as children and have a poorly developed sense of play and negative internal representations of themselves as carers (Fagot and Kavanagh 1991). Maltreatment by a parent or carer is also likely to produce insecure attachments in children, which impact on how they explore and respond to the human and nonhuman elements in their environment through play (Pearce and Pezzot-Pearce 1994). Maltreated children whose home environments lack stimulating play materials have been found to not actively engage in play in other play environments (Giblin, Starr and Agronow 1984).

Conversely, the experience of sexual abuse within the care milieu is likely to be very different to other experiences of maltreatment. Because intra-familial sexual abuse involves developmentally immature children in sexual activities that they are unable to give informed consent to, this not only violates social taboos within the family but also involves secrecy, betrayal of trust, implicit threats and 'grooming' by the perpetrator (Mian, Marton and LeBaron 1996). Fagot et al. (1989) noted that sexually abused preschoolers preferred to play by themselves and were unlikely to be seen as deviant by adult observers. The way in which sexually abused children's play reportedly differs is the frequently observed existence of sexualised play behaviour (Davies, Glaser and Kossoff 2000). No sexualised play was observed in this study, even though half of the maltreated group had been sexually abused.

CONCLUDING COMMENTS

In this chapter, I have illustrated three potential ways that the child therapist can use the conceptualisation of play as a transaction: first, to better understand and define what typical play is; second, to focus clinical observations on play dysfunction and third, as a framework for applying observations to a research process. Observing a child's spontaneous play responses to a therapist's playful interactions can be a useful source of information about the child's developmental skills, playfulness and coping ability. The use of time-limited play sampling methods provide therapists with a viable means of merging structured and naturalistic play observations into the therapy situation. Given the breadth of play theories and the nature of working with children who present with developmental and behavioural problems, the use of a conceptualisation can help inform observations, assessment choices and intervention decisions. Too often, play interventions are ad hoc, have blurred play and therapy goals and lack a theoretical understanding of play.

In the research example, I found that the play transaction was adversely affected by the experience of intra-familial child maltreatment, which places the maltreated preschool child at greater risk for learning and social problems. Utilising structured, play-based early intervention programmes to address underlying developmental deficits is an appropriate treatment strategy for some young maltreated children.

REFERENCES

Alessandri, S. M. (1991) 'Play and social behavior in maltreated preschoolers.' *Development and Psychopathology 3,* 191–205.

Bateson, G. (1972) *Steps to an Ecology of Mind.* New York: Ballantine.

Bledsoe, N. P. and Shepherd, J. T. (1982) 'A study of reliability and validity of a preschool play scale.' *American Journal of Occupational Therapy 36,* 12, 783–788.

Bousha, D. M. and Twentyman, C. T. (1984) 'Mother–child interractional style in abuse, neglect, and control groups: Naturalistic observations in the home.' *Journal of Abnormal Psychology 93,* 1, 106–114.

Bronfenbrenner, U. (1979) 'Ecological Systems Theory.' In R. Vasta (ed.) *Annals of Child Development, vol. 6.* Greenwich, CT: JAI Press.

Bundy, A. C. (1997) 'Play and Playfulness: What to Look for.' In L. D. Parham and L. S. Fazio (eds) *Play in Occupational Therapy for Children.* St Louis: C.V. Mosby.

Caughey, C. (1991) 'Becoming the child's ally – Observations in a classroom for children who have been abused.' *Young Children 46,* 4, 22–28.

Cooper, R. and Sutton, K. (1999) 'The effects of child abuse on preschool children's play.' *Australian Journal of Early Childhood 24,* 2, 10–14.

Cooper, R. J. (2000) 'The impact of child abuse on children's play: a conceptual model.' *Occupational Therapy International 7,* 259–276.

Cooper, R. J. (2001) 'The impact of intra-familial child abuse and neglect on preschool children's play.' Unpublished doctorial thesis, Dept. of Occupational Therapy, University of Queensland.

Darwish, D., Esquivel, G. B., Houtz, J. C. and Alfonso V. C. (2001) 'Play and social skills in maltreated and non-maltreated preschoolers during peer interactions.' *Child Abuse & Neglect 25,* 1, 13–31.

Davies, S. L., Glaser, D. and Kossoff, R. (2000) 'Children's sexual play and behavior in pre-school settings: staff's perceptions, reports, and responses.' *Child Abuse & Neglect 24,* 10, 1329–1343.

Davis, J. (1999) 'Effects of trauma on children: Occupational therapy to support recovery.' *Occupational Therapy International 6,* 2, 126–142.

Dockett, S. and Fleer, M. (2002) *Play and Pedagogy in Early Childhood: Bending the Rules.* Melbourne: Thomson Learning.

Éthier, L. S., Lemelin, J. and Lacharité, C. (2004) 'A longitudinal study of the effects of chronic maltreatment on children's behavioral and emotional problems.' *Child Abuse & Neglect 28,* 126–1278.

Fagot, B. I., Hagan, R., Youngblade, L. M. and Potter, L. (1989) 'A comparison of the play behaviors of sexually abused, physically abused and nonabused preschool children.' *Topics in Early Childhood Special Education 9,* 2, 88–100.

Fagot, B. I. and Kavanagh, K. (1991) 'Play as a Diagnostic Tool with Physically Abusive Parents and their Children.' In C. S. Schaefer, K. Gitlin and A. Sandgrund (eds) *Play Diagnosis and Assessment.* New York: Wiley.

Fleer, M. (1998) 'Universal Fantasy: The Domination of Western Theories of Play.' In E. Dau and E. Jones (eds) *Child's Play: Revisiting Play in Early Childhood Settings*. Sydney: MacLennan and Petty.

Gaudin, J. M., Polansky, N. A., Kilpatrick, A. C. and Shilton, P. (1996) 'Family functioning in neglectful families.' *Child Abuse & Neglect 20*, 4, 363–377.

Giblin, P. T., Starr, R. H. and Agronow, S. J. (1984) 'Affective behavior of abused and control children: Comparisons of parent-child interactions and the influence of home environment variables.' *Journal of Genetic Psychology 144*, 69–82.

Glaser, D. (2000) 'Child abuse and neglect and the brain – A review.' *Journal of Child Psychology 41*, 1, 97–116.

Grille, R. (2008) *Heart to Heart Parenting*. Sydney: ABC Books.

Harper, J. (1988) 'Recognizing sexually abused children through their stories, artwork and play.' *Australian Journal of Early Childhood 13*, 1, 35–38.

Harper, J. (1991) 'Children's play: The differential effects of intrafamilial physical and sexual abuse.' *Child Abuse & Neglect 15*, 89–98.

Howard, A. C. (1986) 'Developmental play ages of physically abused and nonabused children.' *American Journal of Occupational Therapy 40*, 10, 691–695.

Hulme, I. and Lunzer, E. A. (1966) 'Play, language and reasoning in subnormal children.' *Journal of Child Psychology and Psychiatry 7*, 107–123.

Kavanagh, K. A., Youngblade, L., Reid, J. B. and Fagot, B. I. (1988) 'Interaction between children and abusive versus control parents.' *Journal of Clinical Child Psychology 17*, 2, 137–142.

Knox, S. (1997) 'Development and Current Use of the Knox Preschool Play Scale.' In L. D. Parham and L. S. Fanzio (eds) *Play in Occupational Therapy for Children*. St Louis, MO: Mosby.

Krasnor, L. R. and Pepler, D. J. (1980) 'The Study of Children's play: Some Future Directions.' In W. Damon (series ed.) and K. H. Rubin (vol. ed.) *New Directions for Child Development: vol. 9, Children's Play*. San Fransisco: Jossey Bass.

Mian, M., Marton, P., and Le Baron, D. (1996) 'The effects of sexual abuse on 3- to 5-year-old girls.' *Child Abuse & Neglect 20*, 8, 731–745.

Moncher, F. J. (1996) 'The relationship of maternal adult attachment style and risk of physical abuse.' *Journal of Interpersonal Violence 11*, 335–350.

Morton, N. and Browne, K. D. (1998) 'Theory and observation of attachment and its relation to child maltreatment: A review.' *Child Abuse & Neglect 22*, 11, 1093–1104.

Neumann, E.A. (1971) *The Elements of Play*. New York: MSS Information.

Pearce, J. W. and Pezzot-Pearce, T. D. (1994) 'Attachment theory and its implications for psychotherapy with maltreated children.' *Child Abuse & Neglect 18*, 5, 425–438.

Piaget, J. (1962) *Play, Dreams and Imitation in Childhood*. London: Routledge & Kegan Paul.

Rubin, K., Fein, G.G. and Vandenberg, B. (1983) 'Play.' In E.M. Hetherington (ed.) *Handbook of Child Psychology: Social Development,* 4th edn. New York: Wiley.

Scerbo, A. and Kalko, D. J. (1995) 'Child physical abuse and aggression: Preliminary findings on the role of internalizing problems.' *Journal of American Academy of Child and Adolescent Psychiatry 34*, 8, 1060–1066.

Singer, J. L. (1973) *The Child's World of Make-believe: Experimental Studies in Imaginative Play*. New York: Academic Press.

Stagnitti, K. and Unsworth, C. (2000) 'The importance of pretend play in child development: An occupational therapy perspective.' *British Journal of Occupational Therapy 63*, 121–127.

Tizard, B., Philps, J. and Plewis, I. (1976) 'Play in preschool centres - Play measures and their relations to age, sex and I.Q.' *Journal of Child Psychology and Psychiatry 17*, 251–264.

Vygotsky, L. (1976) 'Play and its role in the mental development of the child.' In J. Bruner, A. Jolly and K. Sylva (eds) *Play, its role in Development and Evolution*. Harmondsworth: Penguin.

CHAPTER 3

Children and Playfulness

Reinie Cordier and Anita Bundy

CHAPTER OBJECTIVES

This chapter explores the concept of playfulness. Four elements of playfulness: intrinsic motivation, internal control, suspension of unnecessary constraints of reality, and framing, are discussed against the contribution of the environment to children's play. What happens when playfulness is disrupted is then explored and illustrated using examples of autistic spectrum disorder, attention deficit hyperactivity disorder and physical disability.

WHAT IS PLAYFULNESS?

Children and some adults take a playful approach to life. They play with ideas and with objects, seeming to realise that there is more than one way to solve most problems. Unfortunately, playfulness is sometimes mistaken for silliness. Like play, playfulness is often not taken seriously. However, as Albert Einstein is reputed to have said, 'play is the highest form of research'. Further, play and playfulness have been associated with childhood coping and resilience (Hess and Bundy 2003; Saunders, Goodale and Sayer 1999). Thus play and playfulness may form an important cornerstone of intervention for children facing tremendous life challenges.

Perhaps some of the confusion around playfulness comes from a lack of understanding. What is playfulness? How can playfulness be incorporated into our everyday lives and in therapy interventions? We hope to shed some light on the construct of playfulness and how it can be disrupted by paediatric conditions such as attention deficit hyperactivity disorder (ADHD), autistic spectrum disorder (ASD) and physical disabilities.

Theorists have struggled unsuccessfully for years to reach consensus on a definition of play (Sutton-Smith 1997). Play is a complex behaviour that appears deceptively simple (deRenne-Stephan 1980; Reilly 1974; von Zuben, Crist and Mayberry 1991). This same complexity is characteristic of playfulness. Relatively little has been written about playfulness directly and much of the literature that pertains to play applies also to playfulness. In fact, many authors have written about play and playfulness as though they were synonymous. In this text we separate the terms play and playfulness, referring to playfulness as an approach and play as an occupation or transaction.

Play can be defined as a transaction between the individual and the environment that is intrinsically motivated, internally controlled, free of some unnecessary constraints of reality and well framed (Skard and Bundy 2008). Children bring many things to play: developmental abilities and skills, personal preferences and relative playfulness, to name a few. The immediate environment (physical setting, available play materials and social elements) either encourages or limits play activities.

Mary Reilly (1974), an American occupational therapist, described play as a 'cobweb'. She felt that play was fragile and that dissecting it into component parts might destroy it. Playfulness too, is fragile and easily disrupted. We have chosen to depict playfulness as a spider web in a window. While a spider web, from our perspective, is fragile, it is also very effective for capturing prey. Caught in the web shown in Figure 3.1 are a number of 'observations' that are woven together to comprise the elements of playfulness that sit within the frame that forms playfulness.

DEFINING PLAYFULNESS

Playfulness is the disposition or tendency to play (Barnett 1991). Playfulness is most commonly defined by the characteristics that comprise it. Many of the commonly cited characteristics of play can be categorised loosely under one of the four major traits of playfulness comprising the window frame depicted in Figure 3.1: intrinsic motivation, internal control, suspension of unnecessary constraints of reality and framing. In a sense, taken collectively, the characteristics that comprise them form operational definitions of the traits. That is, they answer one or more questions about how intrinsic motivation, internal control, suspension of reality or framing manifest. Two aspects of these elements of playfulness require particular attention. First, the *elements of playfulness are best represented with continua.* Neumann (1971) and Bundy (1991) described the elements of play as continua (see Figure 3.2). This means an individual or a transaction is

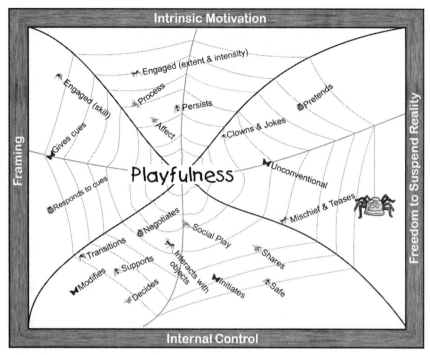

Figure 3.1 Playfulness

relatively more internally than externally controlled, more intrinsically than extrinsically motivated, more free than not free of some constraints of reality, and more clearly framed. Second, *play and non-play also can be represented by a continuum:* taken together, the elements of playfulness 'tip the balance' toward play or non-play. For example, a player's perception that control is more internal than external contributes toward tipping the balance to play. Similarly, if the source of the player's motivation is intrinsic and the player is free from some unnecessary constraints of reality, those also would tip the balance towards play (see Figure 3.2). And while play is relatively intrinsically motivated, internally controlled, and free of any constraints of reality, it is probably not feasible (and perhaps not desirable) for any of those scales to tip completely towards play.

THE ELEMENTS OF PLAYFULNESS

To develop an understanding of playfulness, let us examine the elements of playfulness. Observations that characterise each element are caught in the respective quadrants of the web depicted in Figure 3.1.

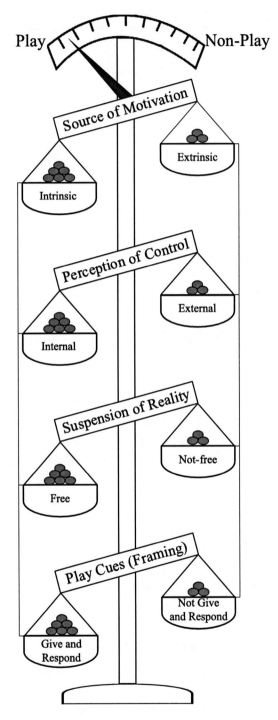

Figure 3.2 The interrelationship of the elements of playfulness

Intrinsic motivation refers to some (unnamed) aspect of the activity itself, rather than an external reward that provides the impetus for the individual's involvement in the activity (Skard and Bundy 2008). That means that players engage in activity simply because they enjoy the process, rather than for a specific outcome (Rubin, Fein and Vandenberg 1983). For example, after a rainstorm children may play in the mud for hours, simply running and splashing in the water, with no particular goal in mind, simply for pleasure. On the other hand, as it relates to competitive games, although winning a game could make play more fun, it may indeed be 'not knowing' who will win the game that encourages players to play for hours on end. When the winner is known, players often stop playing and start another game. And when winning, rather than the process, becomes the primary objective, then the game is no longer play.

Internal control suggests that players are largely 'in charge' of their actions and at least some aspects of the activity outcome (Skard and Bundy 2008). Players make many decisions during play. For instance, whilst playing 'cops-and-robbers', the players decide who will be who, what they will wear to distinguish each group, and how the scene of confrontation will unfold. Some decisions are made on the spot with players even deciding to change sides during the game! The players' sense of being 'in charge' of some of these decisions will influence their engagement in the game.

Freedom from some unnecessary constraints of reality means that players choose how close to objective reality the transaction will be. Players could be playing 'house' pretending to be mum and dad. They may use boxes to represent the house and role play their parents' performing household duties. Often rules are bent and glimpses of clowning and teasing are observed – 'mum' may be allowed to boss 'dad' around even though in reality, the child pretending to be mum would not be allowed to boss the child pretending to be dad.

Framing refers to the ability of players to give and read social cues about how to interact with another. Framing is somewhat more difficult than the other elements of playfulness to operationalise, since the cues that comprise it are so much part of culture. Consequently, framing becomes most obvious when it is impaired. The ability to give and respond to cues is also observed in non-play transactions but is more exaggerated and easier to learn during play (Bateson 1971, 1972). Framing is often observed in situations where players need to convey the message 'what we are doing is play' to enable the play frame to continue.

PLAYFULNESS AND THE ENVIRONMENT

The environment can either support or disrupt play. To support it, first and foremost the environment must be physically and emotionally safe. The emphasis here is on the *player* feeling safe, not on onlookers thinking that the player is safe. Children often carve out a safe space for play, even in situations of war and other trauma (Garbarino *et al.* 1992).

An optimally supportive environment is one that allows for adaptations that keep play challenging and fun, as well as promoting an individual's involvement, attentiveness and performance (Csikszentmihalyi 1990). In short, a positive fit occurs when opportunities provided by the environment meet the needs of the individual and when the ability of the individual matches the demands of the environment (Pervin 1968). A supportive environment matches the motivations of the player. For example, a child whose motivation is for mastery of his physical body will require an environment with lots of space and equipment that challenges balance and motor skills.

HOW IS PLAYFULNESS DISRUPTED?

Playfulness is disrupted when the above requirements are not met: the environment does not speak to the child's motivations, the play is not sufficiently challenging or the play space is not safe. Any of these mean that the child will not be able to get fully engrossed in play.

The main factors within the environment that affect playfulness are caregivers, playmates, objects and space (Skard and Bundy 2008). Restrictions are imposed when caregivers unexpectedly or irrationally change consistent and reasonable boundaries and rules. Playmates can also hamper playfulness when their cues do not support the transaction in the way in which they give and respond to cues. To varying degrees, objects serve as the props in the theatre of play, giving it more life and often providing the impetus for what happens next. However when there are too many or too few objects, it can interfere with playfulness. Consideration should be given to the amount and configuration of a play space, including the sensory environment, physical safety and accessibility.

APPLICATION OF THE PRINCIPLES OF PLAYFULNESS

To illustrate the application of playfulness, applied examples are presented describing children with three different conditions, describing the ways in which these conditions differentially affect playfulness.

Children with ADHD

Attention Deficit Hyperactivity Disorder (ADHD) is characterised by developmentally inappropriate levels of inattention, impulsivity and hyperactivity that cause impairment in day-to-day life; and is associated with a range of behavioural, academic and social problems that may lead to adverse outcomes (American Psychiatric Association 2000). Many children with ADHD will continue to have serious problems with social difficulties throughout adolescence and adulthood (Barkley 1997; Schachar 1991; Wood 1995).

As it relates to play, children with ADHD are likely to be less playful than typically developing children (Leipold and Bundy 2000). The authors' research with ADHD children suggests that they experience difficulties in areas relating to the social components of playfulness: sharing, supporting the play of others, transition between activities, and the intensity with which they engage in social play (all features of internal control), pretend play (freedom from constraints of reality) and responding to play cues (framing) (Cordier *et al.* in preparation). It is therefore evident that children with ADHD struggle to take on others' viewpoints and are overtly focused on having their own needs met. Children with ADHD also have particular strengths compared to typically developing children, such as using mischief and teasing to keep playmates 'hooked' (freedom from constraints of reality), being involved for the process rather than a specific end-product (intrinsic motivation) and the skill to negotiate to have their own play needs met (internal control). The author's new research findings support those of Leipold and Bundy 2000, who found that children with ADHD have strengths in mischief and teasing, joking and clowning, as demonstrated in Figure 3.3.

As most of the affected components relate to internal control, it is important that for the purpose of intervention, that emphasis be given to play activities that are child initiated, where the child controls the outcome and the material to the level of their competency. Directed play may therefore be contra-indicated for children with ADHD initially, as it would directly impact on their sense of control and motivation. Within the play session, components such as sharing and supporting the other players should be encouraged. Many of their difficulties in play also relate to poor social skills compared to their typically developing peers. It is therefore logical to address these skills further along the play intervention pathway.

Children with Autism

Autism, a pervasive developmental disorder, is characterised by the presence of stereotyped or repetitive behaviours and deficits in the areas of

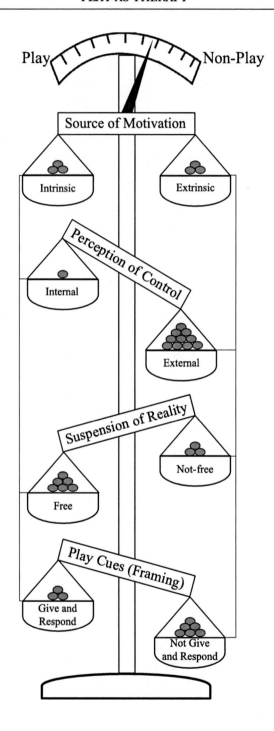

Figure 3.3 Playfulness disrupted in children with ADHD

communication, flexibility and the development of reciprocal social relations (American Psychiatric Association 2000). Social dysfunction has been noted as the most debilitating to the child's quality of life (Batshaw 2002; Newsom 1998). Furthermore, children with autism have impaired abilities to effectively utilise social communication (Marris 1999). Engagement in pretend play is also profoundly affected by autism, with decreased frequency, complexity and novelty of spontaneous pretend play behaviour reported (Rutherford *et al.* 2007).

As it relates to playfulness, it is evident that suspension of reality and framing may be most severely affected in children with autism (see Figure 3.4). Children with autism may appear to be motivated to play by themselves with activities of their choice and have particular strengths and difficulties relating to internal control, thus levelling out. For the purpose of this chapter we will focus on suspension of reality and framing to demonstrate the application of playfulness.

Mischief and teasing (suspension of reality) are observed when the child initiates minor infractions of the rules that may result in a reprimand if caught. Neither reflects meanness as both are done with a 'gleam in the eye' (Skard and Bundy 2008). Children may engage in mischief to shift boundaries in a constraining environment and make play more challenging and fun. This however, is a skill that children with autism struggle with, as it is usually used well by children who are highly skilful at play. Furthermore, children with autism are known for their literal interpretation of situations and the application of objects. Encouragement and guidance may be needed initially to demonstrate how material can be used in unconventional ways in a graded manner.

Framing (giving and responding to social cues) is included in many social skills programmes (Lewis and Boucher 1988). Children with autism may need explicit assistance in interpreting the play cues of players as the play transaction progresses and guidance in appropriate responses to those cues. Imbedded within this is a concerted effort to expand on their repertoire of negotiation skills to have their and their playmates' needs met.

Repetition and intensity within a structured setting are critical to teaching social skills to children with autism (Baron-Cohen and Bolton 1993; McEachin, Smith and Lovaas 1993). Therefore, children with autism may make greater prosocial behavioural gains in direct teaching groups, compared to a play activity group due to the severity of social skills affected (Kroeger, Schultz and Newsom 2007).

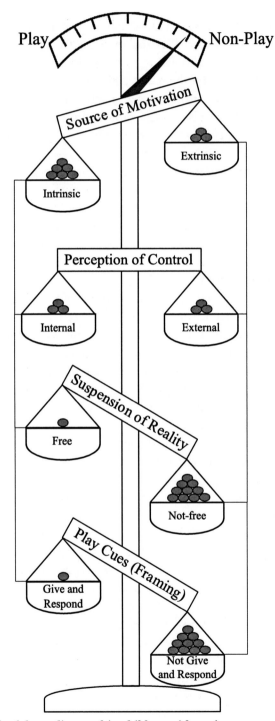

Figure 3.4 Playfulness disrupted in children with autism

Children with physical disabilities

Restricted mobility and accessibility are likely to diminish the opportunities of children with physical disabilities for interactions with potential playmates and the physical environment (Holaday, Swan and Turner-Henson 1997). Children with cerebral palsy receive less feedback from the environment than typically developing children, restricting their capacity to affect the environment. Their ability to give effective non-verbal cues may be restricted, resulting in difficulty for their playmates and caregivers to read their cues, thus cues may be missed or not responded to appropriately. Consequently, this gives the appearance of passivity and unresponsiveness, which in turn may discourage carers and playmates from actively interacting with them (Jennings and MacTurk 1995). This is reflective of decreased internal control, observed as decreased engagement and ability to persist with an activity in the child with a physical disability.

Further implications of disability include the control of the child's physical response by the carer when moving the child's body, impacting on the child's intrinsic motivation and internal control to play. Children with physical disabilities are likely to respond to this by engaging in less eye contact, vocalisation, and independent play (Kogan and Tyler 1973; Lieberman, Padan-Belkin and Harel 1995). As it relates to playfulness, we would expect children with physical disabilities to make fewer decisions about the nature and direction of play, interact less with objects and be less skilled at using objects (Harkness and Bundy 2001), all components of internal control (see Figure 3.5).

Internal control and intrinsic motivation may take precedence in facilitating playfulness for children with physical disabilities. Contrary to the instinct to anticipate the needs of children with physical disabilities, therapeutic emphasis should be given to allow the child to self-initiate play, structuring the environment in such a way to enable easy access and support the child to initiate play activities (see also Chapter 14). This in itself would promote intrinsic motivation, encouraging the child to learn during play activities and become absorbed in play. The principles inherent to internal control serve as an important mediator towards encouraging greater independence for the child and sound inter-dependency between the child, carer and playmates.

CONCLUSION

In summary, the three applied examples demonstrate how the characteristics inherent to different paediatric conditions could result in some components

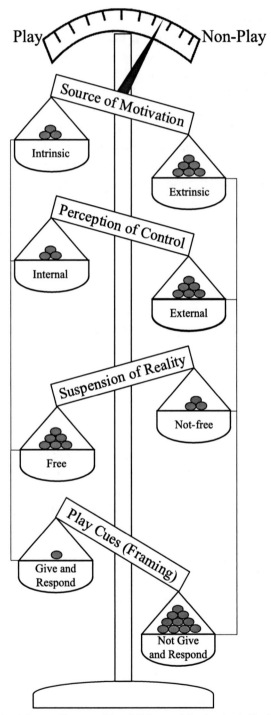

Figure 3.5 Playfulness disrupted in children with physical disabilities

of playfulness being more or less evident during a play transaction. The innately adaptive nature of children encourages them to develop particular strengths in play, compensatory to the difficulties they experience. Subsequently their strengths in play are the observed components of playfulness which got 'caught' in the web of playfulness shown in Figure 3.1. The difficulties they experience are the elusive components of playfulness which escaped the seduction of the web. Through intervention we can encourage them to capture those elusive components by addressing the affected elements of playfulness. The web of playfulness will be spun differently in each play transaction, and together the elements of playfulness will cause the scales to tip the balance between play and non-play.

REFERENCES

American Psychiatric Association (2000) *Diagnostic and Statistical Manual of Mental Disorders,* 4th edn. Washington, DC: Author.

Barkley, R. A. (1997) 'Behavioral inhibition, sustained attention, and executive functions: Constructing a unifying theory of ADHD.' *Psychological Bulletin 121* 1, 65–94.

Barnett, L. (1991) 'Characterizing playfulness: Correlates with individual attributes and personality traits.' *Play and Culture 4,* 371–393.

Baron-Cohen, S. and Bolton, P. (1993) *Autism: The Facts.* New York: Oxford University Press.

Bateson, G. (1971) 'The Message, "This Is Play."' In R. E. Herron and B. Sutton-Smith (eds) *Child's Play.* New York: Wiley & Sons.

Bateson, G. (1972) 'Toward a Theory of Play and Phantasy.' In G. Bateson (ed.) *Steps to an Ecology of the Mind.* New York: Bantam.

Batshaw, M. (2002) *Children with disabilities,* 5th edn. Washington, DC: Paul H. Brookes.

Bundy, A. C. (1991) 'Play Theory and Sensory Integration.' In A. G. Fisher, E. A. Murray and A. C. Bundy (eds) *Sensory Integration Theory and Practice.* Philadelphia: F.A. Davis.

Csikszentmihalyi, M. (1990) *Flow: The Psychology of Optimal Experience.* New York: Harper Perennial.

Cordier, R., Bundy, A., Hocking, C. and Einfeld, S. (in preparation) 'Empathy in the play of children with ADHD.'

deRenne-Stephan, C. (1980) 'Imitation: A mechanism of play behavior.' *American Journal of Occupational Therapy 34,* 95–102.

Garbarino, J., Dubrow, N., Kostelny, K. and Pardo, C. (1992) *Children in Danger: Coping with the Effects of Community Violence.* San Francisco, CA: Jossey-Bass.

Harkness, L. and Bundy, A. C. (2001) 'The Test of Playfulness and children with physical disabilities.' *Occupational Therapy Journal of Research 21,* 2, 73–89.

Hess, L. and Bundy, A.C. (2003) 'The association between playfulness and coping in adolescents.' *Physical and Occupational Therapy in Pediatrics 23,* 2, 5–17.

Holaday, B., Swan, J. H. and Turner-Henson, A. (1997) 'Images of the neighborhood and activity patterns of chronically ill school age children.' *Environment and Behavior 29,* 348–373.

Jennings, K. D. and MacTurk, R. H. (1995) 'The motivational characteristics of infants and children with physical and sensory impairments.' In R. H. MacTurk and G. A. Morgan (eds) *Mastery Motivation: Origins, Conceptualizations and Applications.* Norwood, NJ: Ablex Publishers.

Kogan, K. L. and Tyler, N. (1973) 'Mother–child interaction in young physically handicapped children.' *American Journal of Mental Deficiency 77*, 492–497.

Kroeger K. A., Schultz J. R. and Newsom, C. (2007) 'A comparison of two group-delivered social skills programs for young children with autism.' *Journal of Autism and Developmental Disorders 37*, 808–817.

Leipold, E. E. and Bundy, A. C. (2000) 'Playfulness in children with attention deficit hyperactivity disorder.' *Occupational Therapy Journal of Research 20*, 1, 61–82.

Lewis, V. and Boucher, J. (1988) 'Spontaneous, instructed and elicited play in relatively able autistic children.' *British Journal of Developmental Psychology 6*, 325–339.

Lieberman, D., Padan-Belkin, E. and Harel, S. (1995) 'Maternal directiveness and infant compliance at one year of age: A comparison between mothers and their developmentally-delayed infants and mothers and their nondelayed infants.' *Journal of Child Psychology and Psychiatry 36*, 1091–1096.

Marris, C. (1999) 'Autism: A critical review of psychological theories with particular reference to the development of social understanding.' *Early Child Development and Care 153*, 65–101.

McEachin, J., Smith, T. and Lovaas, O. (1993) 'Long-term outcome for children with autism who received early intensive behavioral treatment.' *American Journal on Mental Retardation 97*, 359–372.

Neumann, E. A. (1971) *The Elements of Play.* New York: MSS Information.

Newsom, C. (1998) 'Autistic disorder.' In E. J. Mash and R. A. Barkley (eds) *Treatment of childhood disorders*, 2nd edn. New York: Guilford.

Pervin, L. A. (1968) 'Performance and satisfaction as a function of individual-environment fit.' *Psychological Bulletin 69*, 56–68.

Reilly, M. (1974) 'An Explanation of Play.' In M. Reilly (ed.) *Play as Exploratory Learning: Studies in Curiosity Behaviour.* Beverly Hills, CA: Sage Publications.

Rubin, K., Fein, G. G. and Vandenberg, B. (1983) 'Play.' In E.M. Hetherington (ed.) *Handbook of Child Psychology: Social Development*, 4th edn. New York: Wiley.

Rutherford, M. D., Young, G. S., Hepburn, S. and Rogers, S. J. (2007) 'A longitudinal study of pretend play in autism.' *Journal of Autism and Developmental Disorders 37*, 6, 1024–1039.

Schachar, R. (1991) 'Childhood hyperactivity.' *Journal of Child Psychology and Psychiatry 32*, 1, 155–191.

Saunders, I., Goodale, A. and Sayer, M. (1999) 'The relationship between playfulness and coping in preschool children: A pilot study.' *American Journal of Occupational Therapy 53*, 2, 221–226.

Skard, G. and Bundy, A. C. (2008) 'Test of Playfulness.' In L. D. Parham and L. S. Fazio (eds) *Play in Occupational Therapy for Children*, 2nd edn. St Louis: Mosby.

Sutton-Smith, B. (1997) *The Ambiguity of Play.* Cambridge, MA: Harvard University Press.

von Zuben, M. V., Crist, P. A. and Mayberry, W. (1991) 'A pilot study of differences in play behavior between children of low and middle socioeconomic status.' *American Journal of Occupational Therapy 45*, 113–119.

Wood, K. (1995) *Attention Deficit Hyperactivity Disorder: A Guide for Professionals.* Melbourne: La Trobe University.

CHAPTER 4

Children and Pretend Play

Karen Stagnitti

CHAPTER OBJECTIVES

This chapter will define pretend play and briefly overview pretend play development. Pretend play (also called imaginative, symbolic, fantasy, representational or make-believe play) is highlighted because it gives us insight into the child's world, is important in the development of the child's language, social skills, problem solving, creativity, and affect and is sensitive to the environment of the child.

INTRODUCTION

In contrast to other chapters in this section, which focus on holistic understandings of play, I will concentrate on one type of play: pretend play. Pretend play ability of children is often dismissed or missed because either adults don't value its contribution to child development or they just don't see it occurring. When we know what pretend play is, it is more likely that we can observe and identify it when watching children play. I often think of pretend play as a great secret, because it is often not recognised for its power and influence in child development. When a child's development in pretend play is delayed it is likely that other aspects of development may be affected. I will begin by identifying pretend play.

DEFINING PRETEND PLAY

Within the literature, there is no dispute that pretend play is play. Pretend play encompasses many of the qualities applied to play in general. Using a cognitive developmental theory approach, the motivation to pretend in play is internally driven with the child voluntarily engaging in the process of playing (Parham and Primeau 1997; Vygotsky 1966). When children pretend in play, they transcend reality by playing out themes such as 'flying to the moon' as well as reflecting reality when they play out events from their own lives. Children are safe when they pretend in play (Sutton-Smith 1967) because they can fight lions and live to tell the tale at the end of the day!

I believe that pretend play is unique because there are three key behaviours that are observed when a child pretends in play, as well as decontextualisation and decentration occurring. The three key behaviours are: substitution of one object to represent another; the attribution of a property to an action or object and reference to an absent object or place (Lewis, Boucher and Astell 1992). These behaviours can be observed when a child plays with toys and/or unstructured objects. For example, substitution of an object can be observed when a child uses a box for a 'bed' or a shoe for a 'telephone'. Attribution of a property can be observed when the child says 'the doll is hungry' or when the child says 'the [box] car is broken down'. Reference to absent objects and places can be observed when a child waves an arm to designate a doorway or refers to a 'planet' the child is 'visiting'. It is also important that children can pretend with both toys and unstructured objects.

Casby (1992) included two additional attributes of pretend play: 'decontextualisation of action' and elements of 'decentration'. Decontextualisation of action is when a child refers to actions, objects or situations that are 'out of context'. For example, the child who sits in a box and pretends to drive a car is decontextualising actions as the box is not a car, whereas 'decentration' is the ability to direct play actions onto something else, outside of the child's self. For example, when a child feeds a doll, the child is directing actions to another object outside of self. The ability to decenter from the self is thought to develop in the child an ability to understand the perspective of others (Baron-Cohen 1996). It is assumed that the child can self-initiate these attributes of play, that is, pretend play is spontaneous. Being able to self-initiate play is a vital component of being able to play.

PRETEND PLAY DEVELOPMENT

The invariant nature of the developmental sequence of pretend play has been well established in the literature (Elder and Pederson 1978; Fein 1981; Lowe 1975; McCune-Nicolich 1977, 1981; Westby 1991). I have detailed this sequence elsewhere (Stagnitti 1997, 1998, 2007). In this chapter I will highlight what I would argue to be the essential components of development in pretend play, which is mostly observed between the ages of 18 months and seven years (Kreye 1987).

What can be confusing for the student of play is that in the literature pretend play is often indirectly discussed as different types of play. For example, 'symbolic play' is discussed in relation to the use of symbols in play (Gowen 1995); 'socio-dramatic play' is when children play out a scene together (Rubin, Fein and Vandenberg 1983); while 'role play' is when children play out roles (Rubin et al. 1983) and 'thematic fantastic play' is when children play out scenes that transcend reality (Wyver and Spence 1995). However, all these play types are increasingly complex expressions of pretend play. When the developmental sequence of pretend play is divided into various stages (i.e. role play, socio-dramatic play), the complexity and common thread of pretend play in a child's development is lost. On the other hand, when pretend play development is viewed as a continuum – with symbolic play, role play, socio-dramatic play and thematic fantastic play seen as expressions of pretend play – then a more complete picture is gained of the child's pretend play abilities. For example, at 20 months a child's play scripts centre around personally experienced events in the home and children imitate adults while just beginning to use the doll in play as separate to themselves, with object substitution beginning with the use of physically similar looking objects to the intended object, though play sequences are still repetitive and often illogical (e.g. a truck is pushed across the floor and then the child finds the logs that should have been in the truck). By four years, however, the child's play scripts reflect personal and fictional events with the child now able to play with others in a negotiated manner with play sequences being logical and complex and pre-planned, the doll has its own character and life, the child is able to hold several roles during the play time and is able to substitute any object for the intended object (Stagnitti 1998). Pretend play is a cognitive play ability and when the continuum of pretend play is divided into separate types of play two important cognitive play skills are lost – sequences of actions and use of symbols in play. I will now examine these two aspects of play development in more detail.

The development of sequential pretend play actions

Initially pretend play develops by children imitating adults and other children. The understanding of simple actions when we observe others is now known to be important for the firing of mirror neurons (Gallese 2007; Rizzolatti, Fogassi and Gallese 2006). These neurons are brain cells which fire when we copy others (mirror them) or when we watch someone else perform the same action (Rizzolatti et al. 2006). It is hypothesised that they help children comprehend other's actions and thus play a role in how children learn about the world, how to act, and how to play.

By two years of age, a child can logically sequence their play actions (Stagnitti 1998). For example, they put the blocks in a truck, push the truck, and then take out the blocks or they feed the doll and put the doll to bed. Logically sequencing play actions reflects the quality of logical thinking. This also means that by two years a child is combining pretend play actions (Westby 1991). Before this time a child's actions are repetitive and often illogical as pretend play is rudimentary in the second year of life. The ability to sequence play actions dictates how long a child plays (i.e. the longer the sequence, the longer the time spent in play) and also reflects the quality or organisation of the child's play.

In the third year of life (24 to 36 months of age) pretend play sequences evolve from a linear sequence (e.g. feed doll, feed teddy, feed mummy) to a hierarchical structure (Lowe 1975). Lowe (1975) explained that a hierarchical structure meant the child was using the doll as an active participant in play. For example, a child may place a cup next to the doll and wait for the doll to have a drink, implying that the doll could drink by itself. This behaviour indicates that the child is decentring – the child is treating the doll as if the doll were alive. By four years of age, the child's sequences in pretend play are complex with the child able to play a sequence of events over several days, sometimes in conjunction with others and usually including sub-plots in the play story (Westby 1991).

In summary, from 18 months to five years (in three and a half years) children's ability to sequence in play moves from imitating a pretend play action to pre-planning a complex story that can be played out over several days or weeks and that incorporates doll figures as active participants in play as well as playmates and objects.

The development of symbols in play

The other important cognitive skill that distinguishes pretend play is the use of symbols in play. This is often referred to as 'symbolic play'. The use of symbols begins when a child uses an object, which is functionally associated with, ambiguous, or physically very similar to the signified object (Stagnitti 1998). In Australia, it is not uncommon for very young children to begin to use a block as a mobile phone by placing a block to their ear and 'listening' to the block. An ambiguous object, such as a block, has least conflict in terms of perceptual and functional qualities with the object it is portraying (Ungerer et al. 1981). I provide more detailed descriptions of the developmental sequence of object substitution in Stagnitti (1998).

After children begin to substitute physically similar or ambiguous objects for the signified object, they begin to become more flexible in their use of objects. That is, they are able to use the same object in substitution for several other objects, (e.g. a box is used as a bed, then a car, then a table). This occurs approximately at two and a half years of age (Stagnitti 1998). While this age group is renowned for temper tantrums and difficulty sharing toys with others, the increasing ability to understand that objects can have several uses lays part of the groundwork for flexibility in joining with others and allowing others to use objects in different ways during play. By four years of age, a child can use any object in substitution. The object does not need to be physically similar (Ungerer *et al.* 1981). Thus a child can use a banana as a telephone or a teddy bear as an aeroplane. After four years, a child uses language to embellish an object's function (Stagnitti 1998).

In summary, the attributes of pretend play (i.e. object substitution, attribution of properties to objects/actions, reference to absent objects, sequencing of play actions, decentration, and ability to play in decontextualised contexts) are unique to children pretending and imagining in play. As children develop their pretend play abilities, they also develop the ability to play alone and with others. By five years of age, a child can assign roles to others, negotiate a play story and play scene, and use a variety of objects in play. To pretend in play, a child requires cognitive play abilities, social interaction skills, language skills, problem-solving skills and emotional self-regulation (Peter 2003; Russ 2005). An example of complex play skills is given in the story of Mary, Bob and Helen.

'Mary, Bob and Helen'

'Mary' was five years old. Her friends 'Bob' and 'Helen' had come over to her house to play. She had an idea that they could play outside pretending to be kings and queens. They would live in a castle (defined by two trees in her backyard), and have adventures riding around their kingdom (on pretend horses) protecting their subjects. Bob was the king and Helen was a princess. Their subjects were the cat and dog. Together they negotiated the play narrative and spent the best part of four hours fighting off enemies of the kingdom, proclaiming new rules of the kingdom and eating great feasts (all imaginary with some support from props such as boxes, sticks and pieces of cloth).

THE IMPORTANCE OF PRETEND PLAY IN CHILD DEVELOPMENT

One of the differences between the view of Piaget (1962) and that of Vygotsky (1997, first published 1934) is that Piaget viewed play as assimilation and thus the child did not create new knowledge by pretending in play, whereas Vygotsky believed that pretend play was a way in which children learnt that one thing could represent another. For Vygotsky, play was causal in a child's development (Pellegrini and Galda 1993). Kreye stated that preschool children spend a substantial part of their waking hours pretending and believed that pretend play 'may in fact be [the child's] primary mode of conceptual organization' (1987, p.305). This is a view shared by Vygotsky (1966) who noted that pretend play was a leading factor in child development.

Pretend play contributes to a child's cognitive and social development in a unique fashion compared to other forms of play behaviour (Doswell *et al.* 1994; Greenspan and Lieberman 1994), as well as giving insight into how the child uses this knowledge in the real world (Westby 1991), and contributes to self-regulation and problem-solving ability (Russ 2005). Pretend play is a window to a child's development and into a young child's mind (Eisert and Lamorey 1996). The importance of pretend play for a child to function in the world is now discussed in more depth.

Pretend play and language

'There is now considerable evidence supporting a relationship between play and language in normally developing children' (Lewis *et al.* 2000, p.117). McCune (1995) found that transitions from one pretend play level to the next preceded language and Lyytinen *et al.* (1999) found that pretend play and vocabulary production of 14-month-old toddlers made a unique contribution to their language skills at two years of age. In the second year of life pretend play actions coincide with two word utterances (Greenspan and Lieberman 1994; McCune-Nicolich 1981). The ability to use language and the ability to pretend play require mental representation and it is this ability to use representational thought that is argued to underlie the link between language and pretend play (Doswell *et al.* 1994; Westby 1991).

Lewis *et al.* (2000), in a study of 40 children aged one to six years, found that symbolising in play (as assessed on the *Test of Pretend Play* (Lewis and Boucher 1997)) was related to expressive and receptive language whereas conceptual knowledge (as assessed by the *Symbolic Play Test* (Lowe and Costello 1988)) was related to expressive language only. From these findings the authors suggested that conceptual knowledge was not sufficient for language development but using symbols in play was of primary importance.

Pretend play and oral language

Pretend play has been linked with literacy skills and academic adjustment in children (Russ 2005; Stagnitti and Jellie 2006). Pretend play and language-literacy both share the use of 'decontextualised language'. When a child uses decontextualised language in play, the child is required to use language to explain to others the meaning of the play (e.g. the story line) as well as meanings of objects used in play. Inability to use decontextualised language has been associated with lack of academic success in children with learning disabilities (Westby 1991). This has led to the conclusion that oral language, school-based literacy (including reading comprehension) and pretend play share the feature of the use of 'cohesive texts' (Pellegrini and Galda 1993). Cohesive texts are used when meaning is conveyed via language and not context (Pellegrini 1985). For example, the meaning is contained *only* in the language and not by use of gestures or context. Cohesive texts (also called literate language) are used during preschool children's pretend play when language minimally relies on context (i.e. more language is required to give meaning to the context). The ability to use cohesive texts is thought to be an important precursor to school-based literacy such as reading and writing (Pellegrini and Galda 1993). In a study of 65 school-aged children Pellegrini (1980) categorised children's play based on Smilansky's play continuum of: functional play, constructive play, dramatic play and games with rules. In this study dramatic play was akin to pretend play because dramatic play was scored when the child pretended to be someone else and language was used to define objects, activities and situations (Pellegrini 1980). Achievement in literacy was measured by word writing fluency and the subtests of pre-reading and school language from the Metropolitan Readiness Test (Nurss and McGauvran 1976). Results of the study indicated that a child's level of pretend play was a significant predictor of achievement performance in reading and writing in the first year of school (Pellegrini 1980).

Williams and Rask (2003) interviewed parents and teachers and found that play was a meaningful context for children to gain metacognitive awareness of why literacy was important. In particular, children enjoyed making up stories in their play and carrying out pretend play in the home using various rooms as different settings for the play. Understanding a story (i.e. a narrative structure) is important for oral language and school-based literacy (Pellegrini and Galda 1993).

Pretend play, narrative competence and social competence

When children pretend in play with others, they are acting out characters in a scene with an unfolding narrative which is reflected in logical sequential actions of the play. Nicolopoulou (2005) argued that pretend play and narrative are a continuum of each other with narratives being the discursive exposition of stories and pretend play being the enactment of story. Jellie (2007) found support for this view when she established that preschool children who had elaborate pretend play used more narrative language with longer sentences and more different words than preschool children who were poorer in their pretend play ability.

Integral to understanding narrative is the understanding of character-appropriate language and how that character is likely to behave – that is, the character's actions, motives, and goals that are consistent with a particular story (Westby 1991). This is part of 'thinking forward', that is, thinking about what might happen next or how a character may act. The ability to think forward and act out a character assists in a child's social competence because it helps the child to understand motives, social causes and consequences (Peter 2003). Children who competently socially interacted with peers (as assessed by teachers using the Penn Interactive Peer Play Scale (Fantuzzo *et al.* 1995)) were found to have more complex levels of pretend play with more elaborate play sequences and use of objects as symbols during pretend play (McAloney and Stagnitti, in press).

A link between pretend play and emotional understanding was found in Lindsay and Colwell's (2003) study when they gathered data on 44 preschool children and found that high levels of pretend play, as assessed by video-tape analysis, were associated with high levels of emotional understanding. Seja and Russ (1999) also found significant relationships between cognitive dimensions of pretend play and ability to describe one's emotional experiences and understanding others' emotional experience. So, children who have high levels of pretend play have been found to be more competent in social interaction with peers, have greater emotional understanding, greater use of narrative language and narrative competence.

CREATIVITY AND PROBLEM SOLVING

Pretend play has been linked with problem solving for several decades now. For example, in 1973 Dansky and Silverman divided the 90 preschool children in their study into three groups. One group played with four objects, one group imitated four behaviours of an adult using the objects, and one group (control group) were asked to colour in some pictures. The children were then asked to provide alternate uses for the four objects they had been playing with. Playing with the objects (group 1) involved object substitution and object manipulation. Children who had had this type of exposure were better at creative thought as assessed on the Associative Fluency Test (Wallach and Kogan 1965). This result supported Dansky and Silverman's hypothesis that pretend play facilitated divergent thinking. In 1995 Wyver and Spence found that preschool children who engaged in high levels of pretend play had higher levels of divergent problem solving and in 1999 Russ, Robins and Christiano followed up 31 children over a four-year period, and found that the quality of a child's pretend play when they were a preschooler predicted divergent problem solving ability over time.

CONCLUSION

In this chapter I have defined and described pretend play. When we can identify it, we can observe whether a child engages in pretend play. Understanding the importance of pretend play to child development increases our understanding of how it links with language, literacy, narrative understanding and social and emotional development. Chapter 6 provides more information on assessing pretend play and Chapter 12 describes a therapeutic technique to help children develop pretend play ability.

Pretend play facilitates the healthy development of emotions, convergent and divergent thought, language-literacy, impulse control, perspective taking, and socialisation (Westby 1991). The benefits to the child of learning how to pretend play can be seen in increased language development, social understanding, and emotional self-regulation (Peter 2003; Russ 2005). In summary, pretend play:

- encompasses and reflects important cognitive skills in the development of the child
- is important to language development
- is associated with social competence
- is important to emotional development.

The healthy development of pretend play is important to a child's health and well-being.

REFERENCES

Baron-Cohen, S. (1996) *Mindblindness. An Essay on Autism and Theory of Mind.* London: MIT Press.
Casby, M. W. (1992) 'Symbolic play: Development and assessment considerations.' *Infants and Young Children 4*, 343–48.

Dansky, J. L. and Silverman, I. W. (1973) 'Effects of play on associative fluency in preschool aged children.' *Developmental Psychology 9*, 38–43.

Doswell, G., Lewis, V., Sylva, K. and Boucher, J. (1994) 'Validation data on the Warwick Symbolic Play Test.' *European Journal of Disorders of Communication 29*, 289–298.

Eisert, D. and Lamorey, S. (1996) 'Play as a window on child development: the relationship between play and other developmental domains.' *Early Education and Development 7*, 221–235.

Elder, J. L. and Pederson, D. R. (1978) 'Preschool children's use of objects in symbolic play.' *Child Development 49*, 500–504.

Fantuzzo, J. W., Sutton-Smith, B., Coolahan, K., Manz, P., Canning, S. and Debnam, D. (1995) 'Assessment of play interaction behaviours in young low-income children: Penn Interactive Peer Play Scale.' *Early Childhood Research Quarterly 10*, 105–120.

Fein, G. (1981) 'Pretend play in childhood. An integrative review.' *Child Development 52*, 1095–1118.

Gallese, V. (2007) 'Before and below 'theory of mind': embodied simulation and the neural correlates of social cognition.' *Philosophical Transactions of the Royal Society B 362*, 659–669.

Gowen, J. W. (1995) 'The early development of symbolic play.' *Young Children 50*, 75–84.

Greenspan, S. I. and Lieberman, A. (1994) 'Representational Elaboration and Differentiation: A Clinical-Quantitative Approach to Clinical Assessment of 2- to 4-year-olds.' In A. W. Slade and D. Wolf (eds) *Children at Play.* New York: Oxford University Press.

Jellie, L. (2007) 'The relationship between pretend play and narrative in preschool children.' Unpublished Master of Science thesis, Flinders University, Australia.

Kreye, M. (1987) *Conceptual Organization in the Play of Preschool Children: Effects of Meaning, Context, and Mother-Child Interaction.* Orlando, FL: Academic Press.

Lewis, V. and Boucher, J. (1997) *The Test of Pretend Play.* London: NFER.

Lewis, V., Boucher, J. and Astell, A. (1992) 'The assessment of symbolic play in young children: A prototype test.' *European Journal of Disorders of Communication 27*, 231–234.

Lewis, V., Boucher, J., Lupton, L. and Watson, S. (2000) 'Notes and discussion. Relationships between symbolic play, functional play, verbal and non-verbal ability in young children.' *International Journal of Language and Communication Disorders 35*, 117–127.

Lindsay, E. W. and Colwell, M. J. (2003) 'Preschoolers' emotional competence: Links to pretend and physical play.' *Child Study Journal 33*, 39–52.

Lowe, M. (1975) 'Trends in the development of representational play in infants from one to three years - an observational study.' *Child Psychology Psychiatry 16*, 33–47.

Lowe, M. and Costello, A. (1988) *The Symbolic Play Test* 2nd edn. Windsor: NFER-Nelson.

Lyytinen, P., Laakso, M-L., Poikkeus, A-M. and Rita, N. (1999) 'The development and predictive relations of play and language across the second year.' *Scandinavian Journal of Psychology 40*, 177–186.

McAloney, K. and Stagnitti, K. (in press) 'Pretend play and social competence. The concurrent validity of the Child-initiated Pretend Play Assessment.' *International Journal of Play Therapy.*

McCune, L. (1995) 'A normative study of representational play at the transition to language.' *Child Development 31*, 198–206.

McCune-Nicolich, L. (1977) 'Beyond sensorimotor intelligence: Assessment of symbolic maturity through analysis of pretend play.' *Merrill-Palmer Quarterly 23*, 89–99.

McCune-Nicolich, L. (1981) 'Toward symbolic functioning: Structure of early pretend games and potential parallels with language.' *Child Development 52*, 785–797.

Nicolopoulou, A. (2005) 'Play and narrative in the process of development: Commonalities, differences, and interrelations.' *Cognitive Development 20*, 495–502.

Nurss, J. R. and McGauvran, M. (1976) *Metropolitan Readiness Tests: Level II Test and Teacher's Manual.* New York: Harcourt Brace Jovanovich.

Parham, L. D. and Primeau, L. A. (1997) 'Play and Occupational Therapy.' In L. D. Parham and L. S. Fazio (eds) *Play in Occupational Therapy for Children.* St Louis MO: Mosby.

Pellegrini, A. D. (1980) 'The relationship between kindergartner's play and achievement in prereading, language and writing.' *Psychology in the Schools 17*, 530–535.

Pellegrini, A. D. (1985) 'The relations between symbolic play and literate behavior: A review and critique of the empirical literature.' *Review of Educational Research 55*, 107–121.

Pellegrini, A. D. and Galda, L. (1993) 'Ten years After: A reexamination of symbolic play and literacy research.' *Reading Research Quarterly 28*, 162–175.

Peter, M. (2003) 'Drama, narrative and early learning.' *British Journal of Special Education 30*, 1, 21–27.

Piaget, J. (1962) *Play, dreams and imitation in childhood.* New York: W. W. Norton.

Rizzolatti, G., Fogassi, L. and Gallese, V. (2006) 'Mirrors in the mind.' *Scientific American 295*, 54–61.

Rubin, K., Fein, G. and Vandenberg, B. (1983) 'Play.' In P. H. Mussen (series ed.) and E. M. Hetherington (vol ed.) *Handbook of Child Psychology: Vol. 4. Socialization, Personality, and Social Development*, 4th edn. New York: Wiley.

Russ, S. (2005) 'Building an Empirical Foundation for the Use of Pretend Play in Therapy.' In C. Shaefer, J. McCormick and A. Ohnogi (eds) *International Handbook of Play Therapy.* New York: Jason Aronson.

Russ, S., Robins, A. and Christiano, B. (1999) 'Pretend play: Longitudinal prediction of creativity and affect in fantasy in children.' *Creativity Research Journal 12*, 129–139.

Seja, A. L. and Russ, S. (1999) 'Children's fantasy play and emotional understanding.' *Journal of Clinical Child Psychology 28*, 269–277.

Stagnitti, K. (1997) *The Development of Imaginative Play.* Poster. Melbourne: Co-ordinates Publications.

Stagnitti, K. (1998) *Learn to Play. A Practical Program to Develop a Child's Imaginative Play Skills.* Melbourne: Co-ordinates Publications.

Stagnitti, K. (2007) *The Child-Initiated Pretend Play Assessment. Manual and Kit.* Melbourne: Co-ordinates Publications.

Stagnitti, K. and Jellie, L. (2006) *Play to Learn. Building Literacy in the Early Years.* Melbourne: Curriculum Corporation.

Sutton-Smith, B. (1967) 'The role of play in cognitive development.' *Young Children* (September), 361–369.

Ungerer, J. A., Zelazo, P. R., Kearsley, R. B. and O'Leary, K. (1981) 'Developmental changes in the representation of objects in symbolic play from 18 to 34 months of age.' *Child Development 52*, 186–195.

Vygotsky, L. S. (1966) 'Play and its role in the mental development of the child.' *Voprosy psikhologii 12*, 62–76.

Vygotsky, L. S. (1997) *Thought and Language*, trans. Alex Kozulin. Cambridge, MA: MIT Press.

Wallach, M. and Kogan, N. (1965) *Modes of Thinking in Young Children: A Study of Creativity-Intelligence Distinction.* New York: Holt, Rinehart and Winston.

Westby, C. (1991) 'A scale for assessing children's pretend play.' In C. Schaefer, K. Gitlin and A. Sandrund (eds) *Play Diagnosis and Assessment.* New York: John Wiley & Sons.

Williams, M. and Rask, H. (2003) 'Literacy through play: How families with able children support their literacy development.' *Early Child Development and Care 173*, 527–533.

Wyver, S. and Spence, S. (1995) 'Cognitive and social play of Australian preschoolers.' *Australian Journal of Early Childhood 20*, 42–46.

SECTION TWO

Play Assessment

CHAPTER 5

Play Assessment:
A Psychometric Overview

Ted Brown and Rachael McDonald

CHAPTER OBJECTIVES

This chapter will provide an overview of psychometric measurement issues in the context of the assessment of children's play. More specifically, the reasons for assessment, stages in the assessment process, types and characteristics of assessment, and contextual influences on play assessment will be discussed. The authors outline measurement properties, reliability and construct validity and demonstrate how effective assessment can facilitate children's optimal participation in play.

REASONS FOR PLAY ASSESSMENT

Children's play is often assessed by child therapists, health care professionals and educators (Bruce 1999; Leech 2007; Parham and Fazio 2008). Rogers and Holm (1989) classified the purposes of assessment as: predictive, discriminative, descriptive and evaluative. *Predictive assessment* provides some indication of expected skill levels in regards to future performance. For example, a child exhibiting poor co-operative play skills in kindergarten might predict that child having later difficulties with team sports participation in primary school. *Discriminative assessment* involves using norms to measure and compare performances for the purpose of diagnosis, placement or establishing the level of function in comparison to the normative group. For example, a child's symbolic play skills can be assessed using a standardised test and compared to matched age-level norms to determine if performance is above or below average. *Descriptive assessment* is simply determining a profile of a child's play skills and interests while *evaluative assessment* involves testing methods that are sensitive enough to detect clinical change when used sequentially. An example would be a child's play skills being evaluated before an intervention programme is started, half way into the programme, and then again at the end of the programme.

There are a number of reasons for conducting play assessment. First, assessment is necessary to establish a baseline of the individual child's performance skills for service planning and therapy intervention. Assessment can be used to inform decisions regarding specific interventions. For instance, a child therapist working in the American primary school system may evaluate a child's play in order to establish goals for that child's Individualised Education Program (IEP). To accomplish this, she might use the *Pediatric Interest Profiles (PIP)* (Henry 2000, 2008) to establish a baseline of a child's play and leisure interests and participation that could inform the IEP process. Second, play assessment can be a means of documenting change in the clinical or developmental status of a child. A therapist might use the *Test of Playfulness (ToP)* (Bundy *et al.* 2001; Skard and Bundy 2008) to observe a child's free play in a naturalistic social play environment in order to monitor the child's progress at different points during a trial of clinical interventions focused on specific play-related abilities. Third, objective play assessment results can be used as a means of supplementing subjective clinical observations. For example, the *Child-Initiated Pretend Play Assessment (ChIPPA)* (Stagnitti 2007) could be used to provide objective and systematic information as well as clinical observations about a child's pretend play skills. Fourth, play assessment results are sometimes used as a goal post or marker for funding thresholds for publicly or privately funded services (i.e. the eligibility for funding for an educational assistant within the classroom). *The Play in Early Childhood Evaluation System* (Kelly-Vance and Ryalls 2005), *Infant-Preschool Play Assessment Scale (I-PAS)* (Flagler 1996a, 1996b) or the *Child Behaviors Inventory of Playfulness (CBIP)* (Rogers *et al.* 1998) might be used as part of a battery of assessments to establish eligibility for additional educational resource funding within a kindergarten classroom for a child with special needs.

Fifth, play assessments are completed as a means to assist with client-centred or family-centred programme planning for children and collaborative goal setting or intervention planning with parents and carers. Play assessment can be used as part of the process of engaging parents and carers in early intervention programmes. Appropriate assessment strategies enable professionals to include individuals and their families in the process of selecting the most compatible and effective interventions for them (Law and

Baum 2005). Sixth, assessment allows therapists to evaluate children's level of play engagement since it is important to know how engaged they are in play to determine the best methods to assist them.

Play assessments can also be used as outcome measures in order to demonstrate that a clinical intervention is effective or to facilitate change that leads to improvement. Services usually need to demonstrate to funding agencies that a contracted service has been provided to a client and to show areas where service development might be required or more resources are needed. In this instance, the *Revised Knox Preschool Play Scale (PPS-R)* (Knox 2008) or the *Penn Interactive Peer Play Scale (PIPPS)* (Fantuzzo and Hampton 2000) could be used to evaluate a play-based early intervention programme designed to promote social and communication skills in children with autism spectrum disorder. Similarly, play assessment using the *ChIPPA* and the *ToP* could provide specific evidence about the efficacy of therapeutic pretend play and playfulness interventions. Play assessment therefore contributes to the knowledge base of practice and theory of different therapeutic disciplines.

In summary, play assessment may be a management, clinical, client-perspective or professional tool. Therapists have both a professional and ethical responsibility to assess the need for service, design interventions based on assessment information and evaluate the results of play-based interventions. This provides an evidence base for therapeutic play interventions. Different types of play assessment are completed at different stages of the assessment process. These stages and types will now be described.

FUNDAMENTALS OF CLINICAL PLAY ASSESSMENT

Stages of the assessment process

The assessment of play can take place at different stages of the therapy process (i.e. initial referral, during the intervention process, post intervention) and in different settings (i.e. child's home, school, childcare centre, kindergarten, community health centre, local playgroup, playground or the hospital/clinical setting). The clinical play assessment and intervention process falls into a continuum of steps outlined in Figure 5.1.

Types of play assessment methods and tools

The development of a play assessment involves a process of improvement and evaluation to ensure that the assessment is reliable, valid, consistent, responsive and useful. There are many different types of play assessment tools which child therapists can use in their clinical practice including

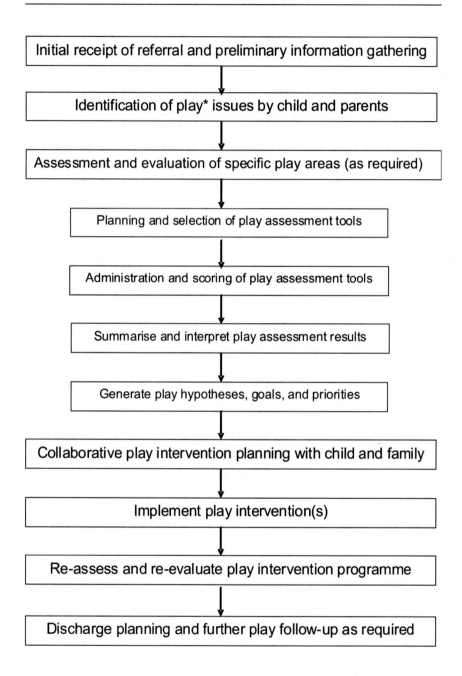

Play: includes play, recreation, and leisure

Figure 5.1 Steps in the play assessment and intervention process

standardised and non-standardised as well as formal and informal play instruments (Parham and Fazio 2008). Some examples include observational play assessments such as the *Assessment of Ludic Behaviors* (Ferland 1997) and the *Test of Environmental Supportiveness* (Bronson and Bundy 2001); play scales completed by parents such as the *Children's Playfulness Scale* (Barnett 1990, 1991); and checklists like the *Transdisciplinary Play-Based Assessment* (Linder 2008), which are used to document the absence or presence of behaviours on a prescribed list. Performance-based assessments usually require a child to complete an activity which is then scored or rated against performance criteria, e.g. *Symbolic Play Test* (Lowe and Costello 1982).

Standardised play assessments have pre-established protocols for administration and scoring of scale items. In the case of children, their performance scores are recorded and then compared to normative data. After administering and scoring the test items, the child's raw score is used to calculate a standard score, which provides a comparison of the child's performance with other children of the same age. A number of scores are associated with standardised assessment including scaled scores, t-scores, percentile ranks, stanines and age-equivalents (Kielhofner 2006). Standardised tests of play are more rigid in their administration protocols and have well-established reliability and validity data.

Formal tests usually have a manual that documents development, theoretical rationale, potential uses, standardisation, reliability and validity testing, and responsiveness to change. They also have a test manual which includes a set of instructions to follow and scoring criteria. In contrast, informal or non-standardised tests can take the form of checklists or assessment task kits, often created by clinicians for their own specific use. Although widely used in the practice context, they lack norms, a test manual and evidence of established reliability and validity. Often informal scales augment the clinical observations made by therapists during the assessment process.

Norm-referenced tests have scale items that are scored and then specifically compared to scores of a large population sample in order to determine how a child's test score compares to the normative sample scores (Anastasi and Urbina 1997). An example of a norm-referenced test of play is the *ChIPPA* (Stagnitti 2007). Norm-referenced tests are often used as scholastic achievement tests. Criterion-referenced tests are those that have scale items based on the published empirical research findings instead of the average performance scores of a normative sample at different age levels. The *PPS-R* (Knox 2008) is an example of a criterion-referenced play assessment.

The final type of test is based on the way they are completed, in other words, the answering format used – interview schedules, surveys with open ended questions, rating scales, true/false scales and Likert scales (McDowell 2006). For example, some tests have scale items where children have to complete a task and then their task performance is scored on a number of specific criteria such as the *Pediatric Activity Card Sort* (Mandich *et al.* 2004).

Characteristics of play assessment tools

Assessment tools need to meet a specific number of criteria in order for their test scores to be considered useable and practical. Psychometric criteria include reliability, validity, responsiveness to change and clinical utility or practicality. *Reliability* is the ability of the items of a test or scale to measure a construct, attribute, or trait on a consistent basis. Specific types of reliability include:

- *Internal consistency* or the degree to which the items of a test are correlated with one another (correlations >0.80), indicating homogeneity between test items.

- *Alternate-form reliability / Equivalent-forms reliability* is the use of alternate or equivalent test forms to obtain correlations between parallel forms of the same test. The results from performance on the first half of the test are correlated with the second half or the scores on all even-numbered items are compared to odd-numbered ones.

- *Split-half reliability* is when the items of a scale are split into two groups and the scores from the two tests are then correlated together.

- *Test-retest reliability* is the ability of a test to exhibit some degree of score stability between two separate administrations of the same test 1–2 weeks apart.

- *Intra-rater reliability* is the ability of the same person to score test items consistently between two administrations.

- *Inter-rater reliability* is the ability of two different people to score test items consistently between two administrations. Correlation coefficients of >0.85 are typically expected to ensure consistency between two raters on the same test.

Content validity describes how well a test measures the scope of the attribute or trait that it purports to evaluate, whereas *face validity* examines whether the scale items appear to address the purpose of the test and the variables that it purports to measure. It is subjective and is based on the local judgement by the author or experts on the topic. *Criterion-related validity*, on the other hand, is when an outside criterion is compared to the test to determine its accuracy in measuring a phenomenon. Two types of criterion-related validity are used:

- *Concurrent / Congruent validity* is when the relationship between the instrument in question and other already validated instruments that measure the same phenomenon is established.

- *Predictive validity* is the ability of an instrument to forecast future behaviour, abilities or performance of participants who complete a test.

Construct validity is how well a test measures the theoretical facets of a construct it purports to measure. Specific types of construct validity include:

- *Convergent validity* is the extent to which a construct is correlated with constructs believed to be similar.

- *Divergent validity* is the extent to which a construct is dissimilar from other constructs believed to be unrelated or different.

- *Discriminant validity* is the ability of a test to differentiate between two groups of participants with known differences (e.g. group with a clinical diagnosis compared with a group who are clinically normal).

- *Factor analysis validity* – items of a test, grouped together, measure the construct they were intended to measure. It also includes the identification of interrelated behaviours or abilities in an individual that contributes to the collective functions.

Clinical validity is how well the scores of a test can be used to predict future clinical performance and health care outcomes. How sensitive a test is to change in the clinical status of a person is called 'responsiveness to change'. This also depends on 'clinical utility' or the clinical usefulness of a tool in terms of length, time to complete (also known as 'respondent burden'), scoring format and complexity of items.

Assessment tools have a number of statistics associated with them and some of these are listed in Table 5.1. One criterion that has recently been revised is the way that test validity is defined.

Table 5.1 Statistical terms used in assessments

Statistic	Definition
Raw Score	A child's score on a test before the score is converted to a comparison scale or normative information.
Frequency Distribution	The tabulation of raw scores into a table or graph to represent groupings of scores into intervals or total tallies.
Norms	The reported test performance of individuals with specific demographic characteristics in the standardisation sample.
1. Normative Sample	The standardisation group.
2. Developmental Norms	The standardisation of group scores reflecting developmental sequence or stages; frequently age-equivalents are stated so that individual performance can be compared to the normative sample.
Measures of Central Tendency	
1. Mean (M)	The average score calculated by adding all scores together and then dividing by the number of the cases.
2. Mode	The most frequent score.
3. Median	The middle-most score when all scores have been arranged in order of small to large.
Normal Distribution	The use of the normal, 'bell-shaped' curve, which has the largest number of responses in the middle.
Measures of Variability	
1. Standard Deviation (SD)	Refers to how far each item score varies from the mean. Regions marked off on the normal curve, starting at the centre, which subdivide scores that vary from the mean or central tendency, 68.26% of the curve is within the area of + 1 SD; + 2 SD is equal to 95.44% of the curve; and + 3 SD is equal to 99.72% of the curve.

Table 5.1 *cont.*

2. Variance	Refers to how far each score varies from the median.
3. Range	Refers to the lowest and highest scores within a group of scores.
Significance level (p)	This identifies the probability that chance influences the results or outcomes. The lower the level, the less confidence in the results. The probability for confidence is usually set at 0.05 or better which means that the probability for a given score or result occurring by chance is less than 5 out of 100.
Error of Measurement	The difference between the real score of a child and the observed score during one session. Error is introduced through different forms of bias and inability to use the test as designed.
Rater Bias	The error introduced by raters when they do not use standardised or consistent procedures and protocols outlined in a test manual when administering it to children.
Standard Error of Measurement (SEM)	The amount that a child will deviate from the true score as a result of irrelevant or chance events as well as sources of error in measurement. It represents the reliability of individual scores.
Standard Error of Estimate (SE)	The degree of predictive validity or margin of error in a person's criterion score. It represents the validity of a test.
Percentile Score / Rank	A score for a child that is reported as the percentage of those children who fall below the child's raw score on a scale.
Standard Score	A derived score that expresses a child's score in terms of distance from the mean.

Statistic	Definition
1. z-score	A child's score that is expressed using the standard deviation from the mean of the normative sample. It is expressed at the mean +1 standard deviation.
2. t-score	A child's score is normalised with 50 representing the mean of the standardisation group and +10 the standard deviation (expressed as 50+10).
3. Stanine	A child's score that is transformed into a score ranging from 1 to 9 with a mean of 5 and + 2 standard deviations approximately (expressed as 5+2).

TEST VALIDITY AND CLINICAL PLAY ASSESSMENT

To ensure that tests are accurately assessing what they purport to measure, they must demonstrate evidence of reliability and validity. Traditionally validity was viewed as a three-part concept made up of content, criterion-related and construct validity (Anastasi and Urbina 1997; Cook and Beckman 2006; Downing 2003). In the most recent edition of the *Standards of Psychological and Educational Testing* (American Educational Research Association [AERA], American Psychological Association [APA], and National Council on Measurement in Education [NCME] 1999), the conceptualisation of validity has markedly changed. The view of validity theory prevailing today is largely based on the seminal work of Messick (1989, 1994, 1995).

The current emphasis is that all validity is subsumed under construct validity and is concerned with 'an overall evaluative judgment of the degree to which empirical evidence and theoretical rationales support the adequacy and appropriateness of interpretations and actions on the basis of test scores or other models of assessment' (Messick 1989, p.741). Although there are numerous methods available to determine validity, validity is now viewed as a unitary concept, meaning that the various approaches to it are related components that can be combined to evaluate what inferences can be made from test scores. Therefore, contemporary play assessment should consider construct validity from a unitary perspective.

The most important issue in the development and evaluation of a play measure is therefore the process of validation which involves the accumulation of evidence to provide a sound empirical foundation for proposed interpretations of test scores. In the contemporary context, validity refers to evidence generated to support or refute the meaning or interpretation assigned to test results. 'Validity is never assumed and is an ongoing process of hypothesis generation, data collection and testing, critical evaluation and logical inference' (Downing 2003, p.831). Therefore, as play scales and instruments are developed, researched and used, a body of knowledge contributing to their construct validity is being established. For example, the *ToP-Version 4* (Skard and Bundy 2008), *Home Observation for Measurement of the Environment (HOME)* (Bradley 1994), and the *PIECES* (Kelly-Vance and Ryalls 2005) all have developing bodies of construct validity evidence.

These conceptualisations of construct validity integrate the traditional components of content, criteria and construct validity. Five subcomponents of construct validity evidence are included as a means of addressing the central issues implicit in the notion of validity as a unified concept. These evidence subcomponents are:

1. content

2. substantive/content

3. structural/response processes

4. generalisability/internal structure/relations to other variables/external

5. consequential aspects of construct validity.

They function either as validity criteria or as standards for all measurement. Therefore, when a new play-based assessment tool is being created or an existing tool is being revised, the test's authors need to report the construct validity-related evidence under the five validity evidence categories. In other words, test authors need to establish a bank of evidence from a variety of sources and obtained in a variety of manners to support or refute the construct validity of a play-based tool.

APPLYING A PRACTICE MODEL TO PLAY ASSESSMENT

Practice-based models often provide the rationale for gathering construct validity evidence. For example, the *International Classification of Functioning (ICF)* model is a universal classification of functioning, disability, and health as experienced by the individual in the context of his or her everyday life (World Health Organization 2001). The ICF is organised into two components: functioning and disability factors (health conditions, body structures and functions of people, the activities people do and the life areas in which they participate) and contextual factors (environmental and personal). Functioning and disability factors can theoretically be applied to all people, while contextual factors are individualised and also political. In this model functioning is an umbrella term relating to the body or body part, the person, or the whole person in a social context (Australian Institute of Health and Welfare 2003). The ICF attributes a person's functioning, disability and health to contextual factors. These comprise the physical, social and attitudinal environment in which people live and conduct their lives, and may act as barriers or facilitators to the person's functioning (Law 2002). The activity, participation, personal factors and environmental factors provide the context for the assessment of children's play skills.

For example, when assessing a child's play skills and level of play engagement, difficulties can be caused by functioning and disability factors of a health condition and the resultant issues with body functions and structures, which in turn impacts on a child's activities and participation. This limits children's play activities and abilities to participate in play-related experiences, particularly in peer situations. In other contexts, the environment can either help or hinder a child's play progression and abilities, and this must therefore also be a consideration in play assessment. Furthermore, personal factors (such as socioeconomic status, cultural values, belief systems, parental and family styles and functioning) will impact a child's opportunities to engage in play and therefore needs to be assessed also. The ICF model considers contextual factors that impact on clinical play assessment.

Contextual influences on play assessment practices
There are a number of societal laws in place that potentially impact on the assessment of children's play. This can be at the level of government (e.g. Department of Education or Health), professional college or registration board as well as the individual work place/clinical setting level (e.g. school, hospital, early intervention programme, private practice, community health centre, child and adolescent psychiatric treatment centres). In Australia (where education is under state jurisdiction) in order for children to be eligible for funding to access extra classroom assistance they have to score at least two standard deviations below average on certain types of mandated assessments. In spite of the evidence about the positive impact of play on

children's development of the skills needed for future life and functioning, play-based scales are still not usually part of this assessment regime.

The service setting also influences the choice of assessment with different assessment priorities existing in schools, early intervention settings, psychosocial treatment programmes and private practice. The amount of time available for the assessment process is in part driven by the type of reimbursement or funding model for professional services. If the time factor for assessment is limited, 'this may mean that an evaluation is limited to initial screening tools, followed by limited specific assessments...comprehensive assessment of all areas of concern is impractical in such a situation...the therapist has to be both focused on the areas to be assessed and skilled enough to choose and administer specific assessments' (Stern and Dutton 1998, p.130). The choice of play assessment, then, needs to be carefully considered if a child's play is to be assessed.

With more focus on accountability by those who fund health care services, the cost of evaluation must be justified. This requires the clinician to limit the selection of assessments to those that deal with the immediate needs of the client, given the setting. The roles and responsibilities in the practice environment also impact the test selection of clinicians. This is particularly true when global outcome measures such as the *Adaptive Behaviour Assessment System* (Harrison and Oakland 2000) are used. Each team member contributes his or her scores to calculate a single composite score for the client. A play-related tool that can be completed with input from a variety of team members is the *Transdisciplinary Play-Based Assessment* (Linder 2008). Unfortunately, the assessment of play is not often included as part of a comprehensive assessment of children.

It has also been emphasised that ecological inventories are a means to bridge assessment and intervention in order to better meet the school aged child's needs. The school version of the *Assessment of Motor and Process Skills (AMPS)* (Fisher, Bryze and Hume 2002) is an example of an ecological assessment tool.

CONCLUSION

This chapter has provided a brief outline of clinical play-related assessment. The stages of the assessment process, types of assessments, and characteristics of assessment tools were presented to provide a context for play assessment for the reader. Using play assessments with strong psychometric measurement properties (validity and reliability) is vital for professionals working with children and their families.

REFERENCES

American Educational Research Association, American Psychological Association, and National Council on Measurement in Education (1999) *Standards for Educational and Psychological Testing.* Washington, DC: American Psychological Association.

Anastasi, A. and Urbina, S. (1997) *Psychological Testing.* Upper Saddle River, NJ: Prentice Hall International.

Australian Institute of Health and Welfare (AIHW) (2003) *ICF Australian User Guide. Version 1.0.* Disability Series, AIHW cat. no. DIS 33. Canberra ACT: AIHW.

Barnett, L. A. (1990) 'Playfulness: Definition, design, and measurement.' *Play and Culture 3,* 319–336.

Barnett, L. A. (1991) 'The playful child: Measurement of a disposition to play.' *Play and Culture 4,* 51–74.

Bradley, R. H. (1994) 'The HOME Inventory: Review and Reflections.' In H. Reese (ed.) *Advances in Child Development and Behaviour.* San Diego CA: Academic.

Bronson, M. and Bundy, A. C. (2001) 'A correlational study of the Test of Playfulness and the Test of Environmental Supportiveness.' *Occupational Therapy Journal of Research 21,* 223–240.

Bruce, T. (1999) *Time to Play in Early Childhood Education.* London: Hodder & Stoughton.

Bundy, A. C., Nelson, L., Metzger, M. and Bingaman, K. (2001) 'Reliability and validity of a test of playfulness.' *Occupational Therapy Journal of Research 21,* 276–292.

Cook, D. A. and Beckman, T. J. (2006) 'Current concepts in validity and reliability for psychometric instruments: Theory and application.' *American Journal of Medicine 119,* 166.e7–e16.

Downing, S. M. (2003) 'Validity: On the meaningful interpretation of assessment data.' *Medical Education 37,* 830–837.

Fantuzzo, J. and Hampton, V. (2000) 'Penn Interactive Peer Play Scale: A Parent and Teacher Rating System for Young Children.' In K. Gitlin-Weiner, A. Sandgrund, and C. Schaefer (eds) *Play Diagnosis and Assessment.* New York: John Wiley & Sons.

Ferland, F. (1997) *Play, Children with Physical Disabilities and Occupational Therapy: The Ludic Model.* Ottawa: University of Ottawa.

Fisher, A. G., Bryze, K. and Hume, V. (2002) *School AMPS: School Version of the Assessment of Motor and Process Skills.* Fort Collins CO: Three Star Press.

Flagler, S. (1996a) *I-PAS Infant-Preschool Play Assessment Scale.* Lewisville, TX: Kaplan.

Flagler, S. (1996b) *Multidimensional Assessment of Young Children Through Play: Preacademic Skills Assessment.* Lewisville, TX: Kaplan.

Harrison, P. and Oakland, T. (2000) *Adaptive Behavior Assessment System.* San Antonio, TX: The Psychological Corporation.

Henry, A. D. (2000) *Pediatric Interest Profiles: Surveys of Play for Children and Adolescents.* San Antonio, TX: Therapy Skill Builders.

Henry, A. D. (2008) 'Assessment of play and leisure in children and adolescents.' In L. D. Parham and L. S. Fazio (eds) *Play in Occupational Therapy for Children.* St Louis, MO: Mosby Elsevier.

Kelly-Vance, L. and Ryalls, B. O. (2005) 'A systematic, reliable approach to play assessment in preschoolers.' *School Psychology International 26,* 398–412.

Kielhofner, G. (2006) 'Developing and evaluating quantitative data collection instruments.' In G. Kielhofner (ed.) *Research in Occupational Therapy: Methods of Inquiry for Enhancing Practice.* Philadelphia: F. A. Davis Company.

Knox, S. (2008) 'Development and Current Use of the Revised Knox Preschool Play Scale.' In
    L. D. Parham and L. S. Fazio (eds) *Play in Occupational Therapy for Children.* St Louis, MO:
    C. V. Mosby.

Law, M. (2002) 'Participation in the occupations of everyday life.' *American Journal of
    Occupational Therapy 56,* 640–649.

Law, M. and Baum, C. (2005) 'Measurement in Occupational Therapy.' In M. Law, C. Baum
    and W. Dunn (eds) *Measuring Occupational Performance: Supporting Best Practice in
    Occupational Therapy.* Thorofare, NJ: Slack Incorporated.

Leech, S.W. (2007) 'Play Assessments.' In I. E. Asher (ed.) *Occupational Therapy Assessment: An
    Annotated Index.* Bethesda, MD: American Occupational Therapy Association.

Linder, T. W. (2008) *Transdisciplinary Play-Based Assessment, (TPBA) Second Edition (TPBA2).*
    Baltimore, MD: Paul H. Brooks.

Lowe, M. and Costello, A. (1982) *The Symbolic Play Test,* 2nd edn. Windsor: NFER Publishing.

Mandich, A., Polatajko, H., Miller, L. and Baum, C. (2004) *Pediatric Activity Card Sort PACS.*
    Ottawa: Canadian Association of Occupational Therapists.

McDowell, I. (2006) *Measuring Health: A Guide to Rating Scales and Questionnaires.* New York:
    Oxford University Press

Messick, S. (1989) 'Validity.' In R. Linn (ed.) *Educational Measurement.* New York: American
    Council on Education and Macmillan Publishing.

Messick, S. (1994) 'The interplay of evidence and consequences in the validation of
    performance assessments.' *Educational Researcher 23,* 13–23.

Messick, S. (1995) 'Validity of psychological assessment: Validation of inferences from persons
    and performances as scientific inquiry into score meaning.' *American Psychologist 50,*
    741–749.

Parham, L. D., and Fazio, L. S. (2008) *Play in Occupational Therapy for Children.* St Louis, MO:
    Mosby Elsevier.

Rogers, C. S., Impara, J. C., Frary, R. B., Harris, T., *et al.* (1998) 'Measuring playfulness:
    Development of the Child Behavior Inventory of Playfulness.' *Play and Culture 4,*
    121–135.

Rogers, J. C. and Holm, M. B. (1989) 'The therapist's thinking behind functional assessment.'
    In C. B. Royeen (ed.) *American Occupational Therapy Association (AOTA) Self-study Series –
    Assessing Function.* Rockville, IN: AOTA.

Skard, G. and Bundy, A. C. (2008) 'Test of Playfulness.' In L. D. Parham and L. S. Fazio (eds)
    Play in Occupational Therapy for Children. St Louis MO: Mosby Elsevier.

Stagnitti, K. (2007) *Manual of the Child-Initiated Pretend Play Assessment (ChIPPA).* Melbourne:
    Co-ordinates Publications.

Stern, K. and Dutton, R. (1998) 'Assessment Selection.' In J. Hinojosa and P. Kramer (eds)
    Evaluation: Obtaining and Interpreting Data. Bethesda, MD: American Occupational Therapy
    Association.

World Health Organization (WHO) (2001) *International Classification of Functioning, Disability
    and Health.* Geneva: WHO.

CHAPTER 6

Pretend Play Assessment

Karen Stagnitti

CHAPTER OBJECTIVES

In this chapter the development of two play assessments is described: the *Symbolic and Imaginative Play Developmental Checklist* and the *Child-Initiated Pretend Play Assessment.* An overview of these assessments is given with evidence of reliability and validity, and an explanation of why pretend play assessments are important when working with children.

INTRODUCTION

The assessment of children's play has proved a difficult undertaking. What appears to be so simple, is in fact one of the most complex of human behaviours and it has been suggested that the difficulty in defining play has further hindered play assessment development (Kalverboer 1977; Kielhofner and Barris 1984). More recently, there has been a shift towards a more focused approach to play assessment with the realisation that play is so complex and broad that an assessment of all that is play is not viable within a reasonable time frame.

There are many play assessments available (Gitlin-Weiner, Sandgrund and Schaefer 2000) and each has its own assumptions of what play is and how play behaviours manifest in children's everyday life. However, I found that the available play assessments didn't lend themselves easily to a clinical situation and so I found myself not assessing children's play, but rather assessing developmental skills and making assumptions about their play. Not surprisingly, when I asked parents and teachers they also gave differing views on a child's play because they see children in different contexts (Sturgess and Ziviani 1995).

DEVELOPING AN ASSESSMENT OF PLAY

I believe that a child's healthy development in play is crucial to that child's well-being. Putting this belief into practice in my workplace required an assessment of play that was accurate and that could be used in the clinical setting. To some, a clinical assessment of play is heresy, especially if the view is taken that play is only influenced by the social context and so multiple observations of a child are needed before any conclusions can be reached about that child's play ability. However, as a busy therapist with a heavy caseload, such a luxury of time was not available to me nor was it practical.

So, I began the process of developing my own play assessment for use in a clinical setting. First, I needed a working definition of play. After a review of the play literature I came to the conclusion that all writers in the area agree that pretend play is play. Moreover, there were essential features that had been identified as only being observed when a child was engaging in pretend play (Lewis, Boucher and Astell 1992). These were: the substitution of objects (e.g. using a banana as a telephone), the attribution of a property to an object or place (e.g. a 'sick' doll) and reference to an absent object or place (e.g. a wave of an arm designates a door space). Pretend play, by its very nature, contains unique behaviours only observed during play. It is the quintessence of play (Stagnitti 2004). Pretend play is a spontaneous self-initiated activity of the child which has meaning for the child (Vygotsky 1966). It increases in complexity as children develop, therefore, pretend play assessment is likely to discriminate the play of developmentally younger children from developmentally older children. Underlying this increasing complexity in pretend play is the assumption that the preschool child prefers pretend play because it is more interesting and challenging than simpler forms of play such as exploration of objects.

WHY ASSESS PRETEND PLAY?

Pretend play ability is a powerful indicator of a child's development and well-being. It reflects the cognitive skills of the child and is related to learning, problem-solving ability and creativity (Russ 2003). It is important for social development (Guralnick, Hammond and Connor 2003), language (McCune 1995), literacy – oral language and narrative language (Nicolopoulou 2005; Pellegrini and Galda 1993), and emotional understanding (Russ, Robins and Christiano 1999). Pretend play development is also sensitive to abusive and neglectful environments with maltreated children showing poorer pretend play ability (Alessandri 1991). Therefore, an assessment of a child's ability to spontaneously initiate pretend play would probably indicate how that child was coping within their environment and how they were developing.

A review of play assessments conducted in the late nineties revealed only two available standardised assessments of pretend play that could be used clinically. One assessment, the *Symbolic Play Test* (Lowe and Costello 1988) does not actually assess symbolic play but rather assesses how the child functionally relates toys together. The other assessment, the *Test of Pretend Play* (Lewis and Boucher 1997) assesses symbolic play and sequences in play actions. Lewis and Boucher recommended that the *Test of Pretend Play* be used with the *Symbolic Play Test* to gain a fuller understanding of the child's pretend play. While both are valuable clinical assessments in their own right, they largely rely on a series of structured tasks presented by the therapist to assess play and do not assess self-initiated spontaneous play. In my own clinical work, I wanted a play assessment that identified: how a child spontaneously played, if the child had a play dysfunction, and guided the interpretation of play dysfunction with respect to a child's development. Consequently, I developed two play assessments: the *Symbolic and Imaginative Play Developmental Checklist (SIP-DC)* (Stagnitti 1998) and the *Child-Initiated Pretend Play Assessment (ChIPPA)* (Stagnitti 2007). The following assumptions underpin these clinically viable play assessments:

1. Play is voluntary (Parham and Primeau 1997).

2. Self-initiation of play is an important cognitive skill.

3. Pretend play is the mature form of play in childhood (Fein 1981).

4. Pretend play is a cognitive play ability (Vygotsky 1966).

5. Pretend play ability is important in social interaction for the pre-schooler (Guralnick *et al.* 2003).

6. Pretend play is about understanding implied meanings in a situation so has cognitive, social, emotional implications (Baron-Cohen 1996).

7. Pretend play gives an insight into a child's inner world (Fein 1981).

8. Pretend play is implicated in creativity and problem solving (Russ 2003).

9. Pretend play is measurable.

10. Without an assessment of pretend play, only part understanding of the child's development is gained.

In any assessment of children's play, it is important to observe what children can do by themselves. To do this the therapist has to be passive. The play assessments described in this chapter measure a child's spontaneous initiation of pretend play and are not therapist-directed.

THE *SYMBOLIC AND IMAGINATIVE PLAY DEVELOPMENTAL CHECKLIST (SIP-DC)* (STAGNITTI 1998)

The *SIP-DC* provides a framework for observing and assessing a child's development in pretend play (see Chapter 4). It can be used in conjunction with the *Learn to Play* programme, which is cross-referenced with the developmental levels of the checklist (see Chapter 12). The *SIP-DC* assesses the development of a child's pretend play up to five years of age across six domains: *play scripts* (previously called themes); *sequences of play actions; object substitution; social interaction; role play;* and *doll/teddy play*. The age categories of the checklist are: 12 months (pre-imaginative play); 18 months; 20 months; 2 years; 2½ years; 3 years; 3½ years; 4 years and 5 years. The checklist is laid out in a grid with play abilities listed across the top and ages listed down the side. Visually, the grid is made up of boxes and if a child can spontaneously initiate play ability/ies then a dot is placed in the appropriate box that corresponds to the child's age and play ability being observed. If the child cannot spontaneously initiate play, then the therapist can begin to model play actions (e.g. give a drink to a doll or place objects in a truck and push it). If the child imitates the therapist's play action then a small square is drawn within the appropriate box. If a child does not display the play ability nor imitate the ability, the box is left blank. When completed, the *SIP-DC* gives a visual profile of the child's spontaneous play abilities, imitated abilities and missing or undeveloped abilities.

To administer the *SIP-DC*, the child can either be observed in a familiar setting such as a playgroup or home with familiar toys or the therapist can present the child with a set of toys (Stagnitti 1998). For children under three years of age, toy suggestions are a truck, teddy, cup, cloth and box. For children over three years, a group of toys can be presented (i.e. a doctor's kit or farm set) in conjunction with unstructured objects. The toys are presented to the child and the therapist invites the child to play with them. The therapist can join the child in play by modelling play actions if the child is losing interest or does not seem able to play with the toys.

The *SIP-DC* can be used for direct observation by therapists or it can be used as a guide for interviewing parents about their child's play abilities. In my clinical work I often found that parents interpreted 'good play' as the child not annoying them or the child entertaining themselves. When using the *SIP-DC* as a guide in interviewing parents, I take out the months on the side of the grid so the parents focus on their child's play ability. This way the parent is not dismayed about their child's development and the parent is focused on what their child does at home. I have found that using the *SIP-DC* with parents helped them become more aware of what to look for in their child's play and often they were able to be very specific about their child's play abilities when they understood what was being asked. The *SIP-DC* includes Developmental Skill Charts for each play ability. The charts have a description and picture of the play ability on each developmental level for each play ability. In this way, both literate and illiterate parents can use the charts effectively.

To date, there has been little research using the *SIP-DC*. A small study by Coombs (2002) found significant positive correlations between the *SIP-DC* sequences of play actions and object substitutions with the cognitive sub-test of the *Bayley Scales of Infant Development* (Bayley 1993).

The value of the *SIP-DC* lies with its clinical application. By using the checklist, a therapist can identify which of a child's abilities within pretend play are weak and which abilities are developing well. Furthermore, becoming skilled at observing a child's pretend play ability using the *SIP-DC* provides a strong basis for play assessment using the *Child-Initiated Pretend Play Assessment (ChIPPA)* (Stagnitti 2007). The *ChIPPA* provides the next level of sophistication for play assessment.

THE *CHILD-INITIATED PRETEND PLAY ASSESSMENT (ChIPPA)* (STAGNITTI 2007)

The *ChIPPA* is a norm-referenced standardised assessment of a child's ability to spontaneously initiate pretend play. It can be used in a clinical, school, community or home setting requiring only a quiet room. A norm-referenced standardised assessment of play provides information on children's skills in relation to their peers. With such an assessment, other professionals working with the child are forced to take play seriously because if the child's play is significantly delayed, then play intervention as an option for the child cannot be ignored.

The age range for the *ChIPPA* is from three years to seven years 11 months. It takes 18 minutes to administer to three-year-olds and 30 minutes to administer to four to seven-year-olds. The *ChIPPA* assesses play in two sessions: an *conventional-imaginative play session* and a *symbolic play session*. At the time of writing, the ChIPPA is the only available assessment that assesses the spontaneous ability of a child to initiate pretend play in both conventional-imaginative play and symbolic play, that is, play with toys as well as unstructured objects. The play assessment materials for the *ChIPPA* have been chosen based on gender neutrality and developmental appropriateness (Stagnitti, Rodger and Clarke 1997). This was important so that the child's play abilities were being assessed, not the child's like or dislike of the toys. For the *conventional-imaginative* play session the toys resemble a farm set for the four to seven-year-olds and for the three-year-olds, a selection of toys including dolls, trucks, animals and tea-set. The play materials for the *ChIPPA* had to be readily recognisable and 'common', so no 'fad' toys make up the play materials. The *ChIPPA* has been used with children in Australia, Singapore, Japan, Switzerland, Finland and England with only a recommendation for the removal of the wrench from the *ChIPPA* when used with Japanese children. (The Japanese children were not familiar with such an object.) As the *ChIPPA* is a pretend play assessment, children do not have to use the toys as they appear. For example, I have seen cows fly over the moon; the truck and trailer turned over to make a bridge; the fences laid out like a house floor plan, and all the animals go to a dance and have a good time! The children with these play ideas were developing strong play skills for their age.

Administration

To administer the *ChIPPA* the therapist prepares a 'cubby house' (called a 'wendy house' in the UK) made from a sheet thrown over two adult chairs so that there is a space between the chairs covered by the sheet. The idea of a 'cubby house' to Australian children is one of fun, enjoyment and play. The therapist and child sit on the floor in front of the 'cubby house', which frames the space for the play area and if the child wishes, gives the child a space to play in. The therapist presents one of the play material sets to the child and invites the child to play, giving no instructions of what to do, how to do it, or any ideas for use of the play materials (see Figures 6.1 6.2). After 15 minutes (or nine minutes for three-year-old children), the other set of play materials is introduced to the child. The *ChIPPA* is child-centred and non-directive, so it is up to the child what they do during the assessment.

ChIPPA items

The measurements or items on the *ChIPPA* are: the *percentage of elaborate pretend play actions (PEPA)*, the *number of object substitutions (NOS)*, and the

Figure 6.1 A child playing with the conventional imaginative play materials of the ChIPPA

Figure 6.2 A child playing with the unstructured play materials of symbolic play of the ChIPPA

number of imitated actions (NIA). Each of these items is scored for each session. There is also a combined score, meaning that nine scores are generated from the assessment. The *PEPA* score gives information on the length of play sequences and the level of complexity of a child's play, that is the elaborateness of the play and the level of organisation. The *NOS* scores gives an indication of whether the child can use symbols in play and the *NIA* score indicates whether the child needs to imitate the therapist in order to play.

Scoring

The scoring of the *ChIPPA* is flexible and adaptable so that no child is un-assessable on the *ChIPPA*. Every action the child makes during the *ChIPPA* sessions is coded, according to one of four play action codes. By the end of the assessment the pattern of play action codes on the score sheet shows how self-organised and consistently the child played out ideas, and whether the child logically sequenced the play. For example, if there were many codes for repetitive and functional actions on the score sheet, then the pattern of scores would indicate that the child only related the objects together in single, unrelated actions (functional actions) and then repeated these actions. With this type of pattern the child's play would lack pretend play elements, with the child moving the play materials around but not really creating a story or complex level of play sequences.

The number of object substitutions is a defining behaviour of pretend play ability. Each object the child uses as a symbol in play is scored. The other two defining behaviours of pretend play (i.e. attribution of properties and reference to absent objects or places) are scored within elaborate actions (see Stagnitti 2007). During each session of the *ChIPPA* there is a segment when the therapist introduces a second doll and randomly models five play actions. This allows for the scoring of the number of imitated actions. There is also a clinical observations form which is filled in after the 30-minute period (or 18-minute period for three-year-olds). The clinical observations form provides qualitative information on the child's play. Play theme analysis can also be carried out with the *ChIPPA* for children who have been emotionally traumatised.

Interpretation of the ChIPPA

The child's *ChIPPA* assessment can be interpreted on several levels. First, the pattern of play codes on the child's score sheet indicates the process of the child's play. It also indicates how the child responded to the therapist's modelling with the second doll and if symbols were used in play and when. The clinical observations form has 'typical indicators of play' and 'indicators of play deficits' with many circles on the latter indicating that the child is struggling in play.

Second, all the elaborate scores (*PEPA*) and object substitution scores (*NOS*) for symbolic play and the combined score can be compared to standard scores of play from the child's aged peer group. There is a choice of two norm comparisons. One is based on z scores and a score of -2 or lower indicates a child is significantly delayed in play ability compared to peers. The other choice is a standard score where 100 is the mean and 15 is the standard deviation. For the standard scores, a score of 70 or below indicates significant delay. For the remaining scores of the *ChIPPA* (i.e. the *NIA* scores and *NOS* object substitution score for the conventional-imaginative session) a range of scores expected for the child's age is given as well as percentiles and mode. The reason for this is that the vast majority of children tested, do not imitate the therapist (therefore they score 0) and use the conventional imaginative play materials in a non-symbolic way. To illustrate how the *ChIPPA* is useful in clinical practice, a case example of 'Harry' is given.

Case Study: Harry

Harry is an Anglo-Australian boy aged four years 8 months. He lives at home with his mother and younger brother. At home Harry needs constant attention and entertaining. He gravitates to the TV and computer games, and when outside kicks a ball around. At preschool he joins in physical play with a group of peers but when observed closely he is following what they do. He knocks down other children's block constructions and has never been observed playing in the sand pit. He can be disruptive to the play of his peers and needs monitoring by an adult. He has difficulty answering questions about a story which has just been read to him. On the *ChIPPA*, Harry performed poorly in both sessions with low scores in elaborate play for conventional-imaginative play and symbolic play. Harry's scores are detailed in Table 6.1. His play themes were not aggressive but he did throw the unstructured objects around because he did not know what to do with them. He was particularly poor at symbolic play scoring 0 per cent for elaborate play. He used two symbols in play which places him in the lowest 10 per cent for his age group. He imitated the therapist four times which is much more than expected for his age. His poor scores in symbolic play suggest he has difficulty playing in unstructured play spaces which is possibly why he avoids (or is disruptive in) the sand pit or block corner.

Table 6.1 Harry's *ChIPPA* score profile

ChIPPA item	Harry's raw scores	Harry's standard scores	Harry's percentile scores
Elaborate play (*PEPA*) in the conventional imaginative play session	39%	-2.05 (69.21)	
Elaborate play (*PEPA*) in the symbolic play session	0%	-2.58 (61.27)	
Elaborate play (*PEPA*) for both sessions	39%	-2.65 (60.22)	
Number of object substitutions (*NOS*) conventional imaginative play session	0		
Number of object substitutions symbolic play session	2	-1.25 (81.18)	10th percentile
Number of object substitutions for both sessions	2	-1.25 (81.18)	10th percentile
Number of imitated actions (*NIA*) for conventional imaginative session	2		5th percentile
Number of imitated actions (*NIA*) for symbolic play session	2		10th percentile
Number of imitated actions (*NIA*) for both sessions	4		5–10th percentile

Harry's *ChIPPA* assessment indicates that he cannot logically sequence and organise his play. He showed no evidence of attribution of properties or reference to absent objects, although he has limited ability to substitute objects. His inability to sequence play actions relates to his inability to understand stories as he does not develop his own stories or sequences in his play. He has difficulty initiating play ideas and his play is experimental and manipulative. His conventional-imaginative play shows many functional actions indicating that he can relate objects together but does not develop his play to a higher level expected for his age. He requires someone to guide him in play, which is possibly the reason for his passivity with his peer group and his imitation of the therapist's modelled actions. It is recommended that Harry have play intervention sessions.

A third way to interpret the *ChIPPA* is play style analysis which is based on the pattern of the *ChIPPA* scores. To date, four play styles for typical players have been found. The general style of a typical player on the *ChIPPA* is within normal to high scores for all *PEPA* scores, within normal to high scores for *NOS* scores in symbolic play and the combined score and no imitations in either session of the *ChIPPA*. Creative children will score *NOS* for the conventional imaginative play session. Of the typical play styles, the 'Narrative play style' is the most common with children self-initiating a story in the play and as they develop the play displaying the ability to logically sequence the play narrative while using objects as symbols and self-initiating all play ideas. Six play styles for children with play deficits have been identified and one of these is the 'Imitator play style' where the child has poor ability to sequence play actions (low *PEPA* scores across both play sessions), low *NOS* scores across both play sessions, and high *NIA* indicating the need to imitate someone else in order to play. Harry's profile is similar to the 'Imitator Play Style', although with many functional actions, Harry's profile would also include the 'Functional Player'. The 'Functional Player' looks busy relating objects together but their play lacks depth and complexity. The play deficit play styles include styles of play where the child is not able to play across the two sessions of the *ChIPPA* or can only play with one set of play materials in one session.

As a general overview the following indicates poor play ability as assessed on the *ChIPPA*:
Low *PEPA* scores indicate one or more of the following:

- The child cannot logically sequence play actions.
- The child cannot elaborate play actions.
- The child is poorly organised in play.
- The child cannot play constructively for periods of time expected of his/her age.
- The child may be at risk of failing at school in literacy.
- The child may be at risk for ability in narrative language.
- The child cannot sustain play, and so playing with others is difficult.
- The child is poorer at problem solving.
- The child is less flexible and adaptable than peers.
- Child is 'internally' chaotic.

Low *NOS* scores indicate one or more of the following:

- The child is at risk for language delay.
- The child is at risk for narrative language delay.
- The child is poor at problem solving.
- The child is a literal thinker and unable to understand alternate uses for objects.
- The child is not as creative as peers.
- The child is unable to use symbols in play.
- The child is less flexible and adaptable than peers.

High *NIA* scores indicate one or more of the following:

- The child needs someone to show them how to play.
- The child has difficulty initiating play ideas.
- The child is less inclined to be able to entertain him/herself.
- The child is more inclined to let peers take the lead in play.

RELIABILITY AND VALIDITY OF THE *ChIPPA*

In Chapter 5 the concepts of reliability and validity are outlined. In this section I report the research on the reliability and validity of the *ChIPPA* to date. There have been two studies on inter-rater reliability. One measured inter-rater reliability by video tape and showed complete agreement (K = 1.00) to excellent agreement (K = .96 to .98) across all *ChIPPA* scores (Stagnitti, Unsworth and Rodger 2000). The second study measured inter-rater reliability in situ and revealed a substantial level of agreement at K = 0.7 across all *ChIPPA* scores (Swindells and Stagnitti 2006). Test-retest reliability with a sample of 38 typical preschool children has been established with ICC's (2,1) showing good reliability at 0.85 to moderate test-retest reliability at 0.56 (Stagnitti and Unsworth 2004).

Stagnitti *et al.* (2000) demonstrated that the *ChIPPA* discriminated pre-schoolers with suspected pre-academic problems from typically developing preschoolers based on their *ChIPPA* scores. Children with developmental delay are significantly different in their play scores from typically developing children with lower elaborate play scores and object substitution scores and higher numbers of imitated actions (Stagnitti 2002). McAloney and Stagnitti (in press) and Uren and Stagnitti (in press) with a sample of 53 preschoolers and 41 primary school aged children, respectively, investigated the concurrent validity of the *ChIPPA* with the *Penn Interaction Peer Play Scale* (Fantuzzo *et al.* 1995). Both studies found that children who can elaborate their play were socially interactive with their peers (McAloney and Stagnitti in press; Uren and Stagnitti in press). Children who were poor at object substitution ability were more likely to disrupt the play of their peers and children with poor elaborate play and object substitution were more likely to be disconnected from their peers (McAloney and Stagnitti in press; Uren and Stagnitti in press). Swindells and Stagnitti (2006) found that children with poor *ChIPPA* scores were rated by parents as co-operative, possibly due to the fact that some children with poor play are passive when playing with others. In a predicative validity study, Stagnitti (2002) found that the quality of a preschool children's pretend play was predictive of their language and narrative re-tell in early primary school. Jellie (2007) also found that the quality of preschool child's pretend play as assessed on the *ChIPPA* was indicative of their narrative language ability, particularly their play with the imaginative conventional play materials.

In conclusion, a child-initiated pretend play assessment reveals a child's abilities as they are, without adult intervention. With this information, the therapist has a clearer understanding of the child's skills and what type of intervention would be most beneficial to the child. Without an assessment of a child's spontaneous pretend play ability, we are missing a crucial aspect of a child's development. With such an assessment, we have greater insight into how and why that child has difficulties or otherwise.

REFERENCES

Alessandri, S. (1991) 'Play and social behaviour in maltreated preschoolers.' *Development and Psychopathology 3*, 191–205.

Baron-Cohen, S. (1996) *Mindblindness*. Cambridge, MA: MIT Press.

Bayley, N. (1993) *Bayley Scales of Infant Development*, 2nd edn. San Antonio, TX: The Psychological Corporation.

Coombs, G. (2002) 'Validation of the Symbolic and Imaginative Play Developmental Checklist.' Unpublished Masters thesis, Master of Psychology (Educational and Developmental), Monash University, Australia.

Fantuzzo, J. W., Sutton-Smith, B., Coolahan, K., Manz, P., Canning, S. and Debnam, D. (1995) 'Assessment of play interaction behaviours in young low-income children: Penn Interactive Peer Play Scale.' *Early Childhood Research Quarterly 10*, 105–120.

Fein, G. (1981) 'Pretend play in childhood. An integrative review.' *Child Development 52*, 1095–1118.

Gitlin-Weiner, K., Sandgrund, A. and Schaefer, C. (eds) (2000) *Play Diagnosis and Assessment*, 2nd edn. New York: John Wiley & Sons.

Guralnick, M., Hammond, M., and Connor, R. (2003) 'Subtypes of non-social play: Comparisons of children with and without developmental delays.' *American Journal of Mental Retardation 108*, 5, 247–362.

Jellie, L. (2007) 'The relationship between pretend play and narrative in preschool children.' Unpublished masters thesis, Flinders University, Adelaide, Australia.

Kalverboer, A. F. (1977) 'Measurement of Play: Clinical Application.' In B. Tizard and D. Harvey (eds) *Biology of Play*. Philadelphia: Lippincott.

Kielhofner, G. and Barris, R. (1984) 'Collecting data on play: a critique of available methods.' *Occupational Therapy Journal of Research 4*, 151–180.

Lewis, V., Boucher, J. and Astell, A. (1992) 'The assessment of symbolic play in young children: A prototype test.' *European Journal of Disorders of Communication 27*, 231–245.

Lewis, V. and Boucher, J. (1997) *The Test of Pretend Play. Manual*. London, Psychological Services.

Lowe, M. and Costello, A. (1988) *The Symbolic Play Test*, 2nd edn. Windsor: NFER-Nelson.

McAloney, K. and Stagnitti, K. (in press) 'Pretend play and social play: The concurrent validity of the Child-Initiated Pretend Play Assessment.' *International Play Therapy Journal*.

McCune, L. (1995) 'A normative study of representational play at the transition to language.' *Child Development 31*, 198–206.

Nicolopoulou, A. (2005) 'Play and narrative in the process of development: Commonalities, differences and interrelations', *Cognitive Development 20*, 4, 495–502.

Parham, L. D. and Primeau, L. A. (1997) 'Play and Occupational Therapy.' In L. D. Parham and L. S. Fazio (eds) *Play in Occupational Therapy for Children*. St Louis, MO: Mosby.

Pellegrini, A. D. and Galda, L. (1993) 'Ten years after: A reexamination of symbolic play and literacy research.' *Reading Research Quarterly 28*, 162–175.

Russ, S. W. (2003) 'Play and creativity: Developmental issues.' *Scandinavian Journal of Educational Research 47*, 291–303.

Russ, S. W., Robins, A. L. and Christiano, B. A. (1999) 'Pretend play: Longitudinal prediction of creativity and affect in fantasy in children.' *Creativity Research Journal 12*, 129–139.

Stagnitti, K. (1998) *Learn to Play. A Program to Develop a Child's Imaginative Play Skills*. Melbourne: Co-ordinates Publications.

Stagnitti, K. (2002). *'The development of a child initiated assessment of pretend play.'* Unpublished doctoral thesis, LaTrobe University, Melbourne, Australia.

Stagnitti, K. (2004) 'Understanding play: implications for play assessment.' *Australian Occupational Therapy Journal 51*, 3–12.

Stagnitti, K. (2007) *The Child-Initiated Pretend Play Assessment.* Manual and kit. Melbourne: Co-ordinates Publications.

Stagnitti, K., Rodger, S. and Clarke, J. (1997) 'Determining gender-neutral toys for assessment of preschoolers imaginative play.' *Australian Occupational Therapy Journal 44*, 119–131.

Stagnitti, K. and Unsworth, C. (2004) 'The test-retest reliability of the Child Initiated Pretend Play Assessment.' *American Journal of Occupational Therapy 58*, 93–99.

Stagnitti, K., Unsworth, C. and Rodger, S. (2000) 'The development of an assessment to identify play behaviours that discriminate between the play of typical preschoolers and preschools with suspected pre-academic problems.' *Canadian Journal of Occupational Therapy 67*, 5, 291–303.

Sturgess, J. and Ziviani, J. (1995) 'Development of a self-report play questionnaire for children aged 5 to 7 years: A preliminary report.' *Australian Occupational Therapy Journal 42*, 107–117.

Swindells, D. and Stagnitti, K. (2006) 'Pretend play and parents' view of social competence: the construct validity of the Child-Initiated Pretend Play Assessment.' *Australian Occupational Therapy Journal 53*, 314–324.

Uren, N. and Stagnitti, K. (in press) 'Pretend play, social competence and involvement in children aged 5–7 years. The concurrent validity of the Child-Initiated Pretend Play Assessment.' *Australian Occupational Therapy Journal.*

Vygotsky, L. S. (1966) 'Play and its role in the mental development of the child.' *Voprosy psikhologii 12*, 62–76.

CHAPTER 7

Play Skill Assessment for Middle Childhood

Jennifer Sturgess

CHAPTER OBJECTIVES

This chapter will provide an understanding of the importance of play in middle childhood and provide a rationale for assessing play in this age group. A review of some assessments is given and a range of play skills which have been found to be valid for middle childhood are discussed. A method for assessing play skills by child self-report is described.

INTRODUCTION

The age group of six to ten-year-olds is under-represented in the literature about children's play and there is even less literature about play and assessment for this age group. This chapter asserts that the middle childhood / early primary school age group is nevertheless highly involved in play, and that particular play skills for this age can be identified. Additionally, this age group is characterised by emerging self-understanding and therefore asking the child about their play could ideally complement play assessment (Sturgess, Rodger and Ozanne 2002).

PLAY AND ASSESSMENT

Play has advantages for assessing children because of its capacity to reflect emerging skills, the spontaneous use of acquired skills, self-regulation, arousal, problem-solving ability, motivation and purposefulness

(Gitlin-Weiner 1998). Play also has the advantage of being able to be used for assessment repeatedly with no learning effect on the part of the child (Gitlin-Weiner 1998). Play is therefore an accepted medium for assessing various capacities of children in a range of contexts.

The concept being examined by many play assessments should be carefully considered. Some play assessments evaluate the developmental level of a child's play skills or the quality of play according to certain criteria. For example, the *Knox Revised Preschool Play Scale* (Knox 1997) is designed to assess play development and the *Test of Playfulness (ToP)* (Bundy 1997) assesses the playfulness of a child. These, however, are examples for a younger age group as very few play assessments for middle childhood exist. Other assessments use play to evaluate non-play capacities such as maturity, cognitive ability and emotional security. For example, Schaefer, Gitlin, and Sandgrund qualified this type of assessment as 'the process by which trained professionals observe play behaviours to understand an individual's or a group of individuals' psychosocial functioning' (1991, p.6).

If a child's play is to be assessed, the reason for assessment should correspond to the aspect of play that the assessment tool explores or evaluates (Bundy 2001; Sturgess 1997). While this may appear self-evident, experience has repeatedly demonstrated that reasons for assessing play are often poorly articulated by the clinician. The intention to evaluate a child's play is based on an understanding of the significance of play to a child's health and occupational roles. Nevertheless, due to the lack of available instruments to choose between, analysing the reason for assessing play and matching this to the correct tool is usually neglected. In Chapter 5 the ICF model is used as an example of thinking through the reasons for assessing play and the type of assessment that would be suitable.

A further consideration in selecting the appropriate play assessment/s for the child is the position on the health–impairment–wellness continuum at which the assessment occurs. The location of the assessment, such as in a hospital ward or in the child's home, will have an effect on the features of an assessment judged as suitable. For example, a different type of play assessment tool would be needed to evaluate the premorbid picture of play for a child who is now confined to bed recovering from severe burns, compared to a child with intellectual impairment being evaluated for the most appropriate schooling option. Some assessments are needed to find out about a child's interests and motivating play scenarios while others need to meticulously examine play abilities and playfulness for a comprehensive developmental overview.

Play assessment can also be used as a method of evaluating change in a child as the result of some specific treatment modality, where theoretical reasoning suggests that a change in play should occur. Schaaf, Merrill and Kinsella (1987) in a case report, hypothesised that change in a child's play behaviour could be indicative of effectiveness of a sensory integration treatment regime. More recently, the *ToP* (Bundy 1997) was used to evaluate the playfulness of children with and without autism in inclusive and non-inclusive preschool programmes (Reed, Dunbar and Bundy 2000). Here the play assessment was used to attempt to evaluate types of intervention.

The evaluation of play as an outcome measure however, requires a wider range of psychometrically sound play measures than is currently available. Russ (1999) suggested play assessment could measure positive features such as joyfulness, openness to emotion and enjoyment of fantasy as well as providing evidence of the quality of a child's transaction with the human and non-human environment. A choice about the aspects of play to assess, which will be most useful, should be made for each individual child.

Some reasons for assessing a child's play are:

- to establish baseline data about a child's underlying skills, such as cognitive, communication, motor and social skills

- to assess the developmental stage of a child's play compared to others of similar age

- to find out about a child's play preferences and range of play interests

- to evaluate environmental factors which influence a child's play

- to determine how well a child is able to engage in playful behaviour in a range of contexts

- to understand a child better, with the assumption that play is an expressive medium (similar to language when a child is limited in his/her verbal language abilities for whatever reason)

- to learn which aspects of play or other issues cause a child discomfort or concern

- to understand which aspects of play a child is keen to have assistance with through technology, carer support, or personal skill development so that participation can be enhanced (Sturgess 1997).

SPECIFIC PLAY ASSESSMENTS FOR MIDDLE CHILDHOOD

One play assessment, the *Assessment of Ludic Behaviours (ALB)*, was developed by Ferland (1997) for use with children with a disability. Although completely standardised for administration within a comprehensive 'ludic' (from the Latin, meaning playful and referring to a model wherein play is the prime purpose of life) model, the assessment has no reported evidence of reliability. However, it is the sole assessment of play available which is useable for all levels of childhood disability and is often cited in therapy literature (e.g. Pollock *et al.* 1997). Like most play assessments, it is structured as adult observations of children's play, albeit in naturalistic or standardised situations.

Paediatric Interest Profiles (Henry 2000) are surveys of play for children and adolescents. They are included here although content covers a wide range of leisure and sporting interests, socialising, classes and other activities. There are three assessments in all that are designed for play assessment: the *Kid Play Profile* for ages 6–9 years, the *Preteen Play Profile* for 9–12 years, and the *Adolescent Leisure Interest Profile* for approximate ages of 12–21 years. The adolescent version was developed first, for a mental health context, and has acceptable psychometrics, whereas there are no psychometric data for the other two profiles for younger groups. The *Kid Play Profile* is in the form of a booklet with line drawings and other graphics, which appear somewhat 'busy' in design for young children. While it has limited usefulness for locations which do not have snow and ice as a regular feature of the environment, the profiles can be considered a welcome start.

Three self-report assessments developed recently by occupational therapists for children include leisure and play activities. Although not specifically designed to assess play, they are the *Children's Assessment of Participation and Enjoyment & Preferences for Activities of Children (CAPE/PAC)* (King *et al.* 2004), the *Perceived Efficacy and Goal Setting System (PEGS)* (Missiuna *et al.* 2004), and the *Paediatric Activity Card Sort (PACS)* (Mandich *et al.* 2004). The PEGS, for example, includes items about playing sport, ball games and video games, while the activities on the PACS include such things as bicycling, drawing/colouring, hopscotch, hockey, board games with friends and trampolining. These three tools are important for assessing play activities within the total range of daily activities of children.

The *Transdisciplinary Play-Based Assessment* (Linder 1990) aims to use play as the medium to assess a child's function. Based on pre-report by parents a structured play session is implemented and observational data about performance from a developmental perspective is collected. This assessment is striking for its multidisciplinary approach and comprehensiveness. It is, however, expensive in terms of time resources and therefore limited in applicability to contexts where long term support and/or intervention are needed such as the therapeutic special education setting.

The need for a wider range of play assessments has been demonstrated repeatedly (Couch, Deitz and Kanny 1998; Rodger, Brown and Brown 2005; Sturgess 1997). The need for context-based play assessment was demonstrated by Way (1999) through research about the influences that different play environments have on the child's play responses due to the action of their sympathetic and parasympathetic nervous systems. A theoretical link was made about the influence of differing play environments on children with post traumatic stress disorder (PTSD). A logical step from this work might be to include a range of environments or contexts in an assessment of children's play, so as to tap variability which might arise from neurological responses. Haight (2004) suggested a need to develop more explicit criteria for the effective use of play therapies. Importantly, Haight recognised a need to be able to identify the emergent play skills in children with special needs and target interventions towards supporting and developing these skills.

The range of play based assessments for middle childhood is limited. The most recent advances have been in clarifying what types of assessments are needed. To date there has been little attempt to ask children themselves about their play skills or their perception of their own play ability. It is only recently with the publication of the *PACS* (Mandich *et al.* 2004) and the *CAPE/PAC* (King *et al.* 2004) that play preference is able to be tapped in a structured fashion. Assessment of play has been primarily adult-driven despite differences having been identified between what adults say they observe and what children say they were doing (Smith *et al.* 1985), with little recognition that play is a child-chosen activity (Sturgess 2003).

Because play is so personal and is imbued with fantasy and/or non-reality, it is conceptually appropriate to ask the player about his/her play. To use a language metaphor, if play is a language, the translation has the most chance of being accurate if it is done by the player/speaker rather than by an observer/listener. Van der Kooij (1989) theorised that observational methods of play did not gather concepts related to play such as internal locus of control and intrinsic motivation as these were intensely personal to the child.

PLAY SKILLS OF MIDDLE CHILDHOOD

In middle childhood the reasons behind assessing a child's play skills are likely to be to shed light on social or behavioural concerns about the child due to concerns about emotional stresses a child is experiencing or, lastly, because a child has a significant illness or physical trauma which will affect his/her transactions with others and with the environment. In these scenarios the child is likely to have an opinion about both his/her play and also about his/her needs within the context where a play assessment is deemed appropriate. Therefore the child should be provided with a real and supported opportunity to talk about his/her play skills and overall play enjoyment.

The author's doctorial research identified play skills appropriate to children in middle childhood from the research literature and evaluated these with both children and their parents (Sturgess 2007). Findings suggested that five to ten-year-old-children were able to evaluate their ability at these play skills as very good, good, quite good or not good. Parents and carers, however, gave different evaluations from their children on more than half of these same play skills. The author proposes that in this age group significant adults should not be the only source of information about a child's play and that the child has a unique and valid perspective to offer.

DEVELOPMENT OF THE *PLAY SKILLS SELF-REPORT QUESTIONNAIRE (PSSRQ)*

Fundamental to the concept of a child self-report questionnaire about play skills are the notions that playing and playfulness are central and beneficial activities in a child's life during the phase from preschool and middle primary school, and that a child is able to comment with unique value about these skills. Play is usually integrated with many aspects of a child's daily life such as in the school playground during breaks, at home with or without siblings while parents are otherwise engaged, during chore-based activities with family such as baking, or during free time with neighbourhood peers. In tandem, involvement in play provides opportunity for honing skills such as physical coordination, language, sociability, thinking and problem solving.

Therefore in any situation in which a child is working with a professional on some aspect of everyday human and non-human transactions, the capacity to ask a child about their play and play skills is valuable. Such play questions can shed light on the child's play skills in various contexts, on the aspects of play or common roles with which the child is experiencing difficulty, and on the activities and roles which are of highest *value* for the child currently – either for pleasure, or where the child would like to feel more capable.

Play may be judged differently by participant and observer (Smith *et al.* 1985). Because of this difference both parent and child perspectives should be included in assessment of play. To address this need the author designed, constructed and developed the *Play Skills Self-Report Questionnaire (PSSRQ)*, a self-report assessment of play skills for children aged between five and ten years, and an associated parent/carer version (Sturgess 2007). Some examples of the items in the children's and the parents/carers' published versions (Sturgess 2008) are presented in Table 7.1 for clarity.

The purpose of the *PSSRQ* children's questionnaire is to gather a 5–10-year-old child's perception of his/her current ability on a set of 29 play skills that were found to have acceptable face and content validity. Three pilot studies were used to develop this face and content validity. The first pilot study asked a group of expert paediatric occupational therapists and speech pathologists to independently rate and provide feedback on 34 draft items and two sets of wording of these items. These 34 draft items were also evaluated in similar fashion by a group of parents. The results were pooled and a set of 30 items with wording similar to the final version was accepted for trial. The third pilot study was to test the questions with a group of children.

Prior to the third pilot study graphics were attached to each question, and an answer structure was chosen. Extensive literature and theory was reviewed to decide that the graphics needed to be black and white so as to be minimally emotive but attractive, to have simple people and ordinary ideas so as not to be too leading, to have a balance of genders in the figures overall, and to adhere to accepted visual literacy practices. The majority of the graphics were created by two adolescent girls aged 13 and 15 with younger male siblings aged eight and ten. The girls were artistic. They were intentionally chosen to be closely linked to childhood perspectives. They were provided with the questions and asked to create drawings which they felt related to the questions (see Figure 7.1). The remaining questions which were unable to be completed by the girls due to time constraints were illustrated by a male occupational therapist with an expert background in play theory and clinical practice who was also an artist. This process ensured a rigorous standard of test development.

For the parent/carer version (see Figure 7.2 for an example) the questions were slightly changed in wording. However in order to ensure a similar concept of the play skill was rated, the parent/carer version was designed to include a minimised version of the same graphic as the child's version.

A full research study was then completed to investigate the validity and test-retest reliability of the *PSSRQ.* One hundred and seventy-six typically

Table 7.1: *Play Skills Self-Report Questionnaire (PSSRQ)* skill items	
Organising to play	• Ability to find something to play when at home • Able to make a collection of things you like for fun • Playing games where you have to follow rules • Able to play card games, board games or computer games
Social play skills in different contexts	• Ability to play with a group of other kids • Able to try and fix up fights or arguments when playing with other kids • Ability to play with just one other child (dyad) and find something to do together • Able to enjoy playtime at school • Able to join a game that other kids have already started playing • Able to find someone to play with at school • Able to talk with friends about a game while playing
Creative and imaginative play skills	• Ability to make things sometimes when playing • Able to draw or make pictures for fun • Able to make up ideas for pretend games • Able to pretend to be someone or something else in a game
Physical and coordination skills in play contexts	• Ability to run, and climb and move when playing • Able to dance or do tricky moves for fun • Able to play in a team for sport • Able to play outside – home, parks, playground • Able to ride bikes, skates, etc. • Able to be careful when playing with little things • Playing rough and tumble for fun
Family and home play	• Ability to play with a grown-up • Ability to enjoy playing with brothers and/or sisters • Able to find something to play when need/want to make self feel better • Able to play quiet inside games • Able to play cubby or tree-house games • Finding a place to play alone at home when he/she wants to

Are you good at making things sometimes when you play?

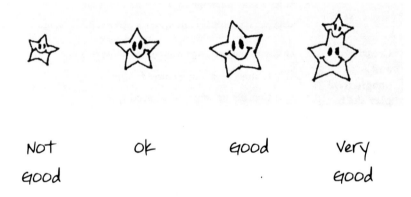

Not   ok   Good   Very
Good   Good

Figure 7.1 An example of a question from the Play Skills Self-Report Questionnaire

developing children and their parents/carers from a range of socio-economic backgrounds were tested using the two versions of the *PSSRQ*. Briefly, there were more items on which parent and child disagreed (n=17) than items on which they agreed (n=13) which was interpreted as supporting the hypothesis that child self-report would produce unique information. Stability over time was shown for a small group (n=16) of parents and children. One item was found to be unreliable and was removed from the questionnaire.

PSSRQ PARENT / CARER REPORT

Name:

Child's Name:

Date:

	1. Is your child good at finding something to play when they are at home?	☐ Not Good	☐ OK	☐ Good	☐ Very Good
	2. Is your child good at making things sometimes when they play?	☐ Not Good	☐ OK	☐ Good	☐ Very Good
	3. Is your child good at playing with a group of other kids?	☐ Not Good	☐ OK	☐ Good	☐ Very Good

Figure 7.2 An example of questions from the Play Skills Self-Report Questionnaire Parent/Carer form

Additionally a range of independent variables was gathered about family details, ethnicity and language, parent education and occupation, child health and development and play opportunity, and effect on agreement between parent/carer and child was examined. Although group numbers were often small, independent variables which exerted an effect on parent–child agreement were school year/grade, some aspects of family composition, language, some aspects of parent education and occupation, teacher identified behaviour problems, current referral for some developmental intervention, available play space, and attendance at outside school hours care that included mornings before school.

The *PSSRQ* was designed to compare a child's ratings on each item against him/herself over time in either an intervention or a research context, hence a meaningful summative score is not the sole aim of the assessment. It is recognised, however, that ability to compare a total *PSSRQ* score between discrete subject groups such as children with attention deficit disorder and those without could provide valuable research data. The purpose of the *PSSRQ* parent/carer version, on the other hand, while similar, aimed to gather parental or carer perception of their child's current ability on the same set of play skills. Thus the parent/carer and child's views can be compared for meaningful difference in either an intervention or research situation, over time (Sturgess 2007). Additionally, the *PSSRQ* has been designed to tap play skills in a range of contexts – home, school, community, with a range of companions, and with a range of material resources (Sturgess 2007). Therefore the purpose is to gather a comprehensive picture of the perceptions of a child's play in most aspects of their daily life.

The 29 play skills listed in Table 7.1 are grouped for conceptual convenience into five play skills: where organisational capacity is primarily at the forefront; where the play skill relates to social situations; where there is a creative and/or imaginative component; where the physical and coordination components are primary, and where a family context is most likely. These play skills can be used independently of the structured *PSSRQ* assessment tool by any person working with children aged 5–10 years who wants to talk with them about their play. Each of the skills is aligned to functions, support skills and play contexts discussed earlier in Chapter 1. For example, each play skill can be framed in a question to the child: How well they can do it? Whether they do it much? If they do it better under certain circumstances rather than others?, etc. Children have been shown to be able to elaborate about their skills (Sturgess 2007; Sturgess and Ziviani 1996).

None of these play skills are limited to the context that they are grouped under. For example, ability to play with a grown up is usually with a parent, grandparent, aunt or uncle but may also be with a coach, a guides/scout leader, teacher or therapist.

CONCLUSION

Ultimately, the usefulness of assessing these play skills appropriate to middle childhood is in being able to use them as a 'hook' through which to help the child clarify whether he or she feels the need for help in becoming more competent with an aspect of play they feel is important to their life. Similarly, the other play and play-related assessments described in this chapter accentuate the need for children at middle childhood to be active participants in providing their opinion about their play and leisure interests and in how their goals in everyday life are enhanced or hindered in play and leisure. The child's own concept of what is or is not play should be respected.

Adults observing or assessing a child's play need to be aware of how their own experience of playing may cloud their judgment about the child's play. This can be ameliorated through carefully determining the outcomes to be achieved through assessing play, and choosing the most appropriate method.

Finally, all children play in one way or another, and play as a child merges into adult play. Children of middle childhood with impairments must also be provided with environments and supports (refer to Chapter 14) which allow and encourage play skills alongside the other skills of everyday life.

REFERENCES

Bundy, A. C. (1997) 'Play and Playfulness: What to Look for.' In L. D. Parham and L. S. Fazio (eds) *Play in Occupational Therapy for Children.* St Louis, MO: Mosby.

Bundy, A. C. (2001) 'Measuring Play Performance.' In M. Law, C. Baum and W. Dunn (eds) *Measuring Occupational Performance: Supporting Best Practice in Occupational Therapy.* Thorofare, NJ: SLACK.

Couch, K. J., Deitz, J. C. and Kanny, E. M. (1998) 'The role of play in paediatric occupational therapy.' *American Journal Occupational Therapy 52*, 111–117.

Ferland, F. (1997) *Play, Children with Physical Difficulties, and Occupational Therapy: The Ludic Model,* trans. P. Aronoff and H. Scott. Ottawa: University of Ottawa Press.

Gitlin-Weiner, K. (1998) 'Clinical Perspectives on Play.' In D. P. Fromberg and D. Bergen (eds) *Play from Birth to Twelve and Beyond.* New York: Garland Publishing.

Haight, W. L. (2004) 'Use and misuse of play intervention.' *PsycCRITIQUES.* New York: American Psychological Association.

Henry, A. D. (2000) *Pediatric Interest Profiles: Surveys of Play for Children and Adolescents.* San Antonio, TX: The Psychological Corporation.

King, G., Law, M., King, S., Hurley, P., Rosenbaum, P., Hanna, S., Kertoy, M. and Young, N. (2004) *CAPE/PAC Children's Assessment of Participation and Enjoyment & Preferences for Activities of Children Manual.* San Antonio, TX: Harcourt Assessment.

Knox, S. (1997) 'Development and Current Use of the Knox Preschool Play Scale.' In L. D. Parham and L. S. Fazio (eds) *Play in Occupational Therapy for Children.* St Louis, MO: Mosby.

Linder, T. W. (1990) *Transdisciplinary Play-based Assessment: A Functional Approach to Working with Young Children.* Baltimore, MD: Paul H. Brooks.

Mandich, A. D., Polatajko, H. J., Miller, L. T. and Baum, C. (2004) *PACS Paediatric Activity Card Sort.* Ottawa: CAOT Publications ACE.

Missiuna, C., Pollock, N. and Law, M. (2004) *PEGS. The Perceived Efficacy and Goal Setting System – Manual.* San Antonio, TX: Psychological Corporation.

Pollock, N., Stewart, D., Law, M., Sahagian-Whalen, S., Harvey, S. and Toal, C. (1997) 'The meaning of play for young people with physical disabilities.' *Canadian Journal of Occupational Therapy 64,* 25–31.

Reed, C. N., Dunbar, S. B. and Bundy, A. C. (2000) 'The effects of an inclusive preschool experience on the playfulness of children with and without autism.' *Physical & Occupational Therapy in Pediatrics 19,* 73–87.

Rodger, S., Brown, G. T. and Brown, A. (2005) 'Profile of paediatric occupational therapy practice in Australia.' *Australian Occupational Therapy Journal 52,* 311–325.

Russ, S. W. (1999) 'Article discussion: Accentuate the positive in assessment.' *Journal of Personality Assessment 72,* 224–227.

Schaaf, R. C., Merrill, S. C. and Kinsella, N. (1987) 'Sensory integration and play behaviour: A case study of the effectiveness of occupational therapy using sensory integrative techniques.' *Occupational Therapy in Health Care 4,* 61–75.

Schaefer, C. E., Gitlin, K. and Sandgrund, A. (eds) (1991) *Play, Diagnosis and Assessment.* New York: John Wiley.

Smith, P. K., Takhvar, M., Gore, N. and Vollstedt, R. (1985) 'Play in Young Children: Problems of Definition, Categorization and Measurement.' In P. Smith (ed.) *Children's Play: Research Developments and Practical Applications.* New York: Gordon and Breach Science Publishers.

Sturgess, J. (1997) 'Current trends in assessing children's play.' *British Journal of Occupational Therapy 60,* 410–414.

Sturgess, J. (2003) 'Viewpoint: A model describing play as a child-chosen activity: Is this still valid in contemporary Australia?' *Australian Occupational Therapy Journal 50,* 104–108.

Sturgess, J. (2007) 'The development of a play skills self-report questionnaire (PSSRQ) for 5–10 year old children and their parents/carers.' Unpublished doctoral thesis, University of Queensland, Australia.

Sturgess, J. (2008) *The Play Skills Self-Report Questionnaire.* Anstead, Queensland: self-published. Available at www.playskillsselfreport.com, accessed 18 September 2008.

Sturgess, J., Rodger, S. and Ozanne, A. (2002) 'A review of the use of self-report assessment with young children.' *British Journal of Occupational Therapy 65,* 108–116.

Sturgess, J. and Ziviani, J. (1996) 'A self-report play skills questionnaire: Technical development.' *Australian Occupational Therapy Journal 43,* 142–145.

Van der Kooij, R. (1989) 'Research on children's play.' *Play & Culture 2,* 20–34.

Way, M. (1999) 'Parasympathetic and sympathetic influences in neuro-occupation pertaining to play.' *Occupational Therapy in Health Care 12,* 71–86.

CHAPTER 8

Assessing Play in a Social Setting

Tiina Lautamo

CHAPTER OBJECTIVES

This chapter will outline the challenges in children's play performance when they need to master social play contexts. The theoretical framework for the *Play Assessment for Group Settings (PAGS)* is introduced and the validation process of the tool is described. Some practical issues when using the *PAGS* in practice are discussed.

PLAY AS A SOCIAL OCCUPATION

To understand play as a social occupation, play can be studied as social performance, not just as 'doing', but as a matter of 'doing with' (Lawlor 2003). By evaluating social play performance, that is, a child's observable 'doing' within a social context, we can gain a wider perspective of a child's competence within a social environment.

Mastery depends on the experience of one's self doing, a sense of causation, and emerging interests and values (Christiansen 1999; Kielhofner 2002). In childhood, children gradually develop a sense of who they are by performing and participating in social occupations such as play. Occupation is seen as a basic human need and engagement in occupation promotes health, wellness, and personal identity (Christiansen 1999; Wilcock 1993). If we approach play as an occupation we can assume that participating in play is essential to children's well-being and is a developmental arena of personal identity. Therefore, play ability becomes an important indicator of the competence of the child.

Play has often been viewed as an indicator of a child's developmental level (Eisert and Lamorey 1996; Knox 1997) and often used only to assess capacities of the child rather than play per se (Bundy *et al.* 2001; Sturgess 1997). In the last decade there has been a shift away from this view of play to a view which explores play as important in itself and how it is supported by both intrapersonal and environmental factors (Parham and Primeau 1997).

Children are social beings and the social play context gives the child the opportunity to engage in social learning through interaction with caregivers and significant others. For example, during the second year of life children begin to show social understanding through pretence by simulating their own daily routines, such as eating or sleeping. During the next few years, these early pretend behaviours expand into more elaborate imaginary make-believe play (Stagnitti 1998). The emerging social pretend play presents challenges for skill acquisition as children learn to take turns, to respond reciprocally to social interactions of other children, to assume a variety of roles and to communicate about the ongoing drama (Fenson 1985).

Play performance includes the ability to use symbols as basic representations (Piaget 1962), and the facilitation of evaluation of one's actions in relation to one's own or others' intentions, beliefs or plans (Nelson *et al.* 2003). According to Harris (1992, 1996) these socio-cognitive abilities demand a process of setting aside your current point of view and imaginatively sharing another's perspective. Social pretend play requires the mutual understanding and sharing of reality with others. Sharing reality and collaborating requires the ability to 'read the minds' of other individuals, and 'see' things from someone else's perspective (Farrant, Fletcher and Mayberry 2006). When children engage in social pretend play, they are building up their own societies. A play society is never a direct copy of objective reality, but there exist socially shared and culturally shaped rules. These informal rules of play must be perceived and understood by the player before the child is capable of joining in or building a new play scenario with other players (Leslie 1987; Sutton-Smith 1997).

Play is an observable process of doing, where a child is engaging in actions or sequences of actions, often in shared reality with other players. These sequences of actions gradually shape and form play narratives (Stagnitti 2007). For example, *lifting and hugging a doll, putting it to bed, covering it and singing a song to it* is a narrative about a doll being put to sleep. These sequences are based on social experiences of the child. When children create and engage in play stories, we can observe a series of organised play actions which result in the construction of a socially shared play narrative. These narratives become more complex by age and have longer sequences of interconnected actions. In more complex play scenes, where two or more players share ideas of the play, the play narrative is built up, adapted and negotiated.

When children pretend play, they create their own ideas and fantasy actions in the context of complementary pretend roles and use toys in a symbolic manner. They adapt their own play performance and adjust to social play scenarios (Elkonin 1971; Fein 1981; Howes 1985; Sutton-Smith 1997). In other words, during the play narrative the social environment and object transformations are changed according to and during the ongoing play process. Therefore, a child learns to adapt to others in order to join this ever changing social process of playing. As the child modifies play stories or actions in relation to others, the child learns how to adapt his/her own doing and how to adjust the environmental conditions of the play. These adaptation skills are fundamental for independent and effective performance in all daily tasks in future life.

Children who are delayed in their development have fewer social opportunities than non-delayed children as they are approached significantly less by play partners, participate in less group social play, and engage in more individual play and onlooking behaviour (Liiva and Cleave 2005). Therefore, to enable participation and optimal learning possibilities for these children it becomes important to assess children's social play and the challenges they face when interacting with others in play.

THEORETICAL ELEMENTS OF THE *PLAY ASSESSMENT FOR GROUP SETTINGS (PAGS)*

The process to develop an assessment tool began with the theoretical framing of the phenomenon. In the *PAGS*, play performance was theoretically conceptualised by three elements influencing the dynamic process of playing: spirit, skills and environment. The dynamic process of playing is theorised as co-operation between the child's internal features (spirit and skills) and the environment where playing occurs.

Spirit is seen as the truest self of the child, something he/she is attempting to express in actions (Egan and DeLaat 1994). The term 'spirit' reflects the concept of 'inner drive', self-direction and self-actualisation which can be observed as excitement, confidence and effort that the child brings into play when he/she can find the 'just right challenge' for him/herself in the process of doing (Ayres 1972; Bundy and Murray 2002; Christiansen 1999). By playing, children learn how they can cause things to happen and the desire to cause effects in their environment becomes a motive for their play (Bundy 1997; Ferland 1997; Kielhofner 2002).

Play is an important arena for optimal *skill acquisition*. Within play performance we can observe a number of discrete, mindful and goal-directed actions. The observable actions that a child performs have been referred to as 'skills within doing' (Fisher 2006; Forsyth and Kielhofner 1999). Human skills have been determined as motor, process, communication and interaction skills (Kielhofner 2002). Motor skills refer to moving self or objects through space and time and process skills refer to logically sequencing and organising actions over time, selecting and using tools and materials and adapting performance (Fisher 2006). Communication and interaction skills refer to conveying intentions and needs and coordinating social actions to act together with people (Forsyth and Kielhofner 1999). Children are learning these skills while participating in everyday occupations, including play.

Environment offers physical and social opportunities, resources, constraints and demands and challenges children to participate in their life arenas. Whether a child notices these challenges or if they influence a child's behaviour depends on the skills, experiences, values, interests and habits of the child (Kielhofner 2002). If environmental challenges are too demanding for the child and he/she cannot cope in the situation, the child may withdraw from the play or just stay an onlooker. When the social environment is supportive the child dares to take risks. Play performance within an environment of supportive peers and adults (called the 'zone of proximal development') is fundamental in the process of skill acquisition (Vygotsky 1976, first published 1934). Environmental factors should always be considered as to how they affect the play situation as environment is not only physical and social but interpreted and shaped by culture (Altman and Chemers 1980). (See Chapter 11 for further discussion on culture and play.)

OPERATIONALISATION OF THE ITEMS OF *PAGS*

Items representing the latent features of play ability in the *PAGS* were constructed based on the theoretical conceptualisations of children's play performance in a social context. To capture the theoretical features of the child's internal play ability in *PAGS*, that is both spirituality and skill acquisition, items were based on the concepts of expressing a playful attitude (i.e. meaningful doing), and creating and engaging in play stories (i.e. mindful doing). Meaningful doing becomes observable when the child approaches social and physical play environments with a playful attitude. Understanding the elements of playfulness enables us to focus on the complex phenomenon of meaningful play activity (Bundy *et al.* 2001; Lieberman 1977). When a child expresses a playful attitude, he or she expresses emotions, shows curiosity, explores, engages spontaneously and exhibits a sense of humour during play (Bundy *et al.* 2001; Ferland 1997; Lieberman 1977). In mindful doing, children use their skills in a way that enables more than just automatic functioning (Langer 1989). It is the process of doing where children create new information in their play world and become aware of the points of view of others (Hasselkus 2002). Through playing children can develop the ability to pretend and the understanding of pretence in others (Leslie 1987). These features are viewed as dynamically developing and interacting with each other and form one unidimensional construct of play ability continuum (Lautamo, Kottorp and Salminen 2005).

The developmental phases of children's play performance change from object-related reality to symbolic-based imagination and role play, and later to more rule-dependent performance (Elkonin 1971; Reilly 1974; Vygotsky 1976). The play items of the *PAGS* describe children's play behaviour as observable play performance. To represent this as a developmental continuum of play ability of children the *PAGS* is designed to measure two to six-year-old children's play. The *PAGS* is not a norm-referenced tool and in order to evaluate whether a child's play performance is competent the rater needs to know how to interpret specific play behaviour of the child. Scoring of the *PAGS* is based on the frequency of certain play behaviours that a child enacts in a social context. The *PAGS* is scored on a 4-point scale indicating the relative amount of time that a child's level of 'doing' is reflected by that item (1=hardly ever; 2=seldom; 3=often, and 4=nearly always; NA= not assessable). In the scoring form there are approximations in percent to give the rater some idea of the likert scores, but they are not meant to be timed exactly. Time-related scoring is based on the fact that when children develop to the next phase of play performance, they still use old play patterns together with new ones (Reilly 1974).

It is important to note that likert scale points are estimations about how much the child's play behaviour reflects a certain item. For researchers I highly recommend using the Rash analysis if *PAGS* is used for research purposes (see Bond and Fox 2001). For clinical applications, *PAGS* can be used as a checklist of the child's play performance in social settings. The scoring form is organised so that the two features of play (that is, meaningful doing and mindful doing) are ranged from easier to harder items in both features of play. The item order is based on previous Rasch analyses from two studies on the *PAGS* validity (Lautamo *et al.* 2005; Lautamo *et al.* in preparation). For example, *PAGS* can be used in clinical work as a guideline to determine what kind of challenges a child has in his/her play performance and if certain play abilities can be set as goals in play interventions.

STEPS OF DEVELOPMENT PROCESS OF THE *PAGS*

The development of the *PAGS* is still an ongoing process. The construction of an assessment is a process where theory guides the statistical analysis and vice versa. Originally there were 54 theoretically constructed play items. In the pilot study (Lautamo *et al.* 2005) we did step-by-step Rasch analysis to remove items that did not fit into the theory or the Rasch model expectations. After critical theoretical consideration, three items were removed and 51 items were analysed. A further four items that did not demonstrate acceptable patterns in Rasch analysis were removed. The pilot study results revealed that the 47 remaining play items of the *PAGS* defined one unidimensional construct of play ability. The *PAGS* was refined further by leaving out items which were descriptions of play behaviour similar to other items and in the same level in the challenge hierarchy. The current version (version 3/2007) of the *PAGS* has 38 items describing observable play behaviour of the child (see Table 8.1).

Table 8.1 The *Play Assessment for Group Settings (PAGS)* play items

What does the child do spontaneously while playing?	1=	2=	3=	4=	NA=
On purpose, the child:	hardly ever	seldom	often	nearly always	not assess-able

Expressing playful attitude:

1. Enjoys activity and play; he or she has fun playing

2. Expresses curiosity towards the environment and the objects

3. Begins a play without the support of an adult

4. Devotes him or herself
   to the process of playing
   and enjoys the activity

5. Explores possibilities of
   the surroundings

6. Takes part in new plays
   with curiosity

7. Plays a trick and makes
   jokes

8. Decides on his or her
   own actions
   independently rather
   than imitates others

9. Takes part in shared play
   as an active participant

10. Embraces activity in new
    surroundings

11. Expresses feelings
    during the play

12. Expresses the feeling of
    competence by, for
    instance, describing
    accomplishments or
    expressing contentment

13. Adapts actions in order
    to make the play more
    challenging or enjoyable

14. Takes risks and seeks
    challenges

15. Teases in positive and
    playful manner

16. Playfully breaks the
    rules of the activity and
    looks for challenges in
    order to accommodate
    the play

Table 8.1 *cont.*

What does the child do spontaneously while playing?	1=	2=	3=	4=	NA=
On purpose, the child:	*hardly ever*	*seldom*	*often*	*nearly always*	*not assessable*

Creating play stories and taking part in them:

17. Plays in organised manner and his or her play has obvious goal

18. Accepts other child's play acts as part of shared play

19. Attributes qualities to objects, e.g. the doll is ill, the car is broken

20. Comes up with his or her own ideas for plays

21. Uses diverse and varying toys and objects while playing

22. Replaces missing objects with imaginary ones, e.g. pretends there is food in the pot

23. Shares toys unity with other players

24. Learns/understands new play rules

25. Builds play surroundings like houses or huts

26. Play-act a theme or a story

27. Invents plays about everyday situations like being at home or in a shop

28. Names a role for him or herself, plays at being someone else

29. Uses objects symbolically, e.g. a box as a table, a block as a car

30. Uses objects in a creative and original way

31. Joins to the ongoing play theme adapting its rules

32. Invents adventure plays like being a princess, a pirate or a spaceman

33. Describes what is going on while playing

34. Actively modifies or adapts the theme as the play progresses

35. Discusses the rules of a play with other playmates

36. Moves from one stage of a play to another easily

37. Invents new plays and shares his or her ideas with playmates

38. Understands the play rules others have set

VALIDITY

To be considered a valid measure, it is critical that an assessment of play performance differentiate between children with limitations in play performance and children without limitations. In the pilot study, the 47 item *PAGS* had a separation index of 4.95 (reliability = 0.96) of the measure of children's ability. This indicated that these 47 items separated the children into at least five different levels of ability in play performance. In addition, the *PAGS* differentiated the children who were at risk or disabled from typically developing children. Eighteen of the 23 at risk or disabled children were among the lower half of all children on the play ability continuum, even though the mean age of the disabled children's group was higher than the typically developed children's group. In another study investigating the play abilities of children with language-related problems (Lautamo *et al.* in preparation) the *PAGS* items were reduced to 40 items. The separation index of items remained stable at 4.71 (reliability = 0.96) which indicated that the reduced set of 40 items on the *PAGS* was equally effective at separating the children into different levels of play ability as the 47 item *PAGS*. Furthermore, independent samples t-test confirmed that the children with language-related problems had significantly (t *(96)* = -3.205, p <0 .01) lower play ability than their peers. These results confirmed that the *PAGS* can be used to differentiate children's play abilities.

Internal scale validity

The pilot study analysis with the 47 item *PAGS* (Lautamo *et al.* 2005) revealed one unidimensional construct with 97.9 per cent of the items demonstrating acceptable patterns of the underlying construct of *PAGS*. All the 47 scale items were well distributed along a linear scale and targeted the play skills of children. A further study with a larger data set found that 38 items met the criterion and demonstrated acceptable patterns (Lautamo *et al.* in preparation).

We also investigated play item difficulty with two groups of children (with and without language-related problems). The comparison of the separately generated play item calibration values revealed that 27 of 40 items had a similar relative position in the hierarchy of play items. Therefore, we concluded that item hierarchy in *PAGS* remained stable and that there were also group specific play items that were relatively easier or harder for children with language-related problems. This reflects possible group differences in play behaviour.

Children with language-related problems had lower play abilities compared to their peers, with greater difficulties in specific areas of play. They had greater difficulties inventing new ideas and sharing them with others and describing what was going on in play situations. They had greater difficulty understanding new play rules and discussing rules with playmates. All these play skills demand both receptive and expressive language abilities as well as the skills to plan and adapt to the process of changing play activity in collaboration with others. When collaborative play activity begins there needs to be a shared idea and then the play story is expanded, adapted and negotiated with the co-players. The children with language problems (SLI) had difficulties initiating play and keeping the focus on the process in order to carry out a sequence of play actions towards shaping a play-script. It seemed that they had difficulties coming up with their own ideas, deciding 'what to do' and planning in advance 'how to do it'. These findings are in accordance with McCabe and associates' studies showing that children with SLI had poor task orientation and delays in controlling their behaviour, and they were more dependent on adults' support in the context of play (McCabe 2005; McCabe and Marshall 2006; Picone and McCabe 2005).

Person-response validity

When examining the response patterns of the children (n=93) in the pilot study (Lautamo *et al.* 2005), 84 of the 93 (90.3%) children demonstrated acceptable patterns in play performance. This was higher than expected and further analysis was undertaken to evaluate if any systematic bias in patterns were found among those children. It was found that children aged 5.10–6.9 years had a higher proportion of scores. In further analysis (n=168) this pattern seemed to continue. Therefore, the response processes of the children must be studied further. At six years, play performance of children changes towards more game-based play as described in several play theories (Reilly 1974) and changes in play performance occur individually. Future studies involving more participants in different age groups are needed to provide further evidence of the validity of the *PAGS* in relation to age.

Inter-rater reliability

Play is acknowledged to be a complex activity that contributes significantly to all aspects of the development of children (Ferland 1997). The complexity of play demands special skills from the persons observing and scoring children's play performance in social and physical environments (Ferland 1997; Wright and Linacre 1989). Sutton-Smith (1997), for example, indicated that female teachers, in particular, can easily misinterpret the noisy and aggressive play of boys. Both teacher attitudes towards play and the institutional context of day-care affects how play manifests in children's groups (Lautamo *et al.* 2005).

We have found preliminary evidence for inter-rater reliability (raters n=12, cases n= 78) (Heikkilä and Lautamo in preparation). We have analysed the rater response processes with Rasch analyses and confirmed all the raters fit in the Rasch model expectations of consistency (separation index < 2.0) and there is no need for calibration of raters. Future research will examine intra-rater reliability of the possible use of the *PAGS* as a clinical measure of changes in child's play ability after interventions. Other research areas are cultural differences, group specific issues or play style differences of the tool.

APPLICATION IN PRACTICE

The *PAGS* is designed as an assessment of play abilities in a social setting. The social environment is one element affecting a child's play ability. The *PAGS* focuses on children's play performance in natural social settings and, therefore, it should be used in familiar settings where the child has opportunities to join in social play. With *PAGS* we can assess if a child can engage in the process of playing alone or with others.

All the observations during the development process of *PAGS* have been done in day-care settings where children were observed over a two-month period. It has been argued that the play abilities of children should always be observed and measured in natural settings (Bundy *et al.* 2001) which are safe and familiar enough to support play performance and enable a playful attitude (Pellegrini, Dupuis and Smith 2007). Environments that challenge a child's capacities tend to evoke involvement, attentiveness and maximal activity (Csikszentmihalyi 1990). We must recognise that natural peer settings are not necessarily equally challenging environments for all children, especially those who have some learning difficulties or developmental problems. Children with difficulties rely much more on adults to help navigate their social environments than their peers (Picone and McCabe 2005) and their difficulties are most evident in the context of peer relationships (Fujiki *et al.* 1999). It is important that when assessing a child's play abilities the physical and social environment is familiar enough but also allows risk taking.

The *PAGS* is designed to be easy to use by all professionals working with children. Ratings of the *PAGS* should be done after observing the child in several different situations which includes social free play situations where the children are playing without adult support. However, observations of a child with developmental challenges should also include comparison of play abilities when the child is supported by a skilled adult to that child's play abilities when playing alone or with other children.

Learning to observe individual children among a group of children demands special skills of the observer to separate out the effect of the environment on the child's play performance. Consequently, the items of *PAGS* have been formed to describe the spirit-environment and skills-environment dynamic in conjunction with a child's play behaviour. Teachers and nurses have noted after ratings that the scoring process of the *PAGS* had increased their awareness of individual children's play behaviour. In addition, they have learned to look more closely at what the individual child really can do or cannot do in free play situations without adult intervention. The structured observation has given them new knowledge about the challenges to and strengths of the child.

REFERENCES

Altman, I. and Chemers, M. (1980) *Culture and Environment.* Monterey, CA: Books/Cole.

Ayres, A. J. (1972) *Sensory Integration and Learning Disorders.* Los Angeles: Western Psychological Services.

Bond, T. G. and Fox, C. M. (2001) *Applying the Rasch Model: Fundamental Measurement in Human Sciences.* New Jersey: LEA.

Bundy, A. C. (1997) 'Play and Playfulness: What to Look for.' In L. D. Parham and L. S. Fazio (eds) *Play in Occupational Therapy for Children.* St Louis MO: Mosby.

Bundy, A. C. and Murray, E. A. (2002) 'Sensory Integration: A. Jean Ayres' Theory Revised.' In A. C. Bundy, S. J. Lane and E. A. Murray (eds) *Sensory Integration, Theory and Practice* 2nd edn. Philadephia: F. A. Davis Company.

Bundy, A. C., Nelson L., Metzger M. and Bingaman K. (2001) 'Validity and reliability of a test of playfulness.' *Occupational Therapy Journal of Research 21,* 276–292.

Christiansen, C. H. (1999) 'Defining lives: Occupational identity: An essay on competence, coherence, and the creation of meaning.' *American Journal of Occupational Therapy 53,* 547–558.

Csikszentmihalyi, M. (1990) *Flow: The Psychology of Optimal Experience.* New York: Harper & Row.

Egan, M. and Delaat, D. (1994) 'Considering spirituality in occupational therpay practice.' *Canadian Journal of Occupational Therapy 61,* 95–101.

Eisert, D. and Lamorey, S. (1996) 'Play as a window on child development: The relationship between play and other developmental domains.' *Early Education and Development 7,* 221–235.

Elkonin, D. B. (1971) 'Symbolics and its Functions in the Play of Children.' In R.E. Herron and B. Sutton-Smith (eds) *Child's Play.* New York: John Wiley.

Farrant, B. M., Fletcher, J. and Mayberry, M. T. (2006) 'Specific language impairment, theory of mind, and visual perspective taking: Evidence for simulation theory and developmental role of language.' *Child Development 77,* 1842–1853.

Fein, G. G. (1981) 'Pretend play: An integrated review.' *Child Development 52,* 1095–1118.

Fenson, L. (1985) 'The developmental progression of exploration and play.' In C. C. Brown and A. W. Gottfried (eds) *Play Interactions: The Roles of Toys and Parental Involvement in Children's Development.* New York: Jonson & Jonson.

Ferland, F. (1997) *PLAY, Children with Physical Disabilities and Occupational Therapy: The Ludic Model.* Ottawa: University of Ottawa Press.

Fisher, A. G. (2006) *AMPS, Assessment of Motor and Process Skills. Volume 1: Development, Standardization, and Administration Manual,* 6th edn. Fort Collins, CO: Three Star Press.

Forsyth, K. and Kielhofner, G. (1999) 'Validity of the assessment of communication and interaction skills.' *British Journal of Occupational Therapy 62,* 69–74.

Fujiki, M., Brinton, B., Hart, C. H. and Fitzgerald, A. H. (1999) 'Peer acceptance and friendship in children with specific language impairment.' *Topics in Language Disorders 19,* 34–48.

Harris, P. L. (1992) 'From stimulation to folk psychology: The case for development.' *Mind and Language 7,* 120–144.

Harris, P. L. (1996) 'Desires, Beliefs, and Language.' In P. Carruthers and P. K. Smith (eds) *Theories of Theories of Mind.* Cambridge: Cambridge University Press.

Hasselkus, B. R. (2002) *The Meaning of Everyday Occupation.* Thorofare, NJ: SLACK.

Heikkilä, M. and Lautamo, T. (in preparation) 'Rater reliability of the Play Assessment for Group Settings, PAGS.'

Howes, C. (1985) 'Sharing fantasy: Social pretended play in toddlers.' *Childs Development 56,* 1253–1258.

Kielhofner, G. (2002) *Model of Human Occupation: Theory and Application,* 3rd edn. Baltimore, MD: Williams & Wilkins.

Knox, S. (1997) 'Development and current use of the Knox preschool play scale.' In L. D. Parham and L. S. Fazio (eds) *Play in Occupational Therapy for Children.* St Louis, MO: Mosby.

Langer, E. J. (1989) *Mindfulness.* New York: Addison-Wesley.

Lautamo, T., Kottorp, A. and Salminen, A-L. (2005) 'Play assessment for group settings: A pilot study to construct an assessment tool.' *Scandinavian Journal of Occupational Therapy 12,* 136–144.

Lautamo, T., Laakso, M-L., Aro, T. and Ahonen, T. (in preparation) 'Play abilities in children with specific language impairment assessed in natural group settings.'

Lawlor, M. C. (2003) 'The significance of being occupied: The social construction of childhood occupations.' *American Journal of Occupational Therapy 5,* 424–434.

Leslie, A. M. (1987) 'Pretense and representation: The origins of 'Theory of Mind'.' *Psychological Review 94,* 412–426.

Lieberman, J. N. (1977) *Playfulness: Its Relationship to Imagination and Creativity.* New York: Academic Press.

Liiva, C. A. and Cleve, P. L. (2005) 'Roles of initiation and responsiveness in access and participation for children with specific language impairment.' *Journal of Speech, Language and Hearing Research 48,* 868–883.

McCabe, P. C. (2005) 'Social and behavioral correlates of preschoolers with specific language impairment.' *Psychology in the Schools 42,* 373–387.

McCabe, P. C. and Marshall, D. J. (2006) 'Measuring the social competence of preschool children with specific language impairment: Correspondence among informant ratings and behavioral observations.' *Topics in Early Special Education 26,* 234–246.

Nelson, K., Skwerer, P., Goldman, S., Henseler, S., Presler, N. and Walkenfeld, F. F. (2003) 'Entering a community of minds: An experimental approach to Theory of Mind.' *Human Development 46,* 24–46.

Parham, L. D. and Primeau, L. A. (1997) 'Play and Occupational Therapy.' In L. D. Parham and L. S. Fazio (eds) *Play in Occupational Therapy for Children.* St Louis, MO: Mosby.

Pellegrini, A. D., Dupuis, D. and Smith, P. K. (2007). 'Play in evolution and development.' *Developmental Review 27*, 261–276.

Piaget, J. (1962) *Play, dreams, and imitation in childhood*. New York: Norton.

Picone, M. and McCabe, P. C. (2005) 'The reliability and discriminant validity of the Social Interactive Coding System with language impaired preschoolers.' *Journal of Early Childhood and Infant Psychology 1*, 113–128.

Reilly, M. (1974) *Play as Exploratory Learning*. Beverly Hills, CA: Sage Publications.

Stagnitti, K. (1998) *Learn to Play: A Practical Program to Develop a Child's Imaginative Play Skills*. Melbourne: Co-ordinates Publications.

Stagnitti, K. (2007) *The Child-Initiated Pretend Play Assessment*. Manual. Melbourne: Co-ordinates Publications.

Sturgess, J. L. (1997) 'Current trends in assessing children's play.' *British Journal of Occupational Therapy 60*, 410–414.

Sutton-Smith, B. (1997) *The Ambiguity of Play*. Cambridge, MA: Harvard.

Vygotsky, L. S. (1976) 'Play and its role in mental development of the child.' In J. S. Bruner, A. Joly and K. Sylva (eds) *Play*. New York: Basis Books.

Wilcock, A. (1993) 'A theory of human need for occupation.' *Journal of Occupational Science 1*, 17–24.

Wright, B. D. and Linacre, J. M. (1989) 'Observations are always ordinal; Measurements, however, must be interval.' *Archives of Physical Medicine and Rehabilitation 70*, 857–860.

SECTION THREE

Play Contexts

CHAPTER 9

Play in the Hospital Environment

Judi Parson

CHAPTER OBJECTIVES

This chapter acknowledges the importance of play for hospitalised children, and considers how the built environment impacts on child-patients' play. Throughout the chapter an appreciation of the normative, therapeutic and educational values of play strategies suitable for children in the hospital setting are identified.

INTRODUCTION

To understand the role of play in the hospital setting it is important for health care professionals to be cognisant of the psychological and social impact hospitalisation may have on children. As the hospital is a complex physical and social structure this chapter illustrates how the built environment impacts on child-patients. The people who work in this setting, such as hospital play specialists, play therapists, psychologists, occupational therapists, social workers, nurses and other health care professionals all use play to help children cope with hospitalisation and medical procedures. Play is important as it ensures ongoing physical, emotional, cognitive and social development for hospitalised children and also provides distraction from the hospital environment. As a creative form of self-expression play is recognised for its normalising, therapeutic and educative values. In this situation, various forms of play activities may include games, role playing, drawing, painting, collage, medical or procedural play and educative preparation play. Play can facilitate comprehension, enhance coping, reduce anxiety and provide emotional support for children undergoing medical treatment. Therefore, it is important for all health professionals working with child patients to communicate with children through a range of play strategies.

THE PSYCHOSOCIAL RESPONSES OF CHILDREN TO HOSPITALISATION

When children enter the hospital environment they may suffer from stress, fear and anxiety (Bowmer 2002; Gariepy and Howe 2003; Hall 1987; Mathiasen and Butterworth 2001; Mitchell, Johnston and Keppell 2004; Parson 2004; Siegel 1976; Visintainer and Wolfer 1975). Golden (1984, cited in Malchiodi 1999), identified the primary sources of stress experienced by hospitalised children as: separation from parents; loss of independence and control; fears and anxieties about medical procedures, which may cause harm or pain; and worry about death. The child's negative reactions to hospitalisation may include crying, withdrawing, regression, separation anxiety, sleep or eating disturbances, anger and aggression (Gaynard et al. 1998; O'Connor-von 2000). Health care professionals should be aware that these behaviours are indicative of the child's distress. Some of the negative effects of hospitalisation may be overcome through the use of play as a therapeutic tool. However, the foreign environment of the built structure must be considered before play can be facilitated.

THE BUILT ENVIRONMENT

Play is extremely important to all hospitalised children. In play, children not only find enjoyment but they also interact with and explore their environment (Armstrong and Aitken 2000). The hospital setting contains a complex social system where pain and suffering are mixed with joy and healing. For children the atmosphere may feel like a sad and scary place and/or a happy, exciting and very busy place. It may look like a place full of strange faces and even stranger machines. Hospital smells are very different from home or school and they are very noisy places. Children play and this helps them intellectually and emotionally process sensory information. Play can help the child improve his or her understanding and interpretation of hospital language, sights and sounds (Haiat, Bar-Mor and Shochat 2003).

Encouragement of play within the hospital structure requires a child-focused space and toys and activities to facilitate play interactions. Four decades ago Butler, Chapman and Stuible (1975) postulated that, in hospital, play should be considered as important as the medical treatment the child receives. Designers of modern hospital structures now consider the impact the built environment has on the health and well being of child-patients. Sherman, Shepley and Varni (2005) examined the literature on child's health and health-related quality of life in relation to the physical environment. These authors showed that children's perceptions of nature, noise, crowding, spatial arrangements, art and decorations, lighting and temperature potentially contribute towards physical, psychological, emotional, cognitive, behavioural and social health outcomes. The child's improved physiological regulation, that is respiratory rate, heart rate and temperature, sleeping and reduced pain levels have been associated with reducing noise, having natural light cycles, ambient music and regulated temperatures (Sherman *et al.* 2005). There has been a positive move towards incorporating sense-sensitive designs for new and refurbishment of hospital structures (NHS Estates 2004). Sight, sound, smell, taste, and touch should be considered in relation to how the child may interpret the hospital environment. Other studies show the therapeutic benefits of providing play spaces in health care settings to support play behaviour and interaction among patients with different types of physical abilities and across different age group (Sadler and Joseph 2008). The important point is that the structural design impacts on children and should not be overlooked as a facilitating factor contributing towards encouraging and supporting the child's most accessible coping behaviour – play.

CHILDREN'S PERCEPTIONS OF HOSPITAL

Children perceive the hospital environment through a mixture of emotional and intellectual understandings, based on the individual child's awareness of hospitals and hospital life from either direct or indirect experiences. The direct experience may be from the child's own hospitalisation or from visiting someone else in hospital. The indirect experience is what the child may glean from other media, such as what is viewed on TV, read in books or comics, or by playing 'make-believe' hospital.

In order to gain an understanding of the child's level of hospital knowledge, the creative arts can be used as a powerful adjunct to play therapy. 'Art therapy and play therapy share a common bond through their natural appeal to children and their healing qualities of creativity, spontaneous expression, make-believe, and non-threatening, developmentally appropriate communication' (Malchiodi 1999 p.22). Simply asking the child to draw what they see in a hospital room provides information on the child's perception of their new environment. Nine-year-old Emily has direct experience of visiting people in hospital, including her mother on two occasions, when her baby brother was born and when her mother had a knee operation. Emily was hospitalised herself as an infant on one occasion and more recently attended a medical centre for burn treatment. Emily's picture, shown in Figure 9.1, suggests her understanding of both positive and negative aspects of hospital life.

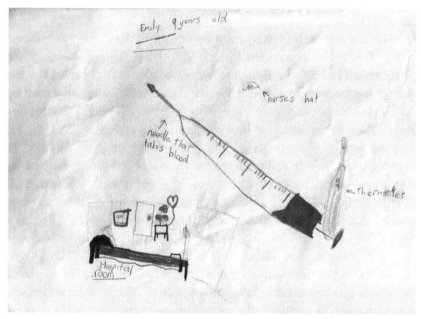

Figure 9.1 Emily's picture of her hospital room

In Emily's picture, the hospital room has some visually attractive features, such as the flowers, balloons and a picture on the wall. However, the size of the needle is significant and the dark colour of the bed may indicate that Emily sees the hospital bed as a dark place to be. The important point is to ask the creator of the artwork their own views. The following anecdote is Emily's explanation of her picture.

She explained the attractive surroundings, such as flowers and the picture on the wall and said '*If I was in hospital, I would be sick and I would want nice things around me because it would make me feel nice.*' The colour of the bed was chosen because that was the colour of the bed in the medical centre she had recently attended and she even explained that '*they are not happy colours*'. This demonstrates the importance of visual sensations and how the physical environment may impact on children. Emily spoke in great detail about her functional idea to attach a bed table/bench that could easily slide up and down the bed so that people could reach things. The slide bar was identified by a blue line under the bed. The 'nurse's hat' is another interesting point because it was assumed that Emily would not have ever seen a nurse wear a nursing cap. However, it was established that the nurse at the medical centre did wear a nurse's hat and Emily spoke fondly about this nurse who treated her. The nurse's cap with a red cross, along with traditional nursing uniforms, remain strong symbols used in children's dress-ups and on pictures denoting what a nurse looks like.

Medical equipment is also strongly present in the drawing, Emily was aware of crutches, intravenous therapy (drips), needles and thermometers. These identify a level of insight into her knowledge of the hospital environment. It is interesting to note that the size of the needle makes it the most significant feature in the picture. Emily stated, '*I don't like needles*'. She spoke at length about many aspects of how the needle and syringe worked, the volume markers on the syringe, the plunger and the '*spiky bit*'. She said her drawing of the needle and syringe was '*really cool*' indicating that she was very proud of her depth of understanding about how they function. Although Emily had no conscious memory of blood being taken, she commented that if she had to have a needle or blood test she would be able to cope if she was given '*chocolate or a lollipop*', thereby providing a preference to a specific coping mechanism.

As health care professionals it is important to bridge established perceptions with current realities as and when required. This process involves listening to and being attuned to the child to understand the child's thoughts and feelings about their illness, treatment and hospitalisation experiences. Coyne (2006) found that school-aged children appeared to rely on various strategies to obtain information such as: asking questions of parents, nurses and doctors; observing and talking to other children on the ward with the same condition or illness; getting books from the local library; comparing experiences with medical television programmes and reflecting on past experiences of visiting relatives in hospital. Whilst children are able to access information from a number of sources, not all children seek information about hospital and medical procedures. Fanurik *et al.* (1993) found that some children cope better with information about medical procedures, whereas others prefer not to be informed at all. Health care professionals should be mindful of the different coping styles of children. Rudolph, Dennig and Weisz (1995) present a full critique of children's coping mechanisms in the medical setting.

THE NEED FOR PLAY IN THE HOSPITAL ENVIRONMENT

Children exhibit behaviours in relation to real or imagined fears when they come into hospital. Research shows that children express distress through crying, shaking, screaming, hostility, lack of cooperation, aggression, withdrawal, anger, vomiting or incontinence in relation to medical procedures (McGrath and Huff 2001; Parson 2008). The negative impact of surgical interventions may cause a traumatised child to avoid future medical health care encounters when they reach adulthood (Justus *et al.* 2006). Fear and distress can be reduced through sensitive educational and therapeutic play. Play may focus on coming to terms with the hospital environment as well as being used to gain mastery and cope with potentially unpleasant and frightening procedures.

In play, children can create an environment where they are in control which facilitates open self expression and emotional growth leading to positive mental health and well being. Landreth (2001) describes play as the child's language, which can be used to bridge the child-adult barrier. A skilled adult can use play to enable clearer, more appropriate, child-centred communication about the hospital world, medical equipment and planned procedures. Thus, play provides an assessment tool for health professionals to access the child's level of understanding. Additionally, when children engage in play they become more available and open to learning that may empower them throughout their hospitalisation experience.

INTEGRATING PLAY IN THE HOSPITAL ENVIRONMENT

Play should be encouraged and integrated throughout the various stages of a child's hospitalisation. The two broad types of adult to child play interactions are 'directed' and 'non-directed' play interventions (Carroll 1998). Directed play may be used to teach and prepare children (Arnold *et al.* 1997), to aid coping (Hall and Reet 2000) before hospitalisation, and before and after medical treatment. Non-directed play (Chambers 1993) occurs when the child controls all aspects of play and may be used to assist in identifying and assessing the child's concerns (see also Chapter 13). Thus, the integration of play in the hospital environment can draw from the understandings of both directed and non-directed play as appropriate to the various phases and to the child's needs. The following play approaches may be helpful in educating children about hospital life and in preparing children for specific medical procedures.

GENERAL EDUCATION ABOUT HOSPITALISATION

Preschool children should be given opportunities to have access to a hospital environment prior to even needing hospitalisation. Hospital tours can and should be organised for well children to visit a hospital children's ward at a time when they are not anxious or distressed due to illness or impending medical procedures. Children should be given opportunity to play with medical equipment in this setting. If this facility is unavailable a simulated environment could be used, for example, a university-based nursing laboratory. Alternatively, medical equipment can be brought to a play group, play centres, child care centres and preschools for 'medical play'.

Medical play is a form of non-directed play that can be used to familiarise children with medical equipment (Wong et al. 1999). It is used to give children an opportunity to safely examine equipment that children may see in hospital (Brennan 1994). Types of disposable equipment could include various sized syringes, tongue depressors, gloves, dressing packs, bandages, bandaids, medicine cups, armbands, oxygen mask and tubing, and intravenous tubing. Non-disposable equipment could also be used in play, for example, a cheap stethoscope, sphygmomanometer, pulse oximeter, tympanic thermometer, ophthalmoscope or otoscope, bedpan and urinal, kidney dish, and the list goes on. Young children may enjoy playing dress-up in hospital attire, such as surgical gown, surgical masks and protective eyewear, theatre hats and shoe covers. Children should be given the opportunity to ask questions about the medical equipment so the adult can explain how and why the equipment is used and thus clarify any misconceptions.

PREPARING CHILDREN FOR PLANNED HOSPITALISATION

Children who are prepared for a planned admission to hospital and medical procedures and who are supported throughout their stay, recover more quickly and have fewer emotional upsets than those who are not prepared (Justus et al. 2006). A range of preparations for hospital programmes exist in varying capacities. It is important for health care professionals to become familiar with local services and make strong links between hospital and community to develop and maintain preparation programmes for children. To do this the following list of questions may be useful as a guide:

- What hospital tours (or simulation) are available for children and when?

- What preadmission programmes are offered to the various age groups of children admitted to the paediatric ward?

- Does the ward provide colouring-in sheets depicting hospital themes at preadmission?

- Does the ward have a list of available children's literature relevant to hospital preparation held in the ward, local library or as web based information?

- What multimedia information about hospital is available for children to access?

- When and where are medical educational puppet shows available, for example, Camp Quality puppet shows (specific to Australia)?

- Does the ward provide practical advice for parents, for example, what to bring to hospital for their child and themselves?

- What parental information is given out and does it consist of their role in assisting their child throughout the hospitalisation experience?

PREPARING CHILDREN FOR MEDICAL PROCEDURES

The need for preparation is based on the understanding that medical procedures may be traumatic for many children and preparation offers a preview or rehearsal in a supportive environment to reduce anxiety, increase knowledge and enhance coping (Justus *et al.* 2006). Whether a child is to undergo a simple medical treatment or complex surgery all children require procedural preparation. Preparation requires initial assessment of the child's perception about what he or she already understands so that the individual child's needs can be met. Once consideration is given to the child's age, temperament, coping style, previous history and current medical condition then various techniques can be phased according to when the procedural play is utilised to facilitate a more positive experience (Blount, Piira and Cohen 2003). Timing of the information giving is also important. For very young children information should be given immediately prior to the medical procedure whereas older children may require more time to process the information. For example, school-age children benefit from information given five days prior to surgery (Kain, Mayes and Caramico 1996).

The types of procedural play interventions would then focus on introducing the child to various aspects of the intended medical treatment as and when required. The following points may be used as a guide to prepare children for medical procedures.

1. The first step involves assessing the child's current perceptions in relation to the anticipated procedure. Explain why the procedure is needed in simple age appropriate terms, i.e. provide clear, concise information about the procedural process, including what, where, when, and how the procedure will occur (Hallowell 2005; Jaaniste, Hayes and von Baeyer 2007; Khan and Weisman 2007; Levine and Kline 2007; Shaw and Demaso 2006; Stanford 1991). To do this it is important to show the child what will happen by demonstrating on a calico doll or stuffed animal toy what is going to happen with 'real' medical equipment. For example, if a child is going to have an intravenous catheter (IVC) inserted, the play preparation would include showing the child on the calico doll how:

    a) the local anaesthetic cream is applied to numb the skin

    b) the tourniquet is applied

    c) the insertion site is cleaned

    d) the IVC is inserted

    e) the needle is removed from the catheter and the plastic tubing is left in place

    f) the IVC is taped and secured in position.

2. Ask the child if they would like to have a play at inserting an IVC on their calico doll.

3. Talk to the child about their role in staying still and discuss ways to help the child keep still.

4. Identify roles for the child, including the medial practitioner, nurse, play therapist, mother/father and the child. This can be achieved by role playing with miniatures in a pretend play treatment room display. Discuss available options for the child, for example, most comfortable position (sit on parent's lap or on the treatment bed). Show the child where people may stand or sit and who will do what. It may also be appropriate to show the child the treatment room prior to procedural interventions.

5. Discuss appropriate coping and distracting techniques, for example:

a) hypnotherapy and guided imagery, such as the 'Magic glove' or 'magic stocking'(Kuttner 1989; Shaw and Demaso 2006).

b) large tactile toys and/or *I spy* books

c) handheld computer games

d) audio and/or visual distractions

e) bubbles

6. In conjunction with procedural play, sensory information should also be incorporated during play sessions to demystify the process (Broome 1985; Gaynard *et al.* 1998; Hallowell 2005; Stanford 1991):

a) Focus on what it may feel, sound, smell like and so on (include colours, size and shape, etc.)

b) When discussing what a sensation feels like, assumptions are *not* helpful, explain that you don't know how it will feel for each individual child – but there are a range of possibilities.

c) Ask the child if it would be all right if it didn't hurt much at all or that it felt okay?

7. Establish the degree of parental (or other support person) involvement. Clearly explain what each member of the health care team will do. Nominate only one person to talk or divert the child's attention during the procedure as multiple voices may overwhelm the child.

8. It may be important to use common medical jargon, but only when medical terminology is clearly and simply explained.

9. Above all be honest.

CONCLUSION

If a child is admitted into hospital it is important that their play is not left behind. Play is increasingly valued by health care professionals because of its normalising, educational and therapeutic effect and usefulness to bridge adult/child communication. Play facilitates comprehension, enhances coping and provides emotional support for children undergoing medical procedures. Consideration has been given to both the structural and the social aspects of hospital life. Sense-sensitive designs are now appreciated in relation to enhancing play activities for hospitalised children. Health care professionals should identify with current hospital-community educational programmes used to inform children about the hospital environment and should be able to integrate a number of play strategies to help facilitate a more positive experience for children of hospitalisation.

ADDITIONAL RESOURCES

- *Going to Hospital: What Will It Be Like?* (Mitchell 2005), an interactive computer game and activity book for children aged 7–11 years and their families.

- A list of books addressing fear of medical procedures can be found at The Pediatric Group, www.pedgroup.com/medtxbk.htm, accessed 19 September 2008.

- The Camp Quality puppet show, can be seen at www.campquality.org.au/community/puppets.cfm?section=program, accessed 19 September 2008.

REFERENCES

Armstrong, T. S. H. and Aitken, H. L. (2000) 'The developing role of play preparation in paediatric anaesthesia.' *Paediatric Anaesthesia 10*, 1–4.

Arnold, M., Mills, M., Peregrina, M., Stout, W. and Wells, D. (1997) 'Creative techniques in paediatric nursing.' *Australian Paediatric Nurse 6*, 1, 12–17.

Blount, R. L., Piira, T. and Cohen, L. L. (2003) 'Management of Pediatric Pain and Distress Due to Medical Procedures.' In M. C. Roberts (ed.) *Handbook of Pediatric Psychology*. New York: Guilford Press.

Bowmer, N. (2002) 'Therapeutic play and the impact on anxiety in hospitalized children.' *Kentucky Nurse 50*, 1, 15.

Brennan, A. (1994) 'Caring for children during procedures: A review of the literature.' *Pediatric Nursing 20*, 5, 451–458, 460–461.

Broome, M. E. (1985) 'The child in pain: A model for assessment and intervention.' *Critical Care Quarterly 8*, 1, 47–55.

Butler, A., Chapman, J. and Stuible, M. (1975) 'Child's play is therapy.' *Canadian Nurse 71*, 12, 35–37.

Carroll, J. (1998) *Introduction to Therapeutic Play*. Oxford: Blackwell Science.

Chambers, M.A. (1993) 'Play as therapy for the hospitalized child.' *Journal of Clinical Nursing 2*, 349–354.

Coyne, I. (2006) 'Consultation with children in hospital: Children, parents' and nurses' perspectives.' *Journal of Clinical Nursing 15*, 1, 61–71.

Fanurik, D., Zeltzer, L., Roberts, M. and Blount, R. (1993) 'The relationship between children's coping styles and psychological interventions for cold pressor pain.' *Pain 53*, 2, 213–222.

Gariepy, N. and Howe, N. (2003) 'The therapeutic power of play: Examining the play of young children with leukaemia.' *Child: Care, Health & Development 29*, 6, 523–537.

Gaynard, L., Wolfer, J., Goldberger, J., Thompson, R. H., Redburn, L. and Laidley, L. (1998) *Psychosocial Care of Children in Hospitals: A Clinical Practice Manual from the ACCH Child Life Research Project,* 2nd edn. Rockville, MD: Child Life Council.

Haiat, H., Bar-Mor, G. and Shochat, M. (2003) 'The world of the child: A world of play even in the hospital.' *Journal of Paediatric Nursing 18,* 3, 209–214.

Hall, C. and Reet, M. (2000) 'Enhancing the state of play in children's nursing.' *Journal of Child Health Care 4,* 2, 49–54.

Hall, D. (1987) 'Social and psychological care before and during hospitalization.' *Social Science and Medicine 25,* 6, 721–732.

Hallowell, L. (2005) 'Choosing the right words – Communicating with hospitalized children.' Paper presented at the Australasian Association for Hospital Play Specialists, Children's Hospital Westmead 21 October.

Jaaniste, T., Hayes, B. and von Baeyer, C. L. (2007) 'Providing children with information about forthcoming medical procedures: A review and synthesis.' *Clinical Psychology: Science and Practice 14,* 2, 124–143.

Justus, R., Wyles, D., Wilson, J., Rode, D., Walther, V. and Lim-Sulit, N. (2006) 'Preparing children and families for surgery: Mount Sinai's multidisciplinary perspective.' *Pediatric Nursing 32,* 1, 35.

Kain, Z. N., Mayes, L. C. and Caramico, L. A. (1996) 'Preoperative preparation in children: A cross-sectional study.' *Journal of Clinical Anesthesia 8,* 6, 508–514.

Khan, K. A. and Weisman, S. J. (2007) 'Nonpharmacologic pain management strategies in the pediatric Emergency Department.' *Clinical Pediatric Emergency Medicine 8,* 4, 240–247.

Kuttner, L. (1989) 'Management of young children's acute pain and anxiety during invasive medical procedures.' *Pediatrician 16,* 39–44.

Landreth, G. (2001) 'Facilitative Dimensions of Play in the Play Therapy Process.' In G. Landreth (ed.) *Innovations in Play Therapy.* London: Brunner-Routledge.

Levine, P. and Kline, M. (2007) *Trauma through a Child's Eyes: Infancy through Adolescence.* Berkeley, CA: North Atlantic Books.

Malchiodi, C. A. (1999) 'Introduction to Medical Art Therapy with Children.' In C. A. Malchiodi (ed.) *Medical Art Therapy with Children.* London: Jessica Kingsley Publishers.

Mathiasen, L. and Butterworth, D. (2001) 'The role of play in the hospitalisation of young children.' *Neonatal, Paediatric & Child Health Nursing 4,* 3, 23–26.

McGrath, P. and Huff, N. (2001) "What is it?": findings on preschoolers' responses to play with medical equipment.' *Child: Care, Health & Development 27,* 5, 451–462.

Mitchell, M. (2005) *Going to Hospital: What Will It Be Like? An Interactive Computer Game and Activity Book.* Melbourne: University of Melbourne and the Royal Children's Hospital, Melbourne.

Mitchell, M., Johnston, L. and Keppell, M. (2004) 'Preparing children and their families for hospitalisation: A review of the literature.' *Neonatal, Paediatric and Child Health Nursing 7,* 2, 5–15.

NHS Estates (2004) 'Improving the patient experience: Friendly healthcare environments for children and young people.' Available at http://195.92.246.148/knowledge_network/documents/publications/children.pdf, accessed 19 September 2008.

O'Connor-von, S. (2000) 'Preparing children for surgery: An integrative research review.' *AORN Journal 71,* 2, 334–343.

Parson, J. (2004) 'Nursing and procedural play strategies for hospitalised children: A review of the literature.' Paper presented at the 2nd Pacific Rim Conference, Growing, Learning, Healing: Partnerships for Children's Well-being, Crowne Plaza, Auckland 27–29 February.

Parson, J. (2008) 'Integration of procedural play for children undergoing cystic fibrosis treatment: A nursing perspective.' Unpublished PhD, Central Queensland University, Brisbane.

Rudolph, K. D., Dennig, M. D. and Weisz, J. R. (1995) 'Determinants and consequences of children's coping in the medical setting: Conceptualization, review, and critique.' *Psychological Bulletin 118*, 3, 328–357.

Sadler, B. and Joseph, A. (2008) 'Evidence for Innovation: Transforming children's health through the physical environment.' Available at www.childrenshospitals.net/AM/Template.cfm?Section=Management_Finance&CONTE NTID=36532&TEMPLATE=/CM/ContentDisplay.cfm, accessed 19 September 2008.

Shaw, R. J. and Demaso, D. R. (2006) *Clinical Manual of Pediatric Psychosomatic Medicine.* Washington, DC: American Psychiatric Publishing.

Sherman, S. A., Shepley, M. M. and Varni, J. W. (2005) 'Children's environments and health-related quality of life: Evidence informing pediatric healthcare environmental design.' *Children, Youth and Environments 15*, 1, 187–222.

Siegel, L. J. (1976) 'Preparation of children for hospitalisation: A selected review of the research literature.' *Journal of Pediatric Psychology 1*, 26–30.

Stanford, G. (1991) 'Beyond honesty: Choosing language for talking to children about pain and procedures.' *Children's Health Care 20*, 4, 261.

Visintainer, M. and Wolfer, J. (1975) 'Psychological preparation for surgical pediatric patients: The effects on childrens' and parents' stress response and adjustments.' *Pediatrics 56*, 187–202.

Wong, D. L., Hockenberry-Eaton, M., Wilson, D., Winnelstein, M. L., Ahmann, E. and Divito-Thomas, P. A. (1999) *Whaley & Wong's Nursing Care of Infants and Children*, 6th edn. St Louis, MO: Mosby.

CHAPTER 10

Parent–Child Play Interactions

Susan A. Esdaile

CHAPTER OBJECTIVES

This chapter includes an introduction to observation of parent–child interaction and play, a more detailed discussion of two key theoretical frameworks: attachment and temperament, and a discussion of key research contributions and the importance of considering cultural contexts. Some comments are provided on avoiding the 'experts' that stress families, and five vignettes are included to illustrate key elements of the chapter.

INTRODUCTION

The most smoothly negotiated and creative parent–child interactions are child initiated. A great deal can be learned from simply watching parents and children in public places that involve waiting, often with nothing specific to do. Airport waiting areas, public transport situations, and waiting rooms of professionals such as doctors, dentists and psychologists afford excellent opportunities for watching children and their caregivers. Religious services and restaurants also afford these opportunities, but these are harder because they involve predetermined expectations of behaviour that truly challenge toddlers' and preschoolers' ability to play happily, constructively and quietly. Visiting friends and relatives with small children can offer insightful opportunities for observing parent–child play interactions. Just remember that what happens at preschoolers' birthday parties and family get-togethers for special holiday occasions that involve gift-giving are likely to display both parents and children at the edge of their emotional control and, alas, often tipped over it.

Things to note include: the age(s) of the child or children, number of children, the space and its constraints, hazards and opportunities for safe play exploration, toys and potential play materials available, the number of adults and caregivers/parents involved. Some people find it difficult to play with children appropriately. The scenarios vary, but can be easily identified because an obviously unhappy child is involved. Children are seldom able to hide their feelings completely. Try to identify how and possibly why, when you see this occur and remember that a child that is screaming loudly may be just overreacting to frustration, perhaps because an adult has inadvertently or deliberately interrupted her play. A tactful professional or understanding relative or friend could help in these situations. A fearfully watchful child may be in a seriously difficult, even dangerous situation. In this kind of situation, observations and actions need to be more carefully considered to ensure that appropriate assistance and support is provided for the child and caregivers.

Some of the most positive examples of parent–child play interactions that I have observed were in public places. The parent(s) remained child-focused, speaking in a low voice, moving rhythmically, had some simple toys and books at hand, but were prepared to let the child initiate the activity that also included moving around within the environment. For example walking down a corridor, or going outdoors and stopping to engage in conversation with the child about things she noticed along the way.

Vignette 1

A mother is feeding her 10-month-old infant, a playful interaction in a routine situation.

The mother is sitting opposite the baby, feeding her yoghurt with a spoon. She is talking to the baby, making a game of her actions, using exaggerated flying motions with the spoon as she scoops the yoghurt and *flies* it to the baby's mouth. She waits for the baby to vocalise in response before giving her the next spoon of yoghurt. The baby dips her finger into the yoghurt jar and offers it to her mother, who pretends to eat it with great enjoyment. The playful feeding–eating interaction continues with both mother and child smiling a lot. Then the mother puts the hand-towel on her lap over her head. She laughs at the baby, indicating that this is a joke. But the baby does not smile and is reluctant to resume eating.

The feeding–eating interaction, modulated by the infant was described by Bruner (1983) in terms of synchronisation and reciprocity in language development. Consider what happened when the mother put the towel on her head. Why wasn't the infant amused?

Vignette 2

A father is playing a vocal game with his four-month-old baby who is lying on the floor in a bouncing rocker.

The father leans over the baby, making gentle cooing sounds; the baby reciprocates making similar sounds. Both are smiling and obviously enjoying themselves. The father, encouraged by the baby's positive response, raises the volume of his vocalisations and includes more complex vocal patterns. The baby joins in the game, imitating his father, kicking his feet and waving his arms energetically. The father continues to enjoy the game as it accelerates, but the baby's vocalisation starts to change and develops into crying that becomes increasingly more distressed.

This interaction between the baby and his father can also be described in terms of synchronisation and reciprocity in language development. Consider why the baby became distressed as the father accelerated the game.

PLAY, PARENTS, CAREGIVERS, CHILDREN AND THE EXPERTS

The nature of play, its development, importance, assessment, environmental and cultural contexts, as well as play-focused interventions, are covered in other chapters of this text. In this chapter, I invite the reader to consider play from the perspectives of parents and caregivers. One can generally assume that parents know that children play. In industrialised consumer societies parents' awareness of play may be influenced by the wide variety of toys that are commercially available. Thus, they may have an instrumental concept of play as something that children do with an object that is colourful, possibly expensive and requires an adult to demonstrate its use. In contrast, families in non-industrialised societies may not associate play with special objects, as they may have no money to buy these, but allow children to handle and explore whatever is safe at hand: utensils, materials and people close to them. In reality, parents' concepts of play are more complex than the simple this or that situations described here. Most parents know that good toys do not have to be expensive or complicated and children in non-industrialised societies also have toys representing cultural traditions, often made by caregivers and relatives.

Play is not just important but essential to optimal child development. We know from an extensive body of research on play that poverty, stress, threat and deprivation have a detrimental effect on play and playfulness (e.g. chapters in Bruner, Jolly and Sylva 1976). However, many families think of play as an add-on, something babies do and others even children, when there is time and available resources, rather like going to a movie or a game. It is not a priority for families under pressure or financial constraint. Research studies involving parent–child interactions with families experiencing stress demonstrate this. Play was not mentioned, or even alluded to, by mothers receiving infant mental health intervention or mothers of children with disabilities in challenging urban environments (Olson 2004; Olson and Esdaile 2000). Even in less stressful situations, parents may need professional support to enhance their awareness of parent–child play interactions and the importance of play in child development. In my experience, toy-making workshops that included games to promote relaxation, proved to be an effective, non-threatening way to enhance parent–child play interactions (Esdaile 1987, 1996, 2004; Esdaile and Sanderson 1987).

Parent–child related factors that impact on relationships and play interactions include the quality of the child's attachment and the temperament, or behavioural style of the child, and how these fit with parental expectations. Therefore, more detailed discussions of attachment and temperament follow.

ATTACHMENT

The term attachment refers to the tendency of infants during the first 24 months to become maximally attached to their primary caregivers, most often the mother, and to be least apprehensive of strange individuals and situations when this person is present. If the infant becomes distressed, she is most readily soothed by this person. The importance of developing secure attachment to a primary caregiver whom the infant can trust to keep her safe enables the infant to explore her environment more freely and engage in play with objects and others. Infants who are less securely attached are more fearful of exploring. Infants who are not attached to a primary caregiver tend to be avoiding and fearful of new situations and people.

Attachment theory developed significantly through the work of Ainsworth and her colleagues (1978). Their carefully structured laboratory-based experiments involving mothers and their 9 to 24-month-old infants, came to be known as the 'Strange Situation'. The two key episodes are when the mother leaves the child, once with the stranger and once alone, and returns several minutes later to be reunited with the child. The child's immediate reaction to the mother's departure, and behaviour on her return, were used by Ainsworth and her colleagues to develop a quality of attachment index. Infants who were only mildly upset when the mother departed and easily comforted when she returned were described as 'securely attached'; infants who showed no distress when the mother left and did not approach her when she returned, were described as 'avoidant'; infants who were seriously upset by the mother's departure and resisted attempts to be soothed on her return, were described as 'resistant' in terms of attachment. The studies conducted by Ainsworth *et al.* have suggested that infants who are described as 'securely attached' become more resilient, curious and adaptive as they develop, ready to explore new situations in play, and are cooperative with others.

Other major contributors to this theory include Bowlby (1969) who argued that attachment to another person is instinctive and endures from infancy to adulthood and that insecure attachment during infancy affects future vulnerability to psychopathology. Harlow and Harlow (1966) studied attachment and deprivation in a series of experiments involving rhesus monkeys. The work of anthropologists, such as Hrdy (1999) and Lorenz (1952), also contributed to the understanding of attachment. The research that has evoked the strongest emotional reactions has been the Harlows' studies of maternal deprivation in rhesus monkeys, illustrated with the poignant photographs of distressed, depressed infant monkeys who were later unable to socialise with their peers. The researchers' reports of their capacity to recover remained less convincing as these reports coincided with other studies of childhood deprivation (e.g. Bowlby 1969).

Subsequently, studies that explored environmental and nurturing influences on infants in terms of neurological development underscored the negative effects of early stress and deprivation. Recovery was not as simple as earlier researchers had suggested (Fox, Calkins and Bell 1994). Attachment theory has been used extensively to study the effects of child abuse as well as early childhood behaviour problems (Bacon and Richardson 2001). It is generally accepted that disorganised infant attachment is a risk factor for problem behaviour and stress management, and additionally poses challenges for later intervention (Bakermans-Kranenburg, Van Ijzendoorn and Juffer 2005). Abused and neglected children are more likely than non-abused children to show delay in play development in terms of decreased skills, playfulness, and behaviour disturbance in play. These deficits present further risks for learning and social development (Cooper 2000).

The importance of early prevention/intervention is increasingly more accepted by the general public as well as funding agencies, though the level of services available is subject to political and economic fluctuations and needs to continue increasing and developing. When I worked with a child and family-based community programme in a multi-ethnic urban environment, clients included mothers on court orders to attend the centre because of convictions for child abuse. Activities that involved toddler-initiated play and relaxation games were part of our programme (Esdaile 1987, 1996; Esdaile and Sanderson 1987).

Vignette 3

Four adults, one male and three female, and one five-year-old boy are in a clinic waiting room; three of them have come for a psychologist's assessment because of custody issues related to the parents' divorce. The adult male and one of the females are the boy's parents; the second female is the boy's aunt, the third is a stranger who also has an appointment at the clinic.

The father engages the boy in an active game involving quick movements and physical contact. His actions suggest that he is very conscious of performing for an audience. Spare furniture is used to represent props and the game accelerates in terms of action and level of noise simulating crashes. The mother and aunt start to become uncomfortable, indicate this to the father, but do not make eye contact with the child. The father insists that they are having fun. As the game gets rougher and louder the boy starts to look anxious and fearful. The psychologist opening her office door and asking the child to come in interrupts the game. The child has not met her before, however, he goes with her without hesitation.

Consider the above scenario in terms of synchronisation and reciprocity and also attachment. How would you describe the interaction between the parents, aunt, psychologist, the stranger and the child?

TEMPERAMENT

An extensive body of research (e.g. Kagan 1984, 1994) has argued that vulnerability to anxiety is an innate, temperamentally determined quality in some children, not necessarily an outcome of insecure attachment. This is an important message for anyone who lives or works with children. Creating an optimal environment is easier with some than others.

Temperament is commonly defined in terms of behavioural style, how an individual behaves, rather than why or what is involved in the behaviour. Chess and Thomas (1986) were the primary researchers responsible for bringing this area of child psychology to the attention of the general public. They described nine temperament characteristics; *activity*, in terms of level and quality; *rhythmicity*, or the regularity of the child's behaviours such as sleeping and eating; *adaptability*, in terms of adjustment to change; *intensity*, in positive and negative reactions; *mood*, both positive and negative; *persistence and attention span* in all activities especially those that involve problem solving; *distractibility* by environmental factors; *sensory threshold*, or the extent to which the child is bothered by external stimuli such as noise. Using a self-report assessment questionnaire that could be completed by parents, caregivers and others involved with the child, temperament type was determined as 'easy' or flexible, if the child was generally calm and happy, with regular habits, adaptable and not easily upset. The child was deemed 'difficult, active', or 'feisty' if her sleeping and feeding patterns were irregular, she was easily upset by new situations sensitive to outside stimuli like noise, and intense in reactions to frustration or hurt. Children were described as 'slow to warm up' or 'cautious' if they were relatively inactive and fussy, tended to withdraw or react negatively to new situations, however, their reactions became more positive over longer exposure to the situation. Chess and Thomas (1986) studied the relationship between child temperament and parent temperament, describing it in terms of 'goodness-of-fit'.

Temperament has been studied extensively during the past 20–30 years, for example in the Australian Temperament Project, now in its twenty-fourth year (Prior, Sanson and Oberklaid 1989; Smart 2007; Smart *et al.* 2007; Smart and Sanson 2006). Children who have been identified 'difficult' may be at greater risk of behavioural adjustment, child abuse and poor scholastic achievement. However, positive environmental and parenting factors may mediate against the 'difficult' child developing behavioural problems. Cultural variability in child temperament was first discussed by Kagan (1984, 1994) and subsequently described in numerous other studies. Asian children tend to have a less active temperament, and are more likely to be described as 'easy'. In contrast, Mediterranean children are more likely to be active and volatile, and thus deemed 'difficult'. However, it is important to return to the issue of goodness-of-fit as, generally, parental expectations are congruent with cultural variability.

The ways in which parents attribute causation for parent–child interaction outcomes affect the quality of their relationships with their children. Thus, causal attributions may lead to behaviours which are either competent or adaptive to a situation, or they may lead to maladaptive behaviours such as inappropriate blame of self or the other person in the interaction (Bugental 1987, 1993). Parents' causal attributions for their children's behaviours are influenced by the degree to which they perceive children to be in control of the situation in which the behaviour occurs, as well as the degree to which they attribute responsibility to the child and/or to themselves for the outcome. Parents' causal attributions also have an affective component; having problems with a difficult task is more acceptable than having problems with one perceived as easy. Thus, we found that mothers were more stressed if they attributed responsibility for negative interaction outcomes to a child they had rated 'easy', than if they attributed responsibility for negative interaction outcomes to a child they had rated 'difficult' (Esdaile and Greenwood 1995). Temperament and caregiver perceptions have implications for the development of prevention and intervention programmes in terms of parental stress as well as child abuse.

Vignette 4

Tracy, a 21-year-old mother of two boys aged 30 months and 12 months, attended a series of community-based toy-making workshops.

Tracy knew little about child development and children's play needs, she tended to interpret her children's behaviour in terms of 'good' and 'bad'. She found her older son's level of energy and curiosity challenging and had rated his temperament 'difficult'. Her situation was exacerbated by the fact that her mother-in-law (her closest relative geographically) and the nurse at the health centre she attended with her children gave her conflicting information. Experts and authority figures intimidated her. The informal but structured process of making age-appropriate toys while her boys were in playgroup, and then using the toys that she made, to play with them at the end of the sessions, suited her style of learning. She also enjoyed the short weekly breaks from watching her children and the companionship of the other mothers in the group, commenting that it was 'good to know she was not alone' and that the toy-making sessions were 'very confidence building'.

Consider why making inexpensive, age-appropriate toys is a useful way to learn about children's play. Why not just talk about toys and look at samples or videos? How might you combine the resources of professionals and volunteers?

PARENT–CHILD PLAY INTERACTIONS IN THE CONTEXT OF CULTURE

Many researchers have contributed to our understanding of parent–child interactions and play. Their works acknowledge differing cultural contexts within families, societies and nations. English child-psychiatrist Winnicott (1964) was one of the first to write about children in a parent-friendly, inclusive manner. Bettleheim (1987), a psychiatrist and child psychologist, was born and trained in Vienna, but worked in the United States. His concept of the 'good-enough-parent' focused on the importance of parental awareness and sensitivity to children's uniqueness and individuality. He had a gift for including succinct and reassuring quotes in his texts, such as the Chinese proverb: 'Nobody's family can hang out the sign "Nothing the matter here".' (1987, p.289). Educational psychologists Tizard and Hughes (1984) challenged earlier assumptions about how children learn, validated parents' role as their children's educators and challenged negative stereotypes about the deficiency of learning in working class families. Bronfenbrenner's (1986) ecological model and Sameroff's (1993) transactional model both envisaged the child and her parents as actively involved, reciprocal participants in the process of their child's development. Bruner and colleagues (1976, 1983, 1990) contributed extensively to the understanding of language, cognition, and play development, adding a more philosophical dimension through exploring action and agency. Sutton-Smith (1997; Sutton-Smith and Sutton-Smith 1974), a play researcher and parent-educator for three decades, was initially concerned with parent-education and use of toys; his later research encompassed cultural interpretations of play, games, sport and festivals. Slaughter (1984), one of the researchers involved in the Head Start Program in the United States during the 1970s and 1980s, developed a series of innovative and effective programmes of toy making and toy-demonstration for parents. She was a strong influence in the development of my community-based work with families (Esdaile 1996). More recently, occupational scientists have explored the way parents create space for play within their homes (Pierce 2004), and the way parents incorporate playfulness in everyday tasks within the home (Primeau 2004).

Considerations of culture in children's play ranges from the relatively simple to the highly complex. At the simple end of the continuum, in many European cultures it is considered appropriate to dress children in their best clothes for meetings with people outside the family, especially professionals. So, children from these families would come to an early intervention play-group dressed in beautifully made clothes that were clearly not for crawling on the floor, and wearing shiny, slippery shoes in which they walked with difficulty. Negotiating a change required careful discussion so that the caregivers were not offended. Kagan provided a succinct example of the complex end of the cultural variation continuum by describing a discussion about attachment theory with a Hindu Brahmin who said that a Great Indian Soul lived in the world, but was not part of it. His spirit does not become attached to people or things. He aims to be like a drop of water on a lotus leaf, moving about on the leaf, but not absorbed in it (1984, p.54).

In order to work effectively with people from diverse cultural backgrounds it is important to be sensitive to differences. Practitioners learn to do this through experience. Recently, I was working with a group of therapists whose clients included teenage mothers and their children with developmental delay. One of the therapists was concerned that she did not know who was the infant's 'real caregiver', as sometimes she came with the mother, other times with her grandmother or her aunt. A more experienced practitioner was quick to point out that it didn't matter; they could all learn the home-programme.

Anyone who has come from one English-speaking country and worked in another can relate to Winston Churchill's comment that England and America are 'divided by a common language'. A lot of it is to do with different values as well as different use of the same words. Even within the same country, there may be different values that affect communications. A parent with an instrumental orientation, playing with a child with a toy truck, will describe its properties, the way the wheels go around, the way the truck tips, its colour and so on. Someone with a more interpersonal orientation may approach the game by commenting on the fact that the truck was a gift and talk about the giver and his relationship to the child as an introduction to play. We see these differences in the dialogues of people from Middle Eastern and many European countries whose concept of polite conversation usually commences in terms of an interpersonal orientation. Thus, if parents with these cultural backgrounds come to see an early intervention specialist with their child, they expect a polite interchange about their health and that of their extended family before honing in on the focus of the visit. They may also expect instructions and plans to include an acknowledgement of God's will in the outcome. More time may be needed, but if the family is offended and not prepared to listen, then time is wasted.

At a workshop for early-intervention specialists that I attended a few years ago, one of the specialists was critical of a Middle Eastern father, who according to her had rejected his disabled daughter and refused to cooperate with staff. She showed a video of the family to make her point. What I observed in the video was a man who carefully held on to a chair his daughter was climbing, making sure she was safe, making eye contact with her. He was turned away from the staff member and appeared to find her manner inappropriate or even offensive within his cultural context.

Some useful issues to consider in regard to culture are: the influences of individualism versus collectivism; whether there are clearly defined gender roles that cannot be transgressed easily or quickly; the decision-making process within the family and the level of involvement with extended family members. It would be useful to find out about the specific games and toys that are traditional to that culture. If you work with clients whose cultural orientation is different from yours, it would be helpful to undertake training to assist you. There are many texts available that have helpful self-assessment questionnaires regarding these issues (e.g. Brislin and Yoshida 1994; also see Chapter 11).

Vignette 5 Gina and her family

When I became Gina's therapist, she was 10 years old and diagnosed with spastic diplegia. Her family was of Italian origin and her mother worked at home, doing sewing on consignment for a garment factory. This was hard work, she was going through menopause, and was additionally stressed by Gina's teenage siblings. So, my home visits and treatment programme unofficially included the family. I listened to all their problems and also recruited them, as well as Gina's friends in the street as part of the home programme – playing games designed to improve her balance, constructing activities to improve her fine-motor coordination and writing skills. When it came time for Gina to enter junior high school, I devised a comprehensive, full-day assessment that required Gina's mother to bring her to the city, where in order to get from the railway station to the street, she had to negotiate many steps. We went to lunch and a movie. All this involved negotiating public transport, walking in a dimly lit movie theatre, eating in a restaurant, meeting new people and retelling the story of the movie. The whole day was also a realistic test of fatigue tolerance. I was able to write a comprehensive report for her teachers. The family didn't think of the day as assessment, just nice that I took Gina to a movie before she started the school year.

We had a productive and enjoyable day, but many professionals prefer to conduct assessments in a more structured setting. What do you think?

PARENTS AND THE EXPERTS

There are many books written for parents about play, child development and selection of toys. Even the best ones may not be in print for long, so parents may need a local guide to assist them in selecting the best that are available. Some are excellent, others frankly commercial, and many are rather unrealistic, putting very high expectations on families' time and resources, emotional and physical as well as financial. It is advisable to avoid these as well as books that tell parents to fill every minute of a child's life with structured play. The Internet has enabled parents to access many excellent informative websites that are research-based, but written for the general public. Some of these are listed at the end of this chapter. There are also community-based programmes for parents in cities and towns in Australia, Canada, the United Kingdom and United States.

The literature and individuals to avoid are what may loosely be described as the 'anxiety makers'. They occur unfortunately in every generation and include the 'experts' that tell parents what they must do, with no options for cultural or individual preferences. For example that they must always sleep with their infants, or that they must not, under any circumstances, do this. Hardyment (1983) gives a very entertaining and insightful account of the way in which 'experts' have stressed parents throughout history with amazingly contradictory injunctions. Common sense and a sense of irony always help to put parenting into perspective. The occupational therapy scholar, Mary Reilly commented succinctly in regard to the parental and often professional tendency to blame parents at every turn: 'A high level of expectation leads many parents to approach child-rearing with such trepidation or hopes that it would have been better if nothing new had been learned in the last century. Never, it would seem, have our child-rearing practices been so inept' (1974, p.25). Although I don't agree with the last sentence, it clearly illustrates the way any current or past child-rearing practices can be viewed negatively or positively. My point in including it here is to acknowledge that we all need to be critical of experts and filter their views to our needs; we have to accept that parents have a right to do this as well. Professionals sometimes underestimate the difficulty of real lives and need to keep compassion at the forefront of their practice. In conclusion, it is important not to lose sight of the fact that parent–child play interactions are meant to be enjoyable for parents as well as children. In order to promote this, professionals need to maintain a sense of playfulness in their own lives.

RESOURCES FOR PARENTS

- Australian Institute of Family Studies, also includes the Australian Temperament Project database, www.aifs.gov.au

- Ohio State University in the United States has an extension programme for families that includes information on understanding temperament (Oliver 2008)

- The United Parenting Association, also in the United States, has many helpful publications for parents, for example about issues of attachment (Nix 2008)

- The European Temperament Network, based in Geneva, Switzerland, has a free online Temperament Profile Service, part of ongoing research, which is available in several languages (Zentner 2006)

REFERENCES

Ainsworth, M. D., Blehard, M. C., Waters, E. and Wall, S. (1978) *Patterns of Attachment.* Hillsdale, NJ: Lawrence Erlbaum.

Bacon, H. and Richardson, S. (2001) 'Attachment theory and child abuse: An overview of literature for practitioners.' *Child Abuse Review 10,* 6, 377–397.

Bakermans-Kranenburg, M. J., Van Ijzendoorn, M. H. and Juffer, F. (2005) 'Disorganized infant attachment and preventive interventions: A review and meta-analysis.' *Infant Mental Health Journal 26,* 3, 191–216.

Bettleheim, B. (1987) *A Good Enough Parent.* London: Pan Books.

Bowlby, J. (1969) *Attachment and Loss. Vol. 1. Attachment.* New York: Basic Books.

Brislin, R. W. and Yoshida, T. (1994) *Improving Intercultural Interactions. Modules for Cross-Cultural Training Programs.* Thousand Oaks, CA: Sage Publications

Bronfenbrenner, U. (1986) 'Ecology of the family as a context for human development: Research perspectives.' *Developmental Psychology 22,* 723–742.

Bruner, J. (1983) *Child's Talk. Learning to Use Language.* Oxford: Oxford University Press.

Bruner, J. (1990) *Acts of Meaning.* Cambridge, MA: Harvard University Press.

Bruner, J. S., Jolly, A. and Sylva, K. (1976) *Play. Its Role in Development and Evolution.* Harmondsworth: Penguin Books.

Bugental, D. B. (1987) 'Attributions as moderator variables within social interaction systems.' *Journal of Social and Clinical Psychology 5,* 469–484.

Bugental, D. B. (1993) 'Communication in abusive relationships.' *American Behavioral Scientist 36,* 288–308.

Chess, S. and Thomas, A. (1986) *Temperament in Clinical Practice.* New York: Guilford Press.

Cooper, R. J. (2000) 'The impact of child abuse on children's play: A conceptual model.' *Occupational Therapy International 7,* 4, 259–276.

Esdaile, S. (1987) 'Relaxation with children: An evaluation of workshops for teachers, parents and students.' *Australian Occupational Therapy Journal 34,* 4–13.

Esdaile, S. (1996) 'A play focused intervention involving mothers of preschoolers.' *American Journal of Occupational Therapy 50,* 2, 113–123.

Esdaile, S. (2004) 'Toys for Shade and the Mother Child Co-occupation of Play.' In S. Esdaile and J. Olson (eds) *Mothering Occupations. Challenge, Agency and Participation.* Philadelphia: F. A. Davis.

Esdaile, S. and Greenwood, K. (1995) 'A survey of mothers' relationship with their preschoolers.' *Occupational Therapy International 2,* 3, 204–219.

Esdaile, S. and Sanderson, A. (1987) *Toys to Make.* Ringwood: Penguin Books Australia.

Fox, N. A., Calkins, S. D. and Bell, M. A. (1994) 'Neural plasticity and development in the first two years of life: Evidence from cognitive and socioemotional domains of research.' *Development and Psychopathology 6,* 677–696.

Hrdy, S. B. (1999) *Mother nature. The History of Mothers, Infants and Natural Selection.* New York: Pantheon Books.

Hardyment, C. (1983) *Dream Babies. Child Care from Locke to Spock.* London: Jonathan Cape.

Harlow, H. F. and Harlow, M. K. (1966) 'Learning to love.' *American Scientist 54,* 3, 244–272.

Kagan, J. (1984) *The Nature of the Child.* New York: Basic Books.

Kagan, J. (1994) *Galen's Prophecy. Temperament in Human Nature.* New York: Basic Books.

Lorenz, K. (1952) *King Solomon's Ring. A New Light on Animal Ways.* New York: Crowell Publications.

Nix, N. (2008) *Attachment Parenting.* United Parenting Publications. Available at http://parenthood.com/articles.html?article_id=7301, accessed 19 September 2008.

Olson, J. (2004) 'Mothering Co-occupations in Caring for Infants and Young Children.' In S. A. Esdaile and J. A. Olson (eds) *Mothering Occupations. Challenge, Agency and Participation.* Philadelphia: F. A. Davis.

Oliver, K. K. (2008) *Understanding your Child's Temperament.* Family and Consumer Sciences: Ohio State University Extension, Columbus OH. Available at www.parenthood.com/articles.html?article_id=7301, accessed 19 September 2008.

Pierce, D. (2004) 'Maternal Management of Home Space and Time to Facilitate Infant/Toddler Play and Development.' In S. A. Esdaile and J. A. Olson (eds) *Mothering Occupations. Challenge, Agency and Participation.* Philadelphia: F. A. Davis.

Primeau, L. (2004) 'Mothering in the Context of Unpaid Work and Play in Families.' In S. A. Esdaile and J. A. Olson (eds) *Mothering Occupations. Challenge, Agency and Participation.* Philadelphia: F. A. Davis.

Prior, M. R., Sanson, A. V. and Oberklaid, F. (1989) 'The Australian Temperament Project.' In G. Kohnstamm, J. Bates and M. Rothbart, H. (eds) *Handbook of Temperament in Childhood.* London:Wiley.

Reilly, M. (ed.) (1974) *Play as Exploratory Learning.* Thousand Oaks, CA: Sage Publications.

Sameroff, A. J. (1993) 'Models of Development and Developmental Risk.' In C. H. Zeanna Jr (ed) *Handbook of Infant Mental Health.* New York: Guilford Press.

Slaughter, D. T. (1984) *Early Intervention and its Effects on Maternal and Child Development.* Society for Research in Child Development, Monograph 48, 4, Serial no. 202.

Smart, D. (2007) *Tailoring Parenting to Fit the Child.* AFRC Briefing paper no. 4. Melbourne: Australian Family Relationships Clearinghouse, Australian Institute of Family Studies.

Smart, D., Hayes, A., Sanson A. V. and Toumbourou, J. W. (2007) 'Mental health and wellbeing of Australian adolescents: Pathways to vulnerability and resilience.' *International Journal of Adolescent Medicine and Health 19,* 263–268.

Smart, D. and Sanson, A. (2006) 'A comparison of children's temperament and adjustment across 20 years.' In *LSAC 2005–06 Annual Report.* Melbourne: Australian Institute of Family Studies.

Sutton-Smith, B. (1997) *The Ambiguity of Play.* Cambridge: Harvard University Press.

Sutton-Smith, B. and Sutton-Smith, S. (1974) *How to Play with Your Children.* New York: Hawthorn Books.

Tizard, B. and Hughes, M. (1984) *Young Children Learning.* London: Fontana Books.

Winnicott, D.W. (1964) *The Child, the Family and the Outside World.* Harmondsworth: Penguin Books.

Zentner, M. (2006) *The European Temperament Network.* Department of Psychology, University of Geneva, Switzerland, available at www.childtemperament.org.index.php?lang=eng, accessed 19 September 2008.

CHAPTER 11

Cultural Considerations

Athena A. Drewes

CHAPTER OBJECTIVES

This chapter explores the place of play in culture, and discusses several cultures and play within those cultures. Two invited vignettes provide examples of children's play in Australian Aboriginal and Japanese cultures. Practical suggestions for culturally appropriate practice are also provided.

PLAY AS CULTURE

Play is a universal, natural and pleasurable experience, as well as an integral part of children's lives. It is a dominant activity throughout all cultures and exerts both a cause and effect on culture (Roopnarine and Johnson 1994). Play has also had a very significant impact on the continuation and development of culture (Monroe 1995), for it is through play that a society is able to express its place in the world and develop such things as poetry, philosophy, music, dance and social structures (Huizinga 1949).

Play is a learned behaviour. It is learned through the interactions with older children and adults within the society and culture that they live in (Fleer 1999). By allowing children opportunities to explore and interact with various objects in the environment and through daily life encounters, along with interactions with individuals, children learn to master their own bodies, their surroundings and how to practise new and old skills and build relationships (Kelly and Godbey 1992; Monroe 1995). Through successful mastery efforts the individual's chances for survival increase, and in turn allow for the successful integration of such mastery into social structures

resulting in cultural survival as well (Monroe 1995). Play is also an important component in the development of values, such as the beliefs, ethics and
actions that guide each person. Through play, children are able to learn
about their society's rules and what is acceptable behaviour (Monroe 1995).
In turn, children can learn to sort out not only their similarities but also what
is different about themselves and others (Levin 2000). Social roles, acceptable play partners and the meaning of play begin to get sorted out through
play. Children within a multicultural society need to become not only competent in their own culture, but also competent within the dominant culture
that they interact with (Fleer 1999). Play helps them to do that.

While play is universal, the way play looks and works, and the degree to
which it is encouraged or attended to varies according to each society and
cultural group (Sutton-Smith 1974, 1999; Vandermaas-Peeler 2002). The
amount of attention devoted by a particular culture to play depends largely
on cultural beliefs about the nature of childhood and specific goals that caregivers have for young children (Vandermaas-Peeler 2002). But across all cultures play can be considered one of the most vital activities for children
(Bloch and Pellegrini 1989). Its importance is seen in children's development of the cognitive skills of symbolism and language use, problem-solving, role play and creativity, along with forming friendships, social
competence and emotional maturity (Vandermaas-Peeler 2002). Play becomes a way to understand the very meaning of human existence (Oke *et al.*
1999). So important is play for a child that the converse, play deprivation,
has serious consequences across all cultures as well. Non-players are ostra-
cised from group activities which results in a lack of learning how to get
along with others within the culture through the social characteristics of
play, a key element (Frost and Jacobs 1996).

Cultural norms and attitudes toward play, along with opportunities for
play, determine how different types of play are stimulated and whether the
adult sees play as a good thing or a waste of children's time (Edwards 2000).
Differences in play and play behaviours across cultures can also be seen in
the degree to which play is viewed as a survival mechanism and to what extent children are permitted or encouraged to take risks, how play fighting
may be viewed, and what the responsibilities are of the children to each
other as well as to adults (Johns 1999). How much freedom the child has to
explore and practise adult roles through play, as well as whether the environment provides easy access to materials for creative and constructive play are
also important cultural considerations (Edwards 2000). Children across all
cultures will engage in various forms of play, whether or not they have actual
toys, or they will create the activities through their own imagination and

creativity. Children around the world find both the time and materials for play (Vandermaas-Peeler 2002).

A developing body of research literature has been emerging on the sociocultural variations of children's play (Farver 1999; Roopnarine, Johnson and Hooper 1994). Such sociocultural variations of play depend on the attitudes of parents, teachers and society in general, along with the amount of play space and time available to children (Roopnarine *et al.* 1998).

CULTURAL DIFFERENCES

While children's play is indeed similar whether they are of the Anglo-European or Indigenous culture, it differs when it comes to being given permission to take risks (Johns 1999). If play is indeed a survival mechanism, then the acceptance of humour, play fighting and the responsibilities of children to each other and to adults are important components that become imbedded in play (Johns 1999). Risk-taking is an important aspect of the learning process for children. Carers, clinicians and child care workers of the Anglo-European cultures may find risk-taking acceptable as long as an adult is nearby for safety and the children know the rule and limits of such behaviour (Johns 1999). For example, it is difficult for staff in day care and school settings, as well as therapists, to stand back and allow a child to experiment on their own and take risks (Johns 1999).

As a survival mechanism, risk-taking play adds to the development of observational skills, for children are constantly tuning into their environment and surroundings (Johns 1999). They need to process where they are heading, both with the land and the surroundings to avoid danger. 'To survive you have to be aware' (Johns 1999, p.63). Play also requires responsibility such as being responsible for themselves, which children achieve through playing and exploring their environment. They are mastering a sense of direction, observing and assessing the situation and seeing what and who is familiar or different, making decisions and calculations as to what to do next, and in following through on their action or plan (Johns 1999).

Children's play fighting, which often can turn physical, may be more prevalent in indigenous cultures, but still remains respectful and caring, knowing there are rules to follow. Therefore it is critical for professionals and caregivers to discuss the cultural views of the families they work with, especially around risk-taking play.

For many cultures, older children are given the responsibility of caring for the younger children with babies treated as though 'real life dolls' by the older children. They are fed, carried around, disciplined and put to bed, but also taught play by joining in the activities (Johns 1999). Such activities by the older children help them learn vital skills and responsibilities through play for their future roles in their society. It is critical to know what the culture's view is about the family for many cultures view the extended family as very important, whereby the family helps the child acquire through play, knowledge about their society. 'They begin to learn who they are, and where they fit in as well as what is expected of them' (Van Diermen and Johns 1995, p.14).

A SAMPLING OF VARIOUS CULTURES AND PLAY

Active parental encouragement and even demonstration by adults of appropriate play activities varies across cultures according to how play is valued (Gil and Drewes 2005). Research by Farver, Kim and Lee (1995) with American, Mexican and Indonesian families found that those mothers who valued play as having educational and cognitive benefits were the ones more likely to join in their child's play and to provide props and suggestions which encouraged pretend play more than mothers who saw their child's play as just amusement or an imitation of adult roles. The same researchers also studied Korean-American and Anglo-American families. They found that those Anglo-American mothers who believed play was critical for children's learning and development engaged in more pretend play than Korean-American mothers, who considered play as just an escape from boredom or a way to amuse them.

INDIGENOUS PEOPLES

When working with children the cultural meanings enacted through their play needs to be considered as well as understanding and valuing the different types of play across cultures. Hamilton's (1981) observations of child rearing practices in Arnhem Land, Australia, found that non-Aboriginal mothers of European heritage used everyday household objects from the environment to distract, pacify and amuse their child as well as to allow the child to explore, whereas Aboriginal mothers seldom did this. The means toward emotional contentment was through the social interaction with the mother, through an oral experience (Fleer 1999). Hamilton (1981) found that Australian Aboriginal children who lived in remote traditional communities did not engage in the fantasy games of similarly aged non-Aboriginal Australian boys which included being explorers, doctors and pirates complete with elaborate role structures and behavioural sequences (Farver 1999). The Anbarra boys' play instead consisted of exploring their environment, risk-taking and developing physical skills (Farver 1999).

Aleesha's story by Alma Dender

Alma is a lecturer at Curtain University in Perth Australia and she is currently developing an Australian Indigenous play assessment.

The Australian Aboriginal culture is an oral culture, where knowledge of the culture, the traditions, the relationships to the land and other people have been passed down in the form of stories. The story of creation and the Dreamtime tell of the beginning and the history of the Australian Aboriginals. Story telling and listening to stories is part of the life of every Aboriginal child.

Aleesha is a vivacious four-year-old, a consummate story teller and an accomplished player. She settles in to play with her four-year-old friend Josiah. Aleesha is captivated by the Australian animals of her region of Australia. Quickly the animals are given life as Aleesha cuddles the kangaroos, and her face lights up as she starts to build a play scene with the toys. She moves them as if they have real life – kangaroos leaping, birds flying and dogs running and barking. She makes their sounds and creates their characters and starts weaving stories about what they are doing and what they are feeling. Her face reflects the antics of the animals and dolls, their fear of the snakes, their joy at leaping, their tenderness when they look at their babies.

Just as Aleesha easily enters into pretence, she brings in the realities of life in an isolated mining town into her play. She loads the dead animals onto the truck and takes them to the hospital, telling the story as the doll drives the truck. She reverses the hospital truck into the garage, making the reversing beeps of the mine trucks she hears every day. All the while she is playing, changing scenes, she narrates the story.

Aleesha brings in her Aboriginality, her understanding of the way creatures of the Dreamtime can take away and bring about life. She sets the scene with the snakes which creep into the horses' way, and when the horses stop, the snakes decide to eat the horses. The snakes slowly eat the horses, until Aleesha declares they are only bones standing up and they are not happy. The horses move forward and beg the snakes to give them back their skin. The snakes eventually agree to give the horses back their skin so they can run and be horses again, and they do so by 'spewing' the skin back on the horses. The horses are happy again. Josiah, her playmate, has sat in absolute silence, enthralled by the story that is so reminiscent of the creation stories he has heard from his communities' elders. But for the Aboriginal child, it is not a pretence, not a fabrication, it is the story of how the Aboriginal world came into being.

United States – Native Americans

Indigenous cultures within the United States of America span over 500 recognised tribes with diversity within and across them. One of the values most frequently associated with these cultures is the pervasive belief in the sacredness of life, where religious experience is constant and surrounds the individual at all times (McDonald and McAvoy 1997). There is a clear, reciprocal and interdependent relationship with all of creation and humans are inseparable from nature. There is also a belief in the cyclical or circular pattern of life, which in turn is recreated at every level of the culture. The use of circles is an important cultural component in Native American cultures, with traditional homes, dances, communication and play all having a circular arrangement and movement occurring in a clockwise fashion (Farrer 1990).

The spoken word is considered important with thinking before speaking expected. Anglo-Europeans may misread the thoughtful pause and silence as withdrawal or as a stereotypical characteristic of a stoic and silent people. Sacred knowledge is passed down in oral forms with elders as the repositories of the knowledge (McDonald and McAvoy 1997). It is also considered impolite to express emotions in public, with parents ignoring minor misbehaviour and rarely correcting their children in a public setting. However, children are expected to behave appropriately, having learned by observing parents, older siblings and other relatives.

Native Americans concentrate more on playing a game well rather than putting down an opponent or being competitive. Competition is seen as a motivating, stimulating force that spurs the group and individual toward greatness (Schroeder 1995). Everyone tries to do their best but not at the others' expense and winning and losing is not seen as relevant. One person's gain is not at the expense of another's loss, with a lack of malice in the games and 'losers' being 'good sports' in how they handled their reactions. Native American children often play in a group with relatives and family members, and this is preferred over solitary play or joining activities with non-Native American children. Activities and physical games are conducted in a circular arrangement.

Physical proximity is also a normal way of communicating for indigenous American children and adults, standing close to the side of the other person with whom you are talking. Eyes are usually kept straight ahead or are cast down and the child's body does not move until the interaction is terminated (Farrer 1990). Adults and children can become offended if the other person (e.g. a therapist or teacher) moves away from their body contact.

PLAY IN OTHER CULTURES

Play in homogeneous agricultural communities in Africa and India show a close link between adult activities and the imitation seen in the children's play (Feitelson 1977). Play activities tend to be very short-lived in these countries, with a lack of complexity and continuity, as compared to Western culture (Fleer 1999).

Play themes originate from the culture of the child, and the interactions between the children are based on their shared or common knowledge (Edwards and Mercer 1987).

Individual and social play is not universal across all cultures but in fact appears to be bound by the culture (Fleer 1999). Mead's (1930) observations of Manus Islander children as reported by Feitelson (1977) found that the children's play lacked imagination, even though there was ample free time and abundant natural materials. Feitelson (1977) also reported how Middle Eastern mothers who were observed actually often interfered, in an active way, whenever imaginative aspects came up in the play situation. These mothers also did not model play or provide play objects.

Mexico

Mayan children's play varied from American children's in several ways (Gaskins and Goncu 1992). The Mayan children from rural Yucatan, Mexico, had play themes that were exclusively about what they saw the adults doing in daily life, along with little elaboration or complexity throughout the play. Roles and play scripts were almost ritualised, with children not deviating from being human and only utilising actual objects (Fleer 1999). There were no imaginary objects or people in the children's play. In turn, the adults did not join in the play, nor seemed particularly entertained by watching the play and did not reward the play by attention or praise (Fleer 1999). Consequently, play was not valued in its own right, with adults preferring the children to observe and learn through watching and engaging in a productive activity or that the play should contain work elements. Children were expected not to interrupt or get in the way, and by the age of five were expected to be self-sufficient in bathing, dressing, grooming, eating and sleeping, resulting in highly independent and competent self-care. There is little social interaction between children and adults and young children do not initiate conversations with adults, and are expected to be silent. Children would talk socially within the same age group, but there were often long periods of silence. Such a lack of contact may look like withdrawal or lack of engagement to Western observers (Gaskins 2000).

Africa

Children in Liberia have over 90 forms of play from make-believe, games, use of toys, story telling, dancing, musical instruments and adult play. Natural materials and objects are turned into toys. Story telling is prominent, with children from age nine upwards telling stories that contained animals talking to each other and to people, humans having access to magical powers and spirits in human form (e.g. witches). Folktales were told by the older children to the younger ones. Hunting games were common in many parts of Africa, serving as imitative play as a prerequisite for actual adult work. Zambian children valued music, making musical instruments from natural materials, writing their own songs, dancing and organising their own bands (Drewes 2005a).

Asia

There is much diversity between and amongst all cultural groups. This diversity is most evident in different Asian ethnic groups and cultures. There is a temptation to view Eastern or Western Asian cultures as one dimensional and homogeneous, rather than multifaceted and pluralistic, whereas there are four distinct geographic Asian groups: Pacific Islanders (e.g. Hawaii, Samoa, Guam); Southeast Asians (e.g. Indonesia, Vietnam, Thailand, Cambodia, Philippines); East Asians (e.g. China, Japan, Korea) and South Asians (e.g. India, Pakistan, Sri Lanka) (Lee and Childress 1999). There are many heterogeneous subgroups within each group, differing in language, religion, customs, history and race (Feng 1994). Therefore clinicians and paediatric professionals need to always ask the child and family about their cultural heritage and where they may have lived previously (Drewes 2005b).

China

In China parents use playtime as a teaching time, demanding mature behaviour, expecting the children to listen attentively to their elders and behave accordingly. Much emphasis is put on helping their children to develop proper conduct for group acceptance and participation (Haight *et al.* 1999). Pretend play is used to teach such conduct and Confucian thought emphasised with role playing social rules and adult customs. Harmonious social interaction through obeying, respecting and submitting to elders, adherence to rules and cooperation is heavily focused on (Chow 1994).

India

Parents in Western India took one of three distinct roles in their children's play: instructive – telling the children what to do; restrictive – cautioning and protecting them from something harmful; or participative – playing with the children (Oke *et al.* 1999). Some universal games, such as tag, hide-and-seek and ball-and-stick games were played but often the children converted almost anything they could find into play materials. Pretend play included being film stars and using dialogues from films, as well as use of festival rituals being played out and sung. Almost three-quarters of the play observed involved physical movement: chasing, jumping over obstacles, racing and dancing, despite limited play spaces (Oke *et al.* 1999).

Korea

In Korea, mothers frequently used food as a way to comfort their young children, offering continuous and immediate gratification. Punishment or removal of objects was used frequently to stop a child's behaviour rather than stopping or redirecting. Mothers had a high expectation for their child's success and believed that play had an important role in promoting this success. Toys were utilised to improve creativity, develop positive feelings and promote and enhance physical and psychological development. Infants were viewed as needing to be protected given their fragility and being at risk from excessive external sensory and psychological stimuli (Hupp, Lam and Jaeger 1992). Therefore mouthing of objects or toys was regarded as risky behaviour.

Japan

Play in Japanese children by Akiko J. Ohnogi, Psy.D.

Akiko is a play therapist and psychologist who runs her own private practice in Tokyo, Japan. She teaches play therapy at International Christian University graduate school and is the co-founder and board director of Japan Association for Play Therapy.

Japanese children's play has changed greatly within the past 20 years and this change can be attributed to the availability of electronic games and societal environmental change. Societal environmental change has impacted play because playing outside has become more dangerous with kidnapping and random assaults and killings of children becoming more rampant; the number of neighbourhood adults 'overseeing' neighbourhood children playing outside has decreased; and open space for children to freely run around without worrying about traffic has also decreased.

Up until about 20 years ago Japanese children's common and traditional play was mainly conducted in groups, either mixed gender or single gender depending on the type of play, with various age groups participating. Most children played outside in parks or open space areas while it was still light, with games of varying degrees of physical exertion (e.g. gomudan, hanetsuki, kinngyosukui). Play behaviours exhibited indoors were physically subdued and usually reserved for play after dark, on rainy days, extra cold or hot days or special occasions (e.g. otedama, hanafuda, oekaki). Toys were made with discarded everyday material (e.g. kannkeri, takeuma), or bought at toy stores catering for children's pocket money (e.g. ohajiki, mennko), or presented by adults (e.g. fukuwarai, kenndama). These objects were used, reused, and passed down to younger siblings or neighbourhood children.

From about 20 years ago (post-electronic games) Japanese children's play has shifted to individual or parallel play with electronic games indoors (e.g. Nintendo Game Cube, Sony Play Station, Wii, etc.). Many children from a very young age are given various electronic game machines, handheld ones and larger ones to be connected to the TV, as well as those downloadable onto the computer. Many of the TV cartoon programmes (TV anime: e.g. Dragon Quest), cartoon magazines (manga: e.g. Dragon Ball) and cartoon movies (anime movies: e.g. Kinnikuman), have become based on characters from these electronic games or vice versa. Drawing these manga/anime/game characters is popular, as in the past, however, the drawings are currently done more in private than in shared groups, and are more often a direct copy of the original anime rather than a fantasised unique version. The drawings are often of humans with supernatural powers or non-earthlings with human characteristics, all in battle, rather than of 'normal' people in everyday life, as drawn pre-electronic game era. If one does not have individual access to a game portal, there are many game centres (e.g. gesen) throughout Japan, readily available to children of all ages. Family playtime has also shifted from going to the park to play baseball together to playing a television wired electronic game made for multiple players. When children play together with a non-electronic game, often it is either trading or playing with anime-based cards (e.g. Pokemon, Mushiking), or taking stickable photos on machines located in various areas (e.g., purikura), trading and collecting them.

When children engage in fantasy role play, the characters they choose to portray have changed from 'real' people (e.g. family members, friends, TV stars, etc.) to those from the electronic games and/or animes/mangas (e.g. Gokuu, Naruto). Play themes often consist of heroes and their counterpart evil enemies, all who have special non-human abilities as well as multiple lives and/or the power to rejuvenate one's life. Boys and girls alike often identify themselves with the strongest and most popular of the 'good guys', defeating the evil and helping their fellow teammates who are not as strong or sophisticated in their special powers as themselves. Character plots are initially always in line with the actual game/manga stories, slowly incorporating 'new' stories that are created in line with what the child him/herself is expressing or fantasising. Competitive games have also changed from physical group oriented activities conducted outdoors (e.g. onigokko, darumasangakoronda), to having various monsters and superhumans battle each other in electronic games or through card games based on the electronic games and/or animes/mangas.

Amongst the majority of Japanese parents and adults, play for children is considered something that is fun and enjoyable, rather than something that is necessary for healthy development, a means of communication or self-expression, or a tool for creativity, socialisation or problem-solving. It is also used as a convenient means of occupying the child when adults are unable to look after them, thus, as long as the children are not bothering adults, and the playing is not interfering with their study time and it is something that the parent feels comfortable with, then it is considered an appropriate way of spending time. Whether a child plays alone or with a group of children is not a major concern for contemporary parents.

IMPLICATIONS FOR EDUCATORS AND CLINICIANS

As families migrate within their country or immigrate to other countries for safety, work and educational benefits, the number of children and families from culturally diverse backgrounds is rapidly increasing across the globe. It is essential for clinicians and paediatric professionals to become more aware of this global shift and its impact on the populations we may serve. We also need to be sensitive to the cultural differences amongst the children we work with (Drewes 2005a).We need to help children embrace these differences (Drewes 2005a). Thus, child therapists and carers need to develop strategies to help children build upon the unique qualities of their cultural identity. Further, we need to ensure that our therapeutic communication and interventions are culturally sensitive, respectful and open to cultural learning.

The implications for educators and clinicians are important, in not assuming that all children play alike or that play is valued in all families. Families should be asked about their upbringing and beliefs with regard to play, and what value play has for them. How the children play with peers, or interact in groups, may also depend on culture and there may be a range of ways that a child plays in a group. The child's play needs to be observed, without expectation or judgment, over time, in light of the value the parent places on play and keeping in mind the child's culture.

It is important to remember that many cultures may not use verbal means for learning, but rather modelling and observational skills. In addition, a period of silence or a long pause may not signal a lack of attention or language problems, but perhaps a cultural norm for communication. Similarly, close physical proximity may be a necessity for communication and play, rather than an intrusion into personal space. Yet a child from a Native American background may resent being touched, especially on the head or hair, by an adult, because in their culture only certain relatives may touch one's head (Rettig 2002), hence the need for cultural awareness education and active seeking of cultural advice for that particular group.

Furthermore, we need to consider that play of children, regardless of type, may be strongly culturally defined, valued, interpreted and perpetuated as a result of cultural practices (Fleer 1999). Theories of play, as defined by Piaget, Smilansky and others, should also be considered in light of the culture in which they were formulated (Fleer 1999), as Western theories may be inappropriate when applied to multicultural or indigenous societies.

CREATING A MULTICULTURAL PLAY ENVIRONMENT

Clinicians and paediatric professionals need to consider their client's cultural backgrounds when including play materials in their offices and therapy rooms so that it reflects cultural diversity. It can be very helpful to invite the child's parent or caregiver into the therapy space to view the play materials that will be used. It is important that the clinician asks questions and becomes educated by the family regarding their cultural and personal metaphors, beliefs; religious views, family's native country, languages spoken at home, and their view towards play. Sensitivity is needed so that items are not included that might be taboo or considered bad luck or evil not only in the therapy room, but also in the clinician's office and waiting room.

Consideration should be given to hanging paintings, prints and photos by artists of various cultures that reflect the cultural diversity of the clientele served (Glover 1999). Inclusion of multicultural sculptures, pottery, baskets and other artefacts and cultural music in the waiting area could also be considered (Drewes 2005b). Arts and crafts supplies, games, dolls, play foods and books are all now available on line and through catalogues representing many different cultures. For example, the non-verbal communication of emotionally loaded material may be typical of many Asian cultures, so items such as origami paper for folding, rice paper for painting and red clay should be available (Drewes 2005b) for children to express themselves with. Pencils, markers, crayons and paints with multicultural skin tones allow children to draw and paint pictures more representative of their self-image and physical characteristics. The inclusion of books and stories that represent the different cultural groups served will be helpful for all the children in being able to learn to appreciate each other's diverse backgrounds as well as their own.

Items that reflect nurturing themes for dramatic play should also be included, such as dishes, cooking utensils and plastic food items from various cultures. Also, items such as empty tea boxes, tea tins, canned foods, cardboard or plastic food containers and various ethnic food utensils should be included. Such items can be inexpensively obtained from stores within the communities of the families or by having the families bring them in or help to obtain them. Dolls of all sizes, shapes and ages can now be purchased in different skin colours, as well as with realistic facial characteristics, different hair colours or styles, and culturally relevant clothing. Scraps of batik fabric, kente cloth or other colourful woven fabric representative of various cultures can also be used as doll blankets or even for dress-up (Drewes 2005b).

The inclusion of ethnic music from the different cultures served can be used in waiting areas or as background music where the children are. The inclusion of a globe or maps of the world or different countries can help spark discussion with the children and families about emigration and immigration, or can help to clarify a family's point of origin (Martinez and Valdez 1992).

It is important that we as clinicians and professionals be able to be proactive in sharing our own cultural background but especially in asking our multicultural clients about themselves, their culture and how it impacts on their child's play, in order to better serve their needs.

REFERENCES

Bloch, M. N. and Pellegrini, A. D. (1989) 'Ways of Looking at Children, Context and Play.' In M. N. Bloch and A. D. Pellegrini (eds) *The Ecological Context of Children's Play*. Norwood, NJ: Ablex.

Chow, R. (1994) 'Beyond parental control and authoritarian parenting style: Understanding Chinese parenting through the cultural notion of training.' *Child Development 65*, 1111–1119.

Drewes, A. A. (2005a) 'Play in Selected Cultures. Diversity and Universality.' In E. Gil and A. A. Drewes (eds) *Cultural Issues in Play Therapy*. New York: Guilford Press.

Drewes, A. A. (2005b) 'Multicultural Play Therapy Resources.' In E. Gil and A. A. Drewes (eds) *Cultural Issues in Play Therapy*. New York: Guilford Press.

Edwards, C. P. (2000) 'Children's play in cross-cultural perspective: A new look at the Six Cultures Study.' *Cross-Cultural Research 34*, 4, 318–338.

Edwards, D. and Mercer, N. (1987) *Common Knowledge*. New York: Methuen.

Farrer, C. R., (1990) *Play and Inter-ethic Communication: A practical ethonography of the Mescalero Apache*. New York, NY: Garland Press.

Farver, J. (1999) 'Activity Setting Analysis: A Model for Examining the Role of Culture in Development.' In A. Goncu (ed.) *Children's Engagement in the World: A Sociocultural Perspective*. Cambridge: Cambridge University Press.

Farver, J. A. M., Kim, Y. K. and Lee, Y. (1995) 'Cultural differences in Korean and Anglo-American preschoolers' social interaction and play behaviours.' *Child Development 66*, 1089–97.

Feitelson, D. (1977) 'Cross-cultural Studies of Representational Play.' In B. Tizard and D. Harvey (eds) *Biology of Play*. London: William Heinemann Medical Books.

Feng, J. (1994) *Asian-American Children: What Teachers Should Know*. Illinois: Early Childhood and Parenting Collaborative, Division of Illinois (ERIC Document Reproduction Service no. ED 369 577).

Fleer, M. (1999) 'Universal Fantasy: the Domination of Western Theories of Play.' In E. Dau (ed.) *Child's Play. Revisiting Play in Early Childhood Setting*. London: Paul Brookes Publishing.

Frost, J. and Jacobs, P. (1996) 'Play deprivation and juvenile violence.' *Play Rights 18*, 4.

Gaskins, S. (2000) 'Children's daily activities in a Mayan village: A culturally grounded description.' *Cross-Cultural Research 34*, 4, 375–389.

Gaskins, S. and Goncu, A. (1992) 'Cultural variation in play: A challenge to Piaget and Vygotsky.' *Quarterly Newsletter of the Laboratory of Comparative Human Cognition 14*, 2, 31–35.

Gil, E. and Drewes, A.A. (2005) *Cultural Issues in Play Therapy*. New York: Guilford Press.

Glover, G. (1999) 'Multicultural considerations in group play therapy.' In D. S. Sweeney and L. E. Homeyer (eds) *The Handbook of Group Play Therapy*. San Francisco: Jossey-Bass.

Haight, W. L., Wang, X., Fung, H. H., Williams, K. and Mintz, J. (1999) 'Universal developmental, and variable aspects of young children's play: A cross-cultural comparison of pretending at home.' *Child Development 70*, 6, 1477–1488.

Hamilton, A. (1981) *Nature, and Nurture: Aboriginal Child Rearing in North-Central Arnhem Land*. Canberra: Australian Institute of Aboriginal Studies.

Huizinga, J. (1949) *Homo Ludens*. London: Routledge & Kegan Paul.

Hupp, S. C., Lam, S. F. and Jaeger, J. (1992) 'Differences in exploration of toys by one-year-old children: A Korean and American comparison.' *Behavior Science Research 26*, 1–4, 123–136.

Johns, V. (1999) 'Embarking on a Journey: Aboriginal Children and Play.' In E. Dau (ed.) *Child's Play. Revisiting Play in Early Childhood Setting.* London: Paul Brookes Publishing.

Kelly, J. R. and Godbey, G. (1992) *Sociology of Leisure.* State College, PA: Venture.

Lee, G. and Childress, M. (1999) 'Promising practices: Playing Korean ethnic games to promote multicultural awareness.' *Multicultural Education 6,* 3, 33–35.

Levin, D. E. (2000) 'Learning about the world through play.' *Early Child Today 15,* 3, 56–64.

Martinez, K. J. and Valdez, D. M. (1992) 'Cultural Considerations in Play Therapy with Hispanic Children.' In L. A. Vargas and J. D. Koss-Chioino (eds) *Working with Culture.* San Francisco: Jossey-Bass.

McDonald, D. and McAvoy, L. (1997) 'Native Americans and leisure: State of the research and future directions.' *Journal of Leisure Research 29,* 2, 145–167.

Monroe, J. E. (1995) 'Developing cultural awareness through play.' *Journal of Physical Education, Recreation and Dance 66,* 8, 24–30.

Oke, M., Khattar, A., Pant, P. and Saraswathi, T. S. (1999) 'A profile of children's play in urban India.' *Childhood 6,* 2, 207–219.

Rettig, M. A. (2002) 'Cultural diversity and play from an ecological perspective.' *Children and Schools 24,* 3, 189–199.

Roopnarine, J. and Johnson, J. (1994) 'A Need to Look at Play in Diverse Cultural Settings.' In J. Roopnarine, J. Johnson, and F. Hooper (eds) *Children's Play in Diverse Cultures.* Albany: State University of New York Press.

Roopnarine, J., Johnson, J. and Hooper, F. (eds) (1994) *Children's Play in Diverse Cultures.* Albany: State University of New York Press.

Roopnarine, J., Lasker, J., Sacks, M. and Stores, M. (1998) 'The Cultural Context of Children's Play.' In O. N. Saracho and B. Spodek (eds) *Multiple Perspectives on Play in Early Childhood Education.* Albany: State University of New York Press.

Schroeder, J. J. (1995) 'Developing self-esteem and leadership skills in Native American women: The role sports and games play.' *Journal of Physical Education, Recreation and Dance 66,* 7, 48–52.

Sutton-Smith, B. (1974) 'The anthropology of play.' *Association for the Anthropological Study of Play 2,* 8–12.

Sutton-Smith, B. (1999) 'Evolving a Consilience of Play Definitions: Playfully.' In S. Reifel (ed.) *Play and Culture Studies,* vol. 2. Stamford, CT: Ablex.

Van Diermen, S. and Johns, V. (1995) *From the Flat Earth: A Guide for Child Care Staff Caring for Aboriginal Children.* Darwin: Children's Services Resource and Advisory Program (Northern Region).

Vandermaas-Peeler, M. (2002) 'Cultural Variations in Parental Support of Children's Play.' In W. J. Lonner, D. L. Dinnel, S. A. Hayes and D. N. Sattler (eds) *Online Readings in Psychology and Culture.* Bellingham: Center for Cross-Cultural Research, Western Washington University. Available at www.wwu.edu/~culture, accessed 19 September 2008.

SECTION FOUR

Play Based Therapies

CHAPTER 12

Play Intervention –
The *Learn to Play* Program

Karen Stagnitti

CHAPTER OBJECTIVES

This chapter introduces the *Learn to Play* program for children by outlining the development of the program, how to use it and things to consider. Illustrations are given of the practical application of the program with case examples.

INTRODUCTION

For many years I worked as an occupational therapist in a specialist early childhood intervention team serving a large rural area in south western Victoria, Australia. As a specialist paediatric team, we saw children under six years of age who had developmental difficulty–the causes for delay ranged from neurological insult to developmental delay (unknown cause) to delay due to inadequate environmental and/or parenting practices. As I worked with the children, it also became clear that many of the non-traumatised children I was seeing did not know how to play (see Section Two for information on play assessment). This chapter outlines a technique called the *Learn to Play* program (Stagnitti 1998), which was developed during my time working with these families and children. It also links into the next chapter where Virginia Ryan discusses non-directive play therapy and how this approach can be used with children who have developmental problems with or without a traumatic history. As a way to relate these two chapters, I will give some background on the development of the *Learn to Play* program.

THE BEGINNING – THE *LEARN TO PLAY* PROGRAM

The theories underpinning the *Learn to Play* program are from Axline (1947), Vygotsky (1997, first published 1934), and the cognitive developmental theories of play. Axline's early work on non-directive play therapy (1947) used a child-centred approach based on Rogerian theory. Axline developed a technique that allowed children a safe space to play while facilitating their development (emotional and social) back to a healthy state (see Chapter 13). There is also an assumption that the child has the capacity to grow. Vygotsky (1997) believed that there was a sociocultural dimension to play and cognition and that the child's social and cultural environment could assist the child to increase their developmental capacities if there were capable adults and peers within their everyday lives. He called it the 'zone of proximal development' (Vygotsky 1997).

Cognitive developmental theories of play describe play as a voluntary activity (Parham and Primeau 1997). Children interact with objects or toys under their control, and through playing children form and manipulate concepts and use symbols in play (Parham and Primeau 1997). Play is thus seen as a cognitive process and through play, problem solving, divergent thinking, adaptability to change and flexibility are developed (Parham and Primeau 1997; Russ 2003). Piaget (1962) and Vygotsky (1997) have been highly influential in the development of cognitive developmental theories (Nicolopoulou 1993). The type of play that is referred to in the cognitive developmental theories is pretend play because when children pretend they impose meaning on a situation (cognitive skill), they use symbols (cognitive skill) and they act 'as if' a situation were different from the literal meaning (a cognitive skill). Many of the children I was working with did not have the pretend play ability expected for their age. So, the work of Casby (1992), Fein (1981), Fenson and Ramsay (1981), Gowen (1995), Greenspan and Lieberman (1994), McCune (1995), Nicolich (1975), Sutton-Smith (1967) and Westby (1991), to name a few, underpin the developmental sequences in the *Learn to Play* program.

The aims of the *Learn to Play* program are to assist children to develop the ability to spontaneously self-initiate their own play, and to develop pretend play skills to or near their expected developmental level for their age so that they can become a 'player' with their peers. The program uses a competent adult (a therapist, teacher and/or parent) to enable the child to develop these skills. The program begins with a directive approach by the therapist and, as the child's play skills develop, and in tune with the child, the therapist then takes a less directive approach as the child begins to spontaneously self-initiate their own play (Stagnitti 1998).

HOW THE PROGRAM WORKS: THE PROGRAM SHEETS

The program is based on a therapist's clear understanding of the child's development in pretend play (see Chapter 4). This understanding is aided by the program being cross-referenced with the Symbolic and Imaginative Play Development Checklist (SIP-DC) (Stagnitti 1998). There are activity sheets for children's developmental abilities in the areas of: play scripts (previously called themes), sequences in play action, object substitution, social interaction, role play and doll/teddy play. Each of these play abilities is described in Stagnitti 1998 with information on the development of the ability plus activities to develop the ability. Each activity has a goal from the child's point of view and several icons (explained in Stagnitti 1998) are used to indicate how to engage the child in the play activity. Each icon is both a prompt and guide on the principles of how to engage a child. The icons indicate how to: get the child's attention, model the play action, talk about the play, repeat the activity, co-actively prompt (i.e. move the child physically to the object) and have fun. It is also important to use the 'more play ideas' as this section details additional play activities at that developmental level.

The play activities are designed as handouts for parents. For therapists, at the bottom of each activity page the details of the play ability and the developmental level from the SIP-DC are provided. For example, in Activity 3 in the chapter on 'Object Substitution', there is detail that this activity is for 'object substitution' and, specifically, for 'using a physically similar object to the intended object' with the SIP-DC cross-reference to 20 months of age.

HOW THE PROGRAM WORKS: THERAPIST-CHILD INTERACTION

The *Learn to Play* program is a dynamic, interactive program, where the therapist works with the child with the aim that the child develops an ability to self-initiate their own play. The program can be carried out with individual sessions between the child and therapist working together, or with the therapist and parent working together with the child, or within a group setting such as a specialised play group where one-on-one assistance to the child is given by the therapist as well as play within groups of children. For information on other methods of using groups to assist a child's play development see Wolfberg and Schuler (1999).

Therapist's role

During implementation the therapist constantly watches, responds to and is completely attuned to the child – it is a bit like a dance between two people moving seamlessly together. To begin with the *Learn to Play* program is directive, with the therapist introducing to the child the play activities one at a time. The therapist engages with the child, and then watches carefully for the child's reaction as to whether he or she can cope with a more advanced play level or whether the directed play activities need to be kept at developmentally younger levels. The therapist is constantly aware of the child's play abilities in play scripts, sequences of play actions, object substitution, social interaction, role play and doll/teddy play.

IMPLEMENTING THE PROGRAM

As a guide to implementation of the program, two explanations are now given. The first explanation of the preparation and process of engagement complexity uses the developmental level of the child's understanding of play scripts as the guide for the implementation of the program over the age groups of 18 months to five years. The second explanation is based on a qualitative research study which investigated in more detail the process of engagement of the therapist with the child.

Explanation 1: Developmental levels of play scripts

The first explanation describes three levels of preparation and engagement with the child. Level 1 is the 18 months to 2½-year level of play scripts, where play stories are centred on the child's body (e.g. drinking, eating, sleeping) and the child's personal experiences in and outside of the home. Level 2 is the 3-year level of play scripts where the child begins to use fictional characters in play stories and Level 3 is the 4–5-year level where the child can play out any story – fictional or non-fictional. Play script developmental levels are used because it was found that the child's play script development limited the type of activities that could be presented to the child. For example, I was once working with a child who had a play script development level on the 2-year level with sequences on the 2–2½-year level, and object substitution on the 18-month level. The play activity was: *the doll family lived in a house, drove the car to the shop, bought some food (plastic food), drove home and ate the food.* The child engaged in the activity, was initiating some play sequences and was emotionally involved. The following week I kept similar toys but exchanged the food items for zoo animals. The sequences were a similar number – *the doll family lived in a house, drove the car to the zoo, the dolls looked at the animals, then the dolls drove home.* During this session, the child did not engage with this play activity because I had changed the play script to a developmentally higher level. That is, the child had not personally experienced going to a zoo and could not comprehend the concept, so the child did not relate to the play.

The following explanation is based on clinical experience working with children on a one-to-one basis for one hour per session. For each child you will usually have a range of developmental levels across sequences of play actions, object substitutions, social interaction, role play and doll/teddy play in conjunction with the play script levels. For example, the child's play scripts may be on a 20-month level with sequences being on a 2-year level, object substitution on an 18-month level and social and role play on a 2-year level with doll play on a 20-month level.

Level 1 – 18 months to 2½ years

Level 1 is the *Learn to Play* process for children who are developmentally between 18 months and 2½ years in their play scripts. For children on this level, the *Learn to Play* program is very intense and directive with the therapist gaining the child's attention, scaffolding and modelling the play. For a one-hour session, you will need five play activities (or scripts such as *feed teddy; teddy goes for a ride in a car; teddy goes to sleep; the child shops for one item; teddy has a drink*) that are developmentally appropriate for the child. Each play activity will need to be repeated at least three times with repetitions of up to eight times for some children. You repeat each activity because children who have poor play skills do not understand what is happening in pretend play and they need time to process. It is a positive sign if a child begins to understand what is happening by the third repetition and joins you in the play. An example of repetition is: *the doll is put to bed and the therapist talks about the doll being in the bed.* The voice of the therapist is quiet. The therapist waits for a minute or so and then takes the doll out of the bed. Therapist then models putting the doll back to bed. This sequence is repeated while the child is engaged with the play. The amount of toys and objects is limited because children with poor play skills cannot cope with a lot of objects/toys all at the same time. So, only use what you essentially need. You encourage the child to attend to the play scene and to imitate what you are doing then wait for the child to respond and invite the child to copy you. It is important to have a variety of pretend play activities on the appropriate developmental level for the child to avoid rote learning by the child. You are aiming to have the child self-initiate play and understand the play (e.g. *putting the doll to sleep*), not just put a doll on a bed. You are attuned to the child and notice the child's reactions. When you feel that the child is ready, you introduce play activities at the next level.

Level 2 – 3 years

Play scripts at this developmental level are play stories with a fictional character, for example, characters the child has seen on television or in a book. Other pretend play abilities of the child may vary from the 3-year script level and so you are conscious of these variations as you plan your sessions with the child. On this level, you will most likely only need three pre-prepared play activities for each one hour session as the child is now playing for longer. You repeat each activity within the session but you may not need to repeat as much as you did when the child was at Level 1. You can include more toys and objects within the play activities because the child's play ability is now more complex and the child can cope with more play materials. A variety of activities is still essential so that the child generalises concepts and does not rote learn without meaning. As a therapist, you pay attention to extending the child's play action sequences – you add more to the story of the play script – and you challenge the child (when ready) to include higher developmental levels of play.

Level 3 – 4 to 5 years

Play scripts at the 4–5-year level include fictional and non-fictional stories with sub-plots. At this level the child's play is very complex. You will only need to prepare one play activity for the session because now the child takes control of the play and you follow the child – you are less directive in your interactions. You can have many objects and toys at your disposal in case the child requires more. You concentrate on adding problems to the play story (e.g. *the doll is sick* or *the dolls are lost*) and encourage the child to problem-solve and add more sequences to the play, thus encouraging the child to add more complexity into the play scenes.

Explanation 2: The *Learn to Play* process of therapist engagement

To understand further the process of the therapist–child interaction during the *Learn to Play* program, a qualitative research study using a multiple case design was undertaken in 2006 with four boys, who were four years old and who had a diagnosis of autism spectrum disorder. This pilot research study was carried out by one of my research students, Siobhan Casey (née Merchant). Ethical approval was gained through Deakin University. The families of the boys volunteered to be in the study and while they undertook their usual early intervention program, the families were also involved in a one-hour *Learn to Play* session once a fortnight, for three months. Three months was chosen because I had noticed in my clinical work that children who were progressing in their play ability were showing noticeable change after seven sessions. I treated the participants using the *Learn to Play* program, which was carried out in the child's home. While I treated the child, my student observed each session and took notes every five minutes on the interaction that had occurred between the therapist (me) and the child. On analysis of the process, Merchant (2006) found that there were three distinct stages depending on the child's progress. These stages are now described as they occurred over seven sessions.

In the initial three sessions I spent a lot of time engaging each child. That is, encouraging the child to look at the toys, to listen and to watch what was happening. Nothing can be assumed about the child's understanding at this stage, in fact you don't assume that the child has any knowledge of the play materials or how to use them in play. I was aware of the child's level of engagement and if the child began to disengage, then I would either lower the developmental expectations of the play activity level, physically bring the child back to the play materials, or change my voice, facial expression, or body posture in order to re-engage the child's interest in the play. In these initial sessions, the therapist needs to be directive, that is, I introduced the toys, I did all the playing, and I modelled pretend play actions. I was the player and the child was the observer who I encouraged to join me in play. The language used in these initial sessions was descriptive, prompting and goal-directed. For example, I would say 'The doll is going to lie on the bed. See, the doll is on the bed. Shhhhhh. Can you see the other doll? That doll can lie on the bed too.'

The second stage occurred during the middle sessions. At this stage, the child was beginning to interact with the toys and was starting to initiate some of the play actions. If the child took initiative in the play, I would encourage and reinforce what the child had done. This was through reflection of what the child had done, for example, 'The doll is in the truck', to imitation of the child's actions. The language I used at this stage changed from descriptive language to language that wove a narrative around the play. So now, I would say 'The doll is tired. The doll wants to go to sleep. [I put the doll on the bed.] The doll is sleeping now. Shhhhhhh. Don't wake up the doll, he is sleeping.' During these middle sessions, the therapist needs to be attuned to the child, being less directive, waiting for the child to respond, responding to the child, reinforcing the child's play. The therapist follows the child's lead.

In the final stage, in this case sessions six and seven, the child takes more and more control of the play and the therapist's interaction becomes less directive. The therapist adds 'problems' to the play narrative so the child is encouraged to add more sequences, to problem-solve and to cope with interruptions and changes to the play. Examples of 'problems' are: *a naughty teddy stealing the doll's treasures, a sick doll*, or *a car that won't go*. The language used by the therapist changes again to match the child's changing play levels. The therapist now questions the child about what is happening (to encourage the child to 'think ahead' and develop the story) and adds to the story of the play. The therapist is aware of the child's play level and is ready to challenge to the next level, or wait, or respond to the child. The therapist follows the child's lead.

CASE EXAMPLES

Two case examples of children who had difficulties in their ability to play are presented. Both children lived with their parents and each had two siblings. There was no history of poor parenting with either child or any developmental diagnosis.

Kelly

'Kelly' was referred from the speech therapist because she had a very unusual language profile. On the *Child-Initiated Pretend Play Assessment* (*ChIPPA*) (Stagnitti 2007) Kelly, aged four years, scored within the low average range for the elaborate play scores in symbolic play and object substitution, however, her scores in elaborate play for the conventional imaginative play session were below the normal range for her age. When a child has this type of play deficit (high fantasy, low conventional play) it is important to teach the child how to play *within* the confines of the conventional toys because this is where the play deficit lies. No other problems were found in sensory motor coordination, visual perception, or problem solving skills. At preschool she was isolated from her peers and did not engage in group play or interaction with the other children.

My intervention involved using only conventional toys in each session. Kelly had difficulty problem solving a narrative (play sequence) within the limits of conventional toys. For example, a common play script for her was to use Superman® (usually imaginary) to save the animals from a lion that had gone mad.

At the beginning of the initial session, I realised I had too many toys because Kelly had difficulty concentrating. I then put aside the train set and only used the people visiting the zoo. Kelly had the lion go mad and kill all the animals and people and Batman® come to the rescue. She concluded all her play scenes in this way – with chaos and rescue. (I have observed that children with poor sequencing in their play, poor understanding of story structure, and who are not suffering from trauma, often have difficulty knowing how to end their play and so they crash all the toys.) In the middle sessions, Kelly's sequencing of her play story was still illogical. For example, she would say the people were going to a party but they would go shopping. In one session I had a farm, blocks to make a house, and people. All was going well until the lady fell through the roof after she had been checking the blocked roof gutters and Batman® came. I however intervened and would not accept Batman® and called the farmer (doll) next door to model an alternative solution in the play story. For the remaining sessions, I continued to model alternative endings using only the toys that I had at my disposal so that Kelly could see there were alternative solutions that did not always need Batman® or Superman®.

Four months later, on reassessment with the *ChIPPA*, Kelly set up the conventional toys as a farm, carried out a non-repetitive play sequence for 15 minutes and expanded a story without resorting to Batman®. Her scores for the conventional imaginative play session were now within normal limits for her age. At preschool she was observed sitting with other girls and leading the conversation. Her teacher reported a huge improvement in her play skills and noted that she could now play within a group.

Owen

'Owen' was a five-year-old boy who was referred because of aggressive behaviour. For example, at preschool he would throw toys and chairs around the room during times of unstructured play (that is, times when children were required to self-initiate and organise their own play activity). He was distractible and needed adult guidance to settle. At home he needed to be entertained and constantly demanded attention resulting in his mum being at the end of her tether. On therapist-directed assessments Owen scored within normal limits, in fact, Owen appeared to be quite bright. On the *ChIPPA* he scored in the low normal range for the imaginative-conventional session but in the symbolic session he had no idea what to do. He could not substitute objects (i.e. he had no concept that you could pretend a piece of paper could be a roof for a block house) or sequence play actions.

During Owen's *Learn to Play* program emphasis was placed on symbolic play. My aims for intervention were to increase his ability to self-initiate play sequences, and to use symbols in play. In initial sessions I used toys but as Owen progressed in this play ability, I introduced more and more unstructured objects into the sessions.

After eight months of working with Owen, every two to three weeks (with his mother using the activities at home) his play skills had improved to the point where he could lead his younger brother in play (it had previously been the other way around), have a friend over to play, and play constructively on his own for 20 minutes. Both his mother and grandmother noted improvements in his behaviour and his mum was very happy with his progress.

BENEFITS OF THE *LEARN TO PLAY* PROGRAM FOR CHILDREN

From my use of the program over the past ten years, the benefits of the *Learn to Play* program with individual children have consistently shown in clinical improvements in children's language, social understanding, initiation of play, use of symbols in play and increased sequences of play actions leading to increased time in self-initiated independent play. The benefits are captured in a case study of a child with autism spectrum disorder (ASD) who was involved in the *Learn to Play* program over 18 months. After the program the child with ASD showed increased language utterances (longer sentences), use of symbols in play, an ability to spontaneously self-initiate play sequences, an ability to co-operatively play with a group of peers, and an ability to pretend in play for long periods of time without adult supervision (Stagnitti 2004).

There are not many publications on specific play programs. Josefi and Ryan (2004) reported a case study of a child with autism and noted improvements in the child's pretend play ability during non-directive play therapy sessions. Specifically, improvements after the ninth session were noted in the child's appropriate use of the toys for pretend play, emotional engagement in play, and ability to initiate play actions. Within the non-directive play sessions, the therapist scaffolded the child's abilities to assist the child to play. The *Learn to Play* program is more directive than this approach and changes in a child's play ability have been noted in seven sessions. Wolfberg and Schuler (1993) proposed a model for Integrated Play Groups (IPG) where the focus of the group is to provide a supportive system for peer play amongst expert (typically developing children) and novice (children with autism) players. They also report changes in the child's developmental play levels.

Further research on the *Learn to Play* program will investigate how to better include parents in the program and how the program can be used to give parents play skills as an avenue to engage and bond with their children. The *Learn to Play* program has been shown to be effective in developing children's pretend play abilities. When a child learns how to play, that child can become a 'player', which can lead to that child belonging to a peer group. This is a great gift to give to a child.

REFERENCES

Axline, V. (1947) *Play Therapy*. New York: Penguin.

Casby, M. W. (1992) 'Symbolic play: development and assessment considerations.' *Infants and Young Children 4*, 343–48.

Fein, G. (1981) 'Pretend play in childhood: an integrative review.' *Child Development 52*, 1095–1118.

Fenson, L. and Ramsay, D. S. (1981) 'Effects of modelling action sequences on the play of twelve, fifteen and nineteen-month-old children.' *Child Development 52*, 1028–1036.

Greenspan, S. I. and Lieberman, A. (1994) 'Representational elaboration and differentiation: a clinical-quantitative approach to clinical assessment of 2- to 4-year-olds.' In A. W. Slade and D. Wolf (eds) *Children at Play*. New York: Oxford University Press.

Gowen, J. W. (1995) 'The early development of symbolic play.' *Young Children 50*, 75–84.

Josefi, O. and Ryan, V. (2004) 'Non-directive play therapy for young children with autism: a case study.' *Clinical Child Psychology and Psychiatry 9*, 4, 533–551.

McCune, L. (1995) 'A normative study of representational play at the transition to language.' *Child Development 31*, 198–206.

Merchant, S. (2006) 'Important markers in the *Learn to Play* program.' Unpublished Honours thesis, Deakin University, Geelong, Australia.

Nicolich, L. M. (1975) *A Longitudinal Study of Representational Play in Relation to Spontaneous Imitation and Development of Multi-Word Utterances*. (Report No. N. I. E. No. NE-11-3-002). Final Report. US Government Report. (ERIC Document Reproduction Service No. ED 103133).

Nicolopoulou, A. (1993) 'Play, cognitive development, and the social world: Piaget, Vygotsky, and beyond.' *Human Development 36*, 1–23.

Parham, L. D. and Primeau, L. A. (1997) 'Play and occupational therapy.' In L. D. Parham and L. S. Fazio (eds), *Play in Occupational Therapy for Children*. St Louis, MO: Mosby.

Piaget, J. (1962) *Play, Dreams and Imitation in Childhood*. New York: W. W. Norton.

Russ, S. W. (2003) 'Play and creativity: developmental issues.' *Scandinavian Journal of Educational Research 47*, 291–303.

Stagnitti, K. (1998) *Learn to Play. A Practical Program to Develop a Child's Imaginative Play*. Melbourne: Co-ordinates Publications.

Stagnitti, K. (2004) 'Occupational performance in pretend play; implications for practice.' In M. Mollineux (ed.) *Occupation for Occupational Therapists*. Blackwell Science: Oxford.

Stagnitti, K. (2007) *The Child-Initiated Pretend Play Assessment*. Manual and Kit. Melbourne. Co-ordinates Publications.

Sutton-Smith, B. (1967) 'The role of play in cognitive development.' *Young Children* (September) 361–369.

Vygotsky, L. (1997). *Thought and Language*, trans A. Kozulin. Cambridge, MA: MIT Press.

Westby, C. (1991) 'A scale for assessing children's pretend play.' In C. Schaefer, K. Gitlin and A. Sandrund (eds) *Play Diagnosis and Assessment*. New York: John Wiley & Sons.

Wolfberg, P. J. and Schuler, A. L. (1993) Integrated play groups: A model for promoting the social and cognitive dimensions of play in children with autism.' *Journal of Autism and Developmental Disorders 23*, 3, 467–489.

Wolfberg, P. J. and Schuler, A. L. (1999) 'Fostering peer interaction, imaginative play and spontaneous language in children with autism.' *Child Language Teaching and Therapy 15*, 1, 41–52.

CHAPTER 13

Playing for Healing and Growth: Exploring Theory and Practice in Non-Directive/Child-Centred Play Therapy

Virginia Ryan

CHAPTER OBJECTIVES

This chapter will focus on the ways in which therapists trained in non-directive play therapy facilitate change with children and families referred for therapy. First, I will look at the ways in which the theoretical underpinnings of non-directive play therapy inform its practice. Next, I will give an example from my own practice to illustrate how change occurs in non-directive play therapy. This extended discussion of non-directive play therapy with a foster child having serious attachment problems due to maltreatment will emphasise the attachment and systemic thinking needed for complex interventions. Finally, the chapter will end with suggestions for practice and research.

INTRODUCTION

So much has been written on why play is essential to development and, more widely, on how play instils hope and happiness into the lives of both humans and animals. Just thinking about playing as we read about it can make us smile with pleasure! It has always made the greatest sense to me that this spontaneous process of playing is best left to itself to develop, where possible. And where additional help is needed and play therapists become involved, it seems very important for us to humbly tap into this complex and satisfying process in respectful ways, disrupting this natural process as little as possible. My attitude has been reinforced by experiences in my own practice, in my supervision of play therapists, and in my training of professionals to qualify as play therapists. All these experiences have strongly affirmed for me the healing and growth children are capable of when play therapists skilfully follow their lead in play. Non-directive play therapy therefore is the right fit for me as a method because of its confidence in children's ability to change, given the right conditions, and because it also fits well with current child development and child psychopathology theory and research.

While this chapter concentrates on the method of non-directive play therapy, other methods of child therapy and play therapy also inform therapists' practice. Depending on the skills and experience of each non-directive play therapist, other methods may be adapted to a non-directive approach within non-directive play therapy sessions. Therapeutic skills also will be used by therapists in working with parents, carers, schools and other important people in children's and adolescents' lives.

THEORETICAL CONSIDERATIONS

Both practitioners and researchers share the need to understand the assumptions and principles underlying non-directive play therapy practice. In this section several different strands that underpin my understanding of non-directive play therapy's current practice will be discussed.

Person-centred counselling

The Rogerian principles of person-centred counselling are basic to this model of therapy, and have been written about since its earliest days (Axline 1947; Dorfman 1951) and continue to be explored into the present (Landreth 2002; Wilson and Ryan 2005). The relationships that play therapists form with children are at the centre of a non-directive approach and Axline's (1947) original practice principles are still followed today. Her principles for therapists include working alongside children by entering into their personal lives and feelings through empathy, attempting to maintain unconditional positive regard, genuineness and transparency during all encounters, and facilitating children in determining their own issues and activities. The therapist does this within limits to anchor therapy within the world of reality. While non-directive play therapists may differ somewhat in the ways they interpret and practise these principles, there seems to be a general agreement with these principles overall.

One interesting and important area of development in my own thinking and practice, and incorporated into my training and supervision of other therapists, is exploring the ways in which therapists show transparency and genuineness in the therapeutic relationships they develop with children. Because many children attending play therapy sessions are able to understand and interpret their therapists' nonverbal expressions and bodily cues, some child-centred play therapists advocate that therapists do not verbally express their own feelings directly within non-directive play therapy (Guerney personal communication, 2003; Landreth 2002). However, certain groups of children do have difficulty understanding others' inner thoughts and feelings. Several groups of children stand out:

1. Children and young people who have disabilities falling along the autistic spectrum, and who therefore have difficulty interpreting the motives and feelings of themselves and others in social situations.

2. Children who have been seriously maltreated and who therefore have developed inadequate or distorted ideas of adults' intentions and beliefs.

3. Younger children, who developmentally are unable to fully take in another's intentions, feelings and thoughts.

4. Children and young people with moderate/more serious learning disabilities, who may find more complex thoughts and emotional reactions in others more difficult to process.

For these groups of children, therapists cannot assume that nonverbal communication of genuineness and transparency within play therapy sessions is sufficient. It seems important for therapists also to verbalise feelings and thoughts directly to these children, as they arise within their interactions together. This additional step seems necessary in order to amplify these therapeutic responses, enabling children and young people to be able to more fully understand normal, adult responses in close relationships (Ryan and Courtney forthcoming).

Other children, who may not have systematic difficulties interpreting others' feelings and motives, may find it difficult sometimes to express their feelings due to experiencing conflicting emotions. Yet others may find it too anxiety provoking to name certain stronger feelings themselves. Both sets of children are likely to benefit from therapists openly and transparently articulating their genuine feelings along with expressing these feelings bodily.

An example of how I responded in a verbally congruent way to a child's feelings expressed in play therapy is with an eight-year-old boy, Dan, who had been maltreated. He drew the same kinds of pictures repeatedly during our sessions, ones filled with destruction and carnage. After several weeks, I eventually said in a concerned tone of voice: 'No one's helping *again. I want* them to get help, but they can't. No one's ever around' (quoted from Ryan and Courtney, forthcoming). This verbally expressed transparency seems especially important for therapists to practise when working with children whose normal reactions have been distorted by abusive relationships with adults. More widely, this example shows how practice skills and decisions are informed by Rogerian principles of empathy and reflection of children's feelings. As well as therapists' responses being informed by findings on maltreatment, other underlying assumptions from a variety of sources also inform practice. One of the most important areas of consideration is the assumptions therapists make about development and psychopathology. The next section looks more closely at these underlying assumptions.

Developmental psychology

In the early practice of non-directive play therapy, as well as in child therapy practice more generally during that era, there was little overlap with child development theory and research. However in current practice most child therapists agree with the importance of using a developmentally sensitive framework for their practice (Wilson and Ryan 2005). There are several reasons for this change. First, that the age groups for practising play therapy have widened to include very young children (e.g. Schaefer *et al.* in press), adolescents (e.g. Gallo-Lopez and Schaefer 2005) and adults (e.g. Schaefer 2002) and therefore a developmentally informed approach is more necessary. Second, there is greater understanding of how to employ play therapy in working with children who have special needs (Alvarez 1996; Josefi and Ryan 2004)

Another reason I emphasise child development in my own writing is to show that non-directive play therapy is highly compatible with current theory and research in child development. Employing Piagetian and attachment theory assumptions along with child development research assumptions and findings, I have set out a model of mental development. This model was then used to show how non-directive play therapy derives its effectiveness and rationale from this developmental framework (see Wilson and Ryan 2005). In this model, play therapy, as an expressive therapy, was conceptualised as working simultaneously on all levels of children's mental functioning – perceptual, cognitive, emotional/social and motor. And non-directive play therapy was viewed as paying particular attention to children's personal, emotional responses in close relationships. Erikson's model of emotional/social development, without its psychosexual underpinnings (in Wilson and Ryan 2005), was also applied to play therapy. Play therapists can use these concepts to understand the emotional and social issues children express in their therapy, distilling play therapy contents into 'themes' as a short-hand means of capturing the essential content. Erikson's theoretical framework allows play therapists to think of these themes developmentally, as well as personally, for each child, while other theoretical formulations of relationships enable therapists to understand the underlying dynamics from differing perspectives. Other research into the normal development of imaginative play conducted by the author (Ryan 1999; Ryan 2004a) has been used to demonstrate applications to non-directive play therapy.

A further practice change that has also gone hand in hand with changes in thinking in child development theory and research is a realisation of the importance of social contexts in all children's development. Early developmental theory emphasised individual development, for example, important changes in children's thinking and personalities due to maturation. In more recent decades, the social context for learning and for development in general has been given increasing importance. Play therapists in turn have become more mindful of the importance of working within children's social contexts, with practitioners increasingly incorporating home and school environments more fully into their work with children and adolescents (Drewes, Carey and Schaefer 2001; Landreth, McGuire and McGuire 2000). Parents now are often given larger roles as active and important partners in therapy, sometimes as co-therapists and other times as the primary therapeutic change agents for their own children (Landreth and Bratton 2006; Ryan and Bratton in press; VanFleet and Guerney 2003). Increasing research support for play therapy and filial therapy (Bratton et al. 2005; Leblanc and Ritchie 2001) add weight to these practice developments.

This emphasis on the importance of parental involvement in therapy has been reinforced by child development embracing attachment theory and research, and its detailing of the importance of parental relationships for children's emotional and social resilience and emotional regulation. Non-directive play therapy, both individual therapy and other models which include parents more fully, seek to understand children's changes in therapy from this attachment perspective (Ryan 2004b; Ryan and Wilson 1995, 2000). Children and adolescents who have had particularly difficult relationships with parental figures, including those who have had statutory involvement as foster or adopted children, are often referred for play therapy to help them with their previous adverse experiences. The next section discusses some ways non-directive play therapy (NDPT) has been influenced by research findings and practice examples with such children.

NDPT and psychopathology

Developmental psychopathology, a newer approach to psychopathology during development that emphasises individual pathways in development, is highly compatible with non-directive play therapy (Cichetti 1989; Wenar and Kerig 2006). Both approaches share the assumption that children and adolescents have multiple pathways towards more optimal development. Non-directive play therapy, within this developmental psychopathology framework, can be defined as the enabling of developmentally needed, individual experiences within a more intensive environment.

Another area of theory and research that has informed therapy practice, and underlined the importance of play therapy as an intervention for children who have developed more serious emotional and social problems, is the trauma literature. Trauma, and particularly chronic traumas such as those that children who have been maltreated often experience, are now viewed as experiences that are incompletely processed mentally and thus not as amenable to cognitively based therapies. This understanding of trauma, coupled with the recognition that play is children's easiest means of processing personal experiences for themselves, has resulted in expressive therapies, such as play therapy, often being the treatment of choice for children who have incompletely processed traumatic memories of highly distressing experiences. Non-directive play therapy, with its emphasis on following children's lead in therapy and ensuring that children's mental defences against anxiety are not undermined by therapy, has been advocated as a particularly safe and effective form of therapy for children who have memories of multiple traumatic and disempowering experiences (Ryan 2007a; Ryan and Needham 2001). By enabling children to work spontaneously and nonverbally, non-directive play therapy allows children and adolescents to address personally important issues of their own choice.

Case study – 'Melanie'

The following case illustration is intended to show how an effective play therapy intervention can be designed and carried out with a child who has significant attachment problems and developmental delays. An added complexity in the following case was that 'Melanie' was a foster child with a court agreed care plan, which meant that social services as well as her school were involved in her intervention, along with her birth parents and foster carers. (All names and some circumstances have been altered to protect anonymity, with consent given by all parties referred to for this case to be discussed.)

Melanie's background

The social services department referred Melanie for therapy when she was 4.6 years old. This referral followed court proceedings where a care order had been agreed for Melanie and her younger two siblings, with the finding that the children had been significantly harmed by their birth parents' neglect. The children's neglect had been documented over the whole of Melanie's lifetime. Despite family support, which included intensive home visits and specialist nursery placements, social services' concerns had escalated. The children's parents resisted social services' help repeatedly; the children were therefore removed and placed in foster care when Melanie was almost four years old.

Melanie was of more concern to professionals than her siblings because she was very seriously delayed in her development, including displaying very poor attention skills, overly high motor activity levels, and a speech delay of at least two years. A psychological assessment had concluded that Melanie had a reactive attachment disorder, disinhibited type, due to her earlier maltreatment (American Psychiatric Association 1994). Melanie had been placed in foster care with her three-year-old sister, with whom she had a very dependent relationship. The sisters had regular supervised visits with their birth parents and their younger brother, who had been placed with another foster family because of space constraints.

Melanie's care plan was for her to remain in her foster placement for two years. During this time Melanie and her foster carers were to receive specialised help for her emotional difficulties. At the end of this work, Melanie's care plan was to be reviewed and a decision on whether to return her to her parents was feasible would be made (social services planned for Melanie's younger siblings to be reunited with their parents earlier than Melanie, if the parents made progress). If it was decided that Melanie's return to her birth parents was not in her best interests, then a specialised, long-term foster placement was to be identified.

Structuring Melanie's play therapy intervention

The social services department asked me to design an intervention to meet Melanie's emotional needs and care plan. The proposed intervention had three main foci:

1. Helping Melanie form more secure attachments to her foster carers then transferring these attachments to new carers or to her birth family. Therefore, a major therapeutic task during my work would be to develop a relationship with Melanie that enhanced, rather than interfered with, the development of her primary attachment relationships with her carers. Careful attention to her carers' role in therapy and to providing Melanie with security, including clear limits, seemed essential aims.

2. Helping Melanie overcome delays in her cognitive, emotional and social development. Given her developmental delay, it was essential that Melanie be helped to play symbolically before she could address emotionally important issues indirectly through play (see Ryan 1999 on promoting symbolic development in developmentally delayed children). In addition, Melanie would need help expressing a full range of emotions appropriately, since her emotional expressions seemed confined to fixed smiles, increased activity levels when aroused emotionally, and whimpering when distressed (James 1994; Pearce and Pezzot-Pearce 1997). Developmentally, Melanie also needed to increase both her competence and independence from her sister and carers and her sense of self-worth overall (Denham 1998).

3   Helping Melanie find ways to work through her emotional distress and life traumas therapeutically, in common with therapists' aims for other children's play therapy (Landreth 2002; West 1996; Wilson and Ryan 2005).

Melanie's earlier psychological assessment had identified her current carers as suitable for working closely with me in order to develop Melanie's primary attachments to them. I had the following aims with Melanie's carers:

1. Helping them manage their own emotional issues when caring for Melanie and when working intensively with her.

2. Teaching them to apply specialised parenting skills to promote Melanie's attachment to them.

3. Teaching the female foster carer, Nancy, to participate in non-directive play sessions, then helping both Melanie and Nancy to transfer special play skills from the playroom to their home. I intended to adapt filial therapy (Guerney 2001; VanFleet and Guerney 2003) in which carers are trained and supervised to

conduct special play sessions with their own children, to Melanie's requirements. An essential feature of filial therapy, which is helping the carers enhance their children's overall development by applying play and parenting skills and other learning about their children's needs to a wide range of situations, would be an important part of this work (Ryan 2007b).

4. Helping the carers transfer their relationship and knowledge of Melanie to new, long-term carers or to her birth parents.

With these aims in mind, the planned two year intervention was designed to include several phases:

1. A brief therapeutic assessment, including my introduction to Melanie at her foster home.

2. Ten weeks of non-directive play therapy with Melanie and Nancy together along with training of Nancy in filial therapy skills. Additionally, fortnightly meetings with Nancy were scheduled, with the social worker attending progress meetings once a month.

3. Twelve weeks of non-directive play therapy with Melanie individually, with Nancy remaining in the waiting room nearby. Nancy to begin weekly, filial therapy play sessions with Melanie at home. Arrangements for meetings continuing.

4. Ongoing individual therapy with Melanie for twenty weeks, with Nancy waiting nearby; ongoing weekly filial therapy sessions at home. Monthly, rather than fortnightly, meetings.

5. Six months of filial therapy play sessions for Melanie at home; individual play therapy sessions in the playroom discontinued. Monthly meetings continuing.

6. Reintroduction of individual play therapy sessions two months before Melanie's scheduled move, to be continued during Melanie's move to new carers. Fortnightly meetings with Nancy, other professionals and then her new carers or parents. Training of new carers in filial therapy.

Early stages of Melanie's intervention

After a referral meeting with Melanie's social worker and reading relevant court papers, I held an initial meeting with Melanie's carer, Nancy, and her social worker to plan our work together, including an agreed working schedule and allocated roles (Wilson, Ryan and Fisher 1995). I introduced myself to Melanie's birth parents separately and explained my role with Melanie and with all the adults involved in her care to them. During my brief therapeutic assessment, I observed Melanie in her foster home and, as predicted from her court assessment, she was overly friendly to me, despite my being a stranger. It was also obvious that she was unable to use her foster carer Nancy as a secure base (Bowlby 1980). Instead, Melanie approached me very eagerly when I arrived, sat very close to me, and began to touch my necklace and hair. She often hurried about the room, always with a fixed smile on her face.

Ten weekly sessions of non-directive play therapy began, with Nancy accompanying Melanie to the playroom after having intro-ductory training on how to interact with Melanie during play therapy sessions. In early sessions Nancy and Melanie increasingly engaged in many playful interaction sequences together. Frequently Nancy extended Melanie's simple actions and minimal words (e.g. Melanie picking up a balloon and bringing it to her) into more meaningful and longer play sequences (e.g. Nancy then blowing up a balloon and Melanie enjoying its release into the room). They also had ritualised games together, such as Melanie or Nancy hiding a hand behind their backs, or pretending to bite each other's finger. From these and other interactions, Nancy seemed highly attuned to Melanie's developmental needs; it was evident that relationship enhancing games were already well established (Binney, McKnight and Broughton 1994). Nancy did not appear to need additional help in transferring play and non-directive play therapy skills into her home. It seemed sufficient that she had watched and participated in our play therapy sessions together for her to take up non-directive play skills readily in her everyday interactions with Melanie. She ensured that child-led play sessions occurred every weekday afternoon with Melanie at home. It seemed counter-productive therefore to restructure or interfere with this naturally developing, playful relationship that was being consolidated. Therefore the original plan to train Nancy in filial therapy was not implemented.

During our initial play therapy sessions with Nancy, Melanie moved quickly and aimlessly from one object to another, sometimes using toys as intended (e.g. putting sand into a doll's hair, then rinsing its hair out with water) and other times seeming to disregard toys' intended functions (e.g. using the toy iron to attempt to flatten a baby's bottle). While she engaged in these activities, I initially tracked her movements (Landreth 2002) then began to see certain consistencies and reflect that

Melanie was doing 'washing…ironing…all jobs for mummies'. This addition of narrative and the enhancement of the meaning to her largely chaotic play sequences seemed to be an important step in her therapeutic progress (Slade and Wolf 1994; Zappella and Messeri 1994). Soon Melanie began to develop rudimentary symbolic play with toys, given this high level of scaffolding from me. Extending her well-established, playful 'bite the finger' routine with her carer, Melanie began to play in the following way after a few sessions:

> Melanie again put the baby doll in the bath, this time washing its face and putting her finger near the hole in the dolls' mouth:
>
> *Melanie (M)*: 'Bite'
>
> *Therapist (T)*: 'She'll bite it!' (laughing)
>
> Melanie took the doll out and got the (real) baby bottle from the sand.
>
> *T*: 'Maybe baby is hungry now?' (with T making a crying sound, adding plaintively, 'she wants her bottle')
>
> Melanie didn't give the baby its bottle, however. Deliberately looking at the doll, she moved the bottle away slowly, with a fleeting, yet stern expression on her face.
>
> *T*: 'She *can't* have it'

This example clearly indicates how Melanie's autonomy and cognitive capacity began increasing, as she began to select a direction for her play and perhaps enact a remembered, difficult, earlier experience at home. She began to show a wider range of emotional responses fleetingly and did not always display her fixed smile. An attachment theme also seemed to be emerging in her rudimentary symbolic play, given my intensive help and increasing attunement to her emotional states (Ryan 1999).

> By her fifth session, Melanie was beginning to enact rudimentary role plays:
>
> She became interested in the play ironing board and then in cleaning the windows in the playroom with a cloth.
>
> *T*: 'You're busy…busy at your house.'
>
> *M (picking up a blanket)*: 'Baby'.

Taking the blanket to the ironing board, Melanie paused, then carefully wrapped it around her head instead, eyes shining and looking at her carer directly.

T: 'You're a mummy!'

T: 'You're Nancy (the carer), maybe.'

Melanie became very excited and kept wrapping the blanket as a 'towel' around her head, laughing with deep delight and looking directly at Nancy first, and then myself. Nancy and I joined in and laughed with her, excited ourselves by this new play and her emotional responsiveness, which was similar to 20–24-month-old toddlers' and their carers' delight when beginning to develop basic role play sequences (First 1994).

This example shows how the development of pretend play enables young children to share their inner world, thus facilitating their attachment relationships. Simultaneously, it advances their understanding of the mental states of significant others ('theory of mind') (Fonagy *et al.* 1997), the development of their internal models of attachment relationships and their advancement in exploration and interest sharing with significant others (Heard and Lake 1997). Indeed, Nancy's presence seems likely to have contributed to Melanie's rapid progress symbolically and to the attachment themes she enacted. This supports developmental hypotheses on the importance of children's motivation to share experiences as a factor in symbolic development (Ryan 1999).

These play sequences in turn demonstrate ways Nancy shared Melanie's highly emotionally charged and meaningful attachment enactments during early therapy sessions. Nancy's participation enabled her to appreciate and share changes in Melanie's play and emotional responses in this highly facilitative environment and seemed to promote rapid changes in their own relationship. Nancy was quickly able to apply attachment concepts and strategies to her thinking and parenting of Melanie from discussions and her participation in play therapy sessions. Our discussions were further informed by using both the attachment dynamic's formulation of defences and principles of non-directive practice (Ryan 2004b).

Nancy's difficulties initially in responding appropriately to Melanie stemmed from her heightened sense of responsibility for a child who was fostered and not her own child (Macaskill 1991), from Melanie's presentation as a very frightened and emotionally damaged child, and from Nancy's own lack of knowledge and experience in working with children who have serious attachment problems. With training and emotional support she became a highly skilled carer. As well as her problem-solving skills and fostering experience, she had a secure attachment style, including a lack of defensiveness in receiving help from me and other professionals. She and her husband displayed reciprocal, secure attachments to one another, easily shared parenting responsibilities, and the family also had strong extended family support. Nancy also developed a secure caregiving and empowering relationship with Melanie's birth parents. All these characteristics appeared to contribute to her excellence as a full partner in Melanie's emotionally demanding intervention.

Melanie's therapeutic progress

The social worker, Nancy, and I all agreed at our meeting after eight non-directive play therapy sessions that Melanie's overall progress was surprisingly rapid. She displayed increasing attachment to her foster carers and a widening range of emotional responses. In addition Melanie had made progress in playing symbolically and in forming a therapeutic relationship with me during her play therapy sessions. We therefore decided to introduce the next phase, preparing Melanie for individual sessions. This phase was intended to increase her independence in an age appropriate manner and enable Melanie to further develop her internal working model of attachment relationships in order to become more securely attached to Nancy. Maintaining Melanie's attachment to her carers, while increasing her use of me as a substitute attachment figure, seemed essential (Ryan and Needham 2001).

Nancy began to leave the playroom early and remained in the waiting room while I continued Melanie's play sessions alone. This transition needed to be managed very sensitively and be responsive to Melanie's needs. It quickly became clear that it needed to be done in a very concrete manner. Melanie initially seemed puzzled by Nancy's departure, even though it had been explained that Nancy would be waiting for her nearby and she had been shown where Nancy would wait. Melanie seemed reassured when Nancy explained that she was having a cup of tea while Melanie and I played without her. As Nancy left the room, Melanie pointed to Nancy's handbag, which was routinely hung on the door at the beginning of each session. As Melanie was allowed to carry Nancy's bag when our play therapy sessions finished, I suggested leaving Nancy's bag on the door until Melanie and I finished. Melanie therefore was able to have this bag as her transitional object, reminding her of Nancy while remaining in the playroom (Winnicott 1971). Melanie seemed highly reassured by being able to look at Nancy's handbag; while she sometimes left our session early during these transitional sessions – always with the handbag! – she was gradually able to make the transition to spending the whole hour on her own with me while Nancy waited nearby.

During this transition I began to provide a higher level of psycho-logical care to Melanie, including helping her regulate her emotional responses, and helping her reunite with Nancy when anxious and needing Nancy's reassuring presence. In these ways I was attempting to reinforce, rather than attenuate, the primacy of Melanie's new and fragile attachment relationship with Nancy. As Melanie became more assertive and autonomous, I began to limit the number of times she was allowed to leave the playroom (Wilson and Ryan 2005). As I set this limit, I talked simply about Nancy waiting for her. After a few sessions Melanie spontaneously began talking about Nancy's absence and what Nancy was doing while she waited. Melanie therefore appeared to be developing and modifying her own internal, supportive attachment system during these heightened, therapeutic experiences of separation. Interestingly, the normal developmental process for children of develop-ing an internal model of their attachment relationships seemed to be unfolding for Melanie in a shorter time than usual, possibly due to the more intense therapeutic experiences of separation and ensuing security she was experiencing weekly in play therapy (Bowlby 1980; Heard and Lake 1997).

Later phases of Melanie's therapy

Over the next six months Melanie continued to develop more secure attachments to her carers. She also became more attached to her parents, albeit insecurely, and less dependent on her younger sister to meet her attachment needs. Melanie slowly increased the length and complexity of her symbolic play to approximately a 2.5 year old level (Westby 2000). Much of my time in therapy and Nancy's time at home was spent supporting Melanie's spontaneous play and developmental progress, now that her attachment relationships seemed more established. My initial plan had been to have a therapy 'holiday' for six months, while continuing monthly meetings with her carer and social worker. At this point I recommended that social services review Melanie's care plan in light of her considerable progress and consider an adoptive placement for her, if Melanie was not to be returned to her birth parents.

Melanie's sister and brother were rehabilitated home during this six-month therapy period, after a favourable psychological assessment. Social services also decided to rehabilitate Melanie to her family at the end of this six-month period. Due to this change in Melanie's care plan, I continued to work with Melanie and her birth parents during her rehabilitation for nine additional months. Unfortunately, due at least in part to her parents' emotional limitations, I was unable to form a strong therapeutic alliance with them. Another factor in our inability to form a productive working relationship seemed to be due to her parents' lack of motivation to change their parenting patterns beyond complying with the statutory requirement that they bring Melanie to her play therapy. Nor did they wish to participate in filial therapy, which had not been required by social services as part of the rehabilitation plan.

Melanie's attachment to her mother and father appeared highly insecure and Melanie's cognitive and emotional development seemed curtailed compared with her earlier, more rapid, developmental progress described above. Sadly therapy ended without her parents reaching the level of competence needed to meet Melanie's emotional and developmental needs in my opinion. I shared these opinions on an ongoing basis with social services and strongly recommended that after Melanie's therapy ended, social services and education monitor and intensively support and supplement her parents' care of Melanie. However I was not hopeful that these recommendations would be followed, given the agencies' limited resources and the lessened priority of Melanie's needs now that the court process had ended. I have not had follow up reports on Melanie, therefore I cannot inform readers about Melanie's future progress after my involvement ended.

PRACTICE AND RESEARCH IMPLICATIONS

Referrals from social services departments, as Melanie's case illustrates, often involve foster children who have more difficult and fragmented lives than children who remain with their families throughout their development. Therapists working with this population need to have realistic aims, as illustrated above, and highly flexible and pragmatic attitudes in order to change their aims and interventions as needed, based on care decisions as well as on therapeutic considerations. Another therapeutic requirement is the ability to adapt interventions to the unique and complex characteristics of each case. Because of changes in circumstances, it is difficult to engage these children in research. One research limitation of the above case, for example, is that while different features discussed above are relevant for practitioners working with similar cases, all of the characteristics of the case are highly unlikely to be replicated again, which makes this type of case difficult to use for research purposes. Child therapy research, in general, finds it difficult to employ the methodologically robust design of collecting outcome data on a comparison of one kind of therapy intervention with another comparable intervention using random sampling. Similarly, play therapy, while showing highly significant results for play therapy and filial therapy studies with control groups (Bratton *et al.* 2005), also finds treatment comparisons particularly challenging. However case studies such as Melanie do provide ways to think about interesting and important research areas for future work. Two such research questions are:

1. What interventions are most effective for developmentally delayed children who are unable to play imaginatively? Is the *Learn to Play* programme (Stagnitti 1998) prior to therapy a more effective way to enhance this process than non-directive play therapy sessions themselves?

2. Are children who attend play therapy who do not have internal models of attachment relationships able to develop these models more quickly than comparable children who have other interventions? (See also Ryan 2007b.)

CONCLUSION

This chapter started with a discussion of congruence, and of children who need additional help in developing their relationships with important adults in their lives. The chapter has shown how non-directive play therapy lends itself to meeting children's varied needs. It can be adapted to complex cases where developmental delay, attachment disorders and maltreatment all have impacted on children's development. The case presented, while showing some signs of progress and hopeful outcomes, also demonstrates that 'life is a perilous journey' where other factors may influence outcomes more powerfully than any therapeutic intervention is able to achieve.

REFERENCES

Alvarez, A. (1996) 'Addressing the element of deficit in children with autism: Psychotherapy which is both psychoanalytically and developmentally informed.' *Clinical Child Psychology and Psychiatry 1*, 4, 525–537.

American Psychiatric Association (APA) (1994) *Diagnostic and Statistical Manual of Mental Disorders*, 4th edn. Washington, DC: American Psychiatric Press.

Axline, V. (1947) *Play Therapy*. London: Churchill Livingstone.

Binney, V., McKnight, I. and Broughton, S. (1994) *Relationship Play Therapy for Attachment Disturbances in Four to Seven Year Old Children*. The Clinical Application of Ethology and Attachment Theory, Occasional Papers no. 9. London: ACCP.

Bowlby, J. (1980) *Attachment and Loss, Vols I-III*. London: Hogarth Press.

Bratton, S., Ray, D., Rhine, T. and Jones, L. (2005) 'The efficacy of play therapy with children: A meta-analytic review of treatment outcomes.' *Professional Psychology: Research and Practice 36*, 4, 376–390.

Cicchetti, D. (1989) 'How research on child maltreatment has informed the study of child development: perspectives from developmental psychopathology.' In D. Cicchetti and V. Carlson (eds) *Child Maltreatment: Theory and Research on the Causes and Consequences of Child Abuse and Neglect*. Cambridge: Cambridge University Press.

Denham, S. A. (1998) *Emotional Development in Young Children*. London: Guilford.

Dorfman, E. (1951) 'Play Therapy.' In C. Rogers, *Client-Centred Therapy*. London: Constable.

Drewes, A., Carey, L. and Schaefer, C. E. (eds) (2001) *School-based Play Therapy*. New York: Wiley.

First, E. (1994) 'The leaving game, or I'll play you and you play me: the emergence of dramatic role play in 2-year-olds.' In A. Slade and D. P. Wolf (eds) *Children at Play: Clinical and Developmental Approaches to Meaning and Representation*. Oxford: Oxford University Press.

Fonagy, P., Steele, H., Steele, M. and Holder, J. (1997) *Attachment and Theory of Mind: Overlapping Constructs? Bonding and Attachment: Current Issues in Research and Practice, Occasional Papers no. 14*. London: ACCP.

Gallo-Lopez, L. and Schaefer, C.E. (eds) (2005) *Play Therapy with Adolescents*. New York: Jason Aronson.

Guerney, L. (2001) 'Child centered play therapy.' *International Journal of Play Therapy 10*, 2, 13–31.

Heard, D. and Lake, B. (1997) *The Challenge of Attachment for Caregivers*. London: Routledge.

James, B. (1994) *Handbook for Treatment of Attachment-Trauma Problems in Children*. New York: Lexington Books.

Josefi, O. and Ryan, V. (2004) 'Non-directive play therapy for young children with autism: A case study.' *Clinical Child Psychology and Psychiatry 9*, 4, 533–551.

Landreth, G. (2002) *Play Therapy: The Art of the Relationship*, 2nd edn. New York: Brunner Routledge.

Landreth, G. and Bratton, S. C. (2006) *Child Parent Relationship Therapy (CPRT): A 10 Session Filial Therapy Model*. London: Routledge.

Landreth, G. L., McGuire, D. K. and Mc Guire, D. E. (2000) *Linking Parents to Play Therapy: Applications, Interventions and Case Studies*. New York: Brunner Routledge.

Leblanc, M. and Ritchie, M. (2001) 'A meta-analysis of play therapy outcomes.' *Counselling Psychology Quarterly 14*, 2, 149–162.

Macaskill, C. (1991) *Adopting or Fostering a Sexually Abused Child*. London: B T Batsford.

Pearce, J. W. and Pezzot-Pearce, T. D. (1997) *Psychotherapy of Abused and Neglected Children.* London: Guilford.

Ryan, V. (1999) 'Developmental delay, symbolic play and non-directive play therapy: essentials in atypical and normal development.' *Clinical Child Psychology and Psychiatry 4,* 2, 167–185.

Ryan, V. (2004a) '"My new mum"': How drawing can help children rework their internal models of attachment relationship in non-directive play therapy.' *British Journal of Play Therapy 1,* 1, 35–46.

Ryan, V. (2004b) 'Adapting non-directive play therapy interventions for children with attachment disorders.' *Clinical Child Psychology and Psychiatry 9,* 1, 75–87.

Ryan, V. (2007a) 'Non-directive play therapy with abused children and adolescents.' In K. Wilson and A. James (eds) *The Child Protection Handbook,* 3rd edn. London: Bailliere Tindall.

Ryan, V. (2007b) 'Filial therapy: Helping children and new carers to form secure attachment relationships.' *British Journal of Social Work 37,* 643–657.

Ryan, V. and Bratton, S. (in press) 'Child-centered/non-directive play therapy for very young children.' In C. E. Schaefer, S. Kelly-Zion, J. McCormick and A. Ohnogi (eds) *Play Therapy For Very Young Children.* Lanham, MD: Rowman and Littlefield.

Ryan, V. and Courtney, A. (forthcoming) 'Therapists' use of congruence in child-centered/non-directive play therapy and filial therapy.' *International Journal of Play Therapy.*

Ryan, V. and Needham, C. (2001) 'Non-directive play therapy with children experiencing psychic trauma.' *Clinical Child Psychology and Psychiatry 6,* 3, 437–453.

Ryan V. and Wilson, K. (1995) 'Non-directive play therapy as a means of recreating optimal infant socialisation patterns.' *Early Development and Parenting 4,* 29–38.

Ryan, V. and Wilson, K. (2000) *Case Studies in Non-Directive Play Therapy.* London: Jessica Kingsley Publishers.

Schaefer, C. E. (ed.) (2002) *Play Therapy with Adults.* New York: Wiley.

Schaefer, C. E., Kelly-Zion, S., McCormick, J. and Ohnogi, A. (eds) (in press) *Play Therapy for Very Young Children.* Lanham, MD: Rowman and Littlefield.

Slade, A. and Wolf, D. P. (eds) (1994) *Children at Play: Clinical and Developmental Approaches to Meaning and Representation.* Oxford: Oxford University Press.

Stagnitti, K. (1998) *Learn to Play: A Practical Program to Develop a Child's Imagination.* Melbourne, Australia: Co-ordinates Publications.

VanFleet, R. and Guerney, L. (eds) (2003) *Casebook of Filial Therapy.* Boiling Springs, PA: Play Therapy Press.

Wenar, C. and Kerig, P. (2006) *Developmental Psychopathology: From Infancy through Adolescence.* New York: McGraw Hill.

West, J. (1996) *Child Centred Play Therapy,* 2nd edn. London: Arnold.

Westby, C. (2000) 'A scale for assessing development of play.' In K. Gitlin-Weiner, A. Sandgrund and C. Schaefer (eds) *Play Diagnosis and Assessment,* 2nd edn. Chichester: Wiley.

Wilson, K. and Ryan, V. (2005) *Play Therapy: A Non-Directive Approach for Children and Adolescents,* 2nd edn. London: Elsevier Science.

Wilson, K., Ryan, V. and Fisher, T. (1995) 'Partnerships in therapeutic work with children.' *Journal of Social Work Practise 9,* 2, 131–140.

Winnicott, D. (1971) *Playing and Reality.* Harmondsworth: Penguin.

Zappella, M. and Messeri, P. (1994) *Shared Emotions and Rapid Recovery in Children with Delayed Development.* The Clinical Application of Ethology and Attachment Theory, Occasional Papers no 9. London: ACCP.

CHAPTER 14

Challenging Bodies: Enabling Physically Disabled Children to Participate in Play

Rachael McDonald and Ted Brown

CHAPTER OBJECTIVES

This chapter will illustrate how to enable a child with a physical disability to participate in play using assistive technologies by describing how to modify the environment to improve access to play. The adaptation of activities for children with disabilities is also described.

INTRODUCTION

Although play is regarded as essential to human development, physical, sensory and communication problems can interrupt the development of play skills (Harkness and Bundy 2001). For children who have physical, sensory or cognitive impairment, access to play is often denied in their daily experiences. Some authors even postulate that children with physical disabilities develop a 'secondary disability' of play deprivation (Missiuna and Pollock 1991; Olds, Sadler and Kitzman 2007). In this chapter we look specifically at children with physical disabilities, who, because of their impaired ability and activity limitations, are prevented from achieving play independence.

Play development is about children gaining control over their world. For children with physical disabilities, however, play exploration is hindered by reduced mobility and impaired function, requiring modifications to the activity or the environment in order to enable their engagement in play. Adults working with severely physically impaired children, whether professionals or non-professionals, require both an adequate knowledge of child development, and a willingness to create environments that encourage and support play. For the child with a physical disability, the right to play can be taken for granted or overlooked because of the focus on their physical dysfunction or other peoples' reactions towards them. It is the responsibility of people caring for or assisting children with physical disabilities to ensure that the child has access to meaningful play opportunities. In order to promote play, a variety of factors must be considered, including the child's own abilities and impairment, the influence of parents/carers or other adults, access and quality of peer relationships, the adaptation of toys and the impact of the environment.

IMPACTS OF HEALTH CONDITIONS THAT MAKE PLAY CHALLENGING

Health conditions that effect children's physical (motor) skills tend to have neuromuscular (cerebral palsy), traumatic injury (acquired brain injury, spinal cord injury) or musculoskeletal (juvenile idiopathic arthritis, arthrogryposis) origins. Literature on this group of children has concentrated on physical activities and activity limitations (Harvey et al. 2008). Much literature describes play as a therapeutic tool (Gupta and Bhargava 2008; Hoare et al. 2007). This chapter will focus on enabling disabled children's access to independent play and will refer primarily to children with cerebral palsy (CP), although the principles applied here can be used for children with other physical disabilities. Cerebral palsy can be defined as a disorder of movement and posture caused by a non-progressive defect or lesion to the immature brain, and is often a term of convenience applied to a group of motor disorders that result in chronic disability (Sankar and Mundkur 2005). Although a motor disorder is the primary prerequisite for the diagnosis of CP, a number of associated features also exist, including learning disabilities, behavioural difficulties, epilepsy, sensory disturbance, hydrocephalus, eating and swallowing problems and speech difficulties (Sankar and Mundkur 2005; Stavness 2006).

HOW PHYSICAL DISABILITIES INFLUENCE PLAY

For children with cerebral palsy, their motor impairment will often hinder or prevent them from fully engaging in play, while their physical environment often presents insurmountable barriers (Harkness and Bundy 2001; Missiuna and Pollock 1991). Playing with conventional toys presents a huge challenge (Ruffino and Mistrett 2007).

Children develop from independently learning about their world through their senses, and at the same time develop sophisticated gross and fine motor, problem solving and communication skills. In the first year of life sensorimotor play predominates. This becomes of secondary importance as the child develops functional pretend play skills. For the child with CP, their play may not develop and so it is important to recognise that children with physical disabilities may not be experiencing a full range of sensorimotor stimulation from an early age, and will often need help to enable them to access play opportunities (Apache 2005; Schaffer *et al.* 1989).

Delayed gross motor development is often the first obvious sign that a child has a physical disability (Palisano, Snider and Orlin 2004). Delays in gross motor development mean that the child will need extra supports and positioning in order to access activities (Ahl *et al.* 2005; Palisano *et al.* 2004). Tamm and Skar (2000) demonstrated that children who have mobility restrictions tend to play either alone or as onlookers rather than actively play with other children or adults.

Children use their hands to access toys, participate in messy play and manipulate objects (Eliasson 2005; Hanna *et al.* 2003; Odding, Roebroeck and Stam 2006). Children with CP however, often have poor fine motor skills. This can be for a number of reasons: first, if a child's core stability is compromised due to underlying gross motor impairment, they often do not have enough stability to use their hands (McDonald and Surtees 2007) and second, their upper limbs may also be affected, which means that they will be unable or less able to access activities without help.

Children with CP are also likely to have some intellectual impairment (Odding *et al.* 2006), meaning that development of play is often slower and activities need to be modified to suit the child's learning capacity (Chiarello, Huntington and Bundy 2006). Communication challenges, especially for children who are non-verbal (Meyers and Vipond 2005) further restrict participation in pretend co-operative play (Sandberg and Lilliedahl 2008).

ENABLEMENT OF PLAY

Given these challenges, there are three main areas to consider when enabling a child with physical disabilities to participate in play. These include changes to the physical environment, modification of the activity itself and supports from people.

The physical environment

The physical environment is one of the main reasons that a child with CP cannot fully participate in play – their bodies don't move the way they want

them to and their everyday environment is not designed for these challenges
(Copley and Ziviani 2004; Hoenig *et al.* 2003). Children with disabilities
have been observed to be more playful at home than at school (Rigby and
Gaik 2007), which seems to be linked to increased opportunities and fewer
physical barriers as well as intensive interaction with another person (Appl,
Fahl-Gooler and McCollum 1997; Chiarello *et al.* 2006).

Simple changes to the child's environment may help enable greater
participation in play. For example, adjusting heights of tables for wheelchairs increases the CP child's access to tabletop play activities. Children
with poor vision or cognitive abilities may benefit from a room arranged in a
constant way. Some children with physical disabilities have not had the same
opportunities to develop, so add sensory stimulation into the environment,
remembering that they may even need extra stimulation due to their underlying sensory problems (hearing, vision, touch). Conversely, an environment
can be too stimulating and lead to sensory overload; therefore quiet environments where the child can concentrate are also necessary. Utilisation of
postural management equipment to encourage the development of skills
increases individual play opportunities (Cox 2003).

Modification of the play activity

When children are unable to access play opportunities one way of assisting
play is to modify the activity itself. This may involve choosing play
equipment the child can access (Hanser 2006), or changing the activity
(Valvano 2004). The idea is to provide play activities that are developmentally appropriate, and can be matched to the child's own physical,
communicative and cognitive ability (Gibbs, Miles and Lloyd 2005).

Modification of an activity to increase the disabled child's assisted or independent play could include:

1. Breaking the play activity down into small steps so that the child
    can achieve it on their own or with minimal help.

2. Providing opportunities for the child to independently achieve
    some play success, even if this appears very small.

3. Modifying toys in order for the child to be able to use them. For
    example, a Play Station console can be modified so that a child
    with physical difficulty can independently play computer games.

4. Choosing toys and play activities that are developed for children
    with special needs.

Supports from people

Encouraging adults (parents, teachers, classroom assistants) to play with a disabled child at the child's developmental level is extremely important, given that children with special needs can be play deprived or play on their own (Harkness and Bundy 2001; Missiuna and Pollock 1991; Tamm and Skar 2000). Parents will often instinctively know what their child wants, but helping them and other caregivers to better understand the developmental level their child is operating at has a number of positive outcomes including strengthening the child/parent bond and empowering them. Parental influence is crucial in helping the disabled child to play with playfulness related to the child's own developmental abilities and parents' responsiveness (Chiarello et al. 2006; Pennington and McConachie 1999). Therefore, encouraging parents to interact with and to play with their physically disabled child needs be a priority for any therapeutic intervention.

Specific strategies for playing with children who have physical disabilities include teaching the child specific skills, modelling play behaviours and following the child's lead. Identify the child's strengths, and get the child to actively participate. Reward success, no matter how small, and modify activities to suit the child. Allow for repetition – all children need to practise to achieve activities, and children with physical disabilities will need more time to practise.

Positioning for play

Children with physical disabilities, particularly those of neurological origins, have difficulty attaining and maintaining a stable position, which means that they have difficulty using their hands and eyes to play (Lacoste et al. 2006; McDonald and Surtees 2007; Rigby and Gaik 2007). A crucial part of enabling children with physical difficulties to play is to enable them to be stable. Adaptive seating systems, for example, are designed to improve the posture and stability of children who are unable to sit by themselves (Stavness 2006; Washington et al. 2002). Once the child is supported in a stable position, their ability to use their eyes, hands, and fingers is optimised, allowing them to functionally manipulate play objects.

Electronic assistive technology

There have been rapid improvements in technology over the last few years, yet most people are unaware of the availability, use and benefits which electronic assistive technology can give when matched to the needs of a physically disabled child (Berry and Ignash 2003; Jutai et al. 2005). Much assistive technology is subject to non-compliance, non-use and is not well used to facilitate child-initiated play (McDonald et al. 2008; Verza et al.

2006). For children, the appeal of the activity or game needs to be considered. Adults can see the benefits, but children who are developing their skills often don't have that insight or understanding, particularly when the access is not straightforward (Light and Drager 2007).

Electronic assistive technology can include powered mobility, technology to assist communication (Augmentative and Alternative Communication), personal computers and software, environmental control and adapted toys. For the young child with a physical disability, their ability to access the devices is paramount to their ability to use and play with them. This is more complex than it seems. Electronic assistive technologies also have high support needs from staff. Providing the equipment is not sufficient enough to guarantee successful use of the equipment (McDonald *et al.* 2008; Verza *et al.* 2006). The cognitive demands of the task increase as the physical demands decrease.

Furthermore, much of the information on access and use of assistive technology was developed for adults with acquired disabilities, which needs to be modified for young children and made fun (Drager *et al.* 2003). Children learn to communicate and develop through play and experimentation, and using an electronic assistive device is no different (Light and Drager 2002). Barriers to success can be minimised first by allowing children to access technology in an age appropriate way but at their developmental level. Second, the device must be easily accessible. Finally, the device or activity must have appropriate support for learning, additional to provision of the device itself (McDonald *et al.* 2008).

Types of assistive technology

Switch adapted toys

These are toys which are battery operated and/or sensory, which are modified so that a switch can be plugged in and the child operates the toy by activating or hitting the switch. For children with profound disabilities, this is often their only way of operating the toy. The major advantage of the switch toy is that if the child can touch the switch, they are operating the toy independently and therefore are able to play with it (Daniels *et al.* 1995; Nilsson and Nyberg 1999). Children can learn cause and effect relationships, independence and control. Once the child has developed switch skills, they are able to apply this to more sophisticated devices. Sometimes however, the switch adapted toy requires the user to hold down the switch and the toy stops when the switch is released. This can be frustrating for a child, so further modification, such as a flexi-timer module, which enables one switch press to keep the toy going for a period of time, can give a reward and extend the play time.

Powered wheelchairs

A powered wheelchair is essentially a wheelchair which is electric, and operated not by pushing on the wheels, but by an input device such as a joystick. There has been great evidence that powered mobility, which gives independence to people with physical disabilities, has a great impact on participation of children even at a very young age (Nisbet 2002; Wiart *et al.* 2003). Studies for children with complex disabilities and less direct access (Nilsson and Nyberg 2003; Nisbet 2002) have shown that these devices, together with alternative access, are a good way for children to gain some independence in movement, and therefore fun. Access to independent mobility enables a child to participate in team games – such as balloon basketball and wheelchair soccer.

Environmental control units

Environmental control units help people with limited physical ability to access equipment around their environment (McDonald, Surtees and Wirz 2004; Stineman *et al.* 2007). Through accessing the device directly or via a switch, the user can operate lights, televisions and any other electronic equipment. One of the benefits is the reduced load on caregivers but, for our purposes, it is a useful way of motivating a child - what could be more fun than changing the channel on the television or radio to annoy your brother!

Communication aids

Communication aids are used to assist a person who has complex communication needs by supplementing or replacing their verbal speech output. This includes aided and unaided methods, but for our purposes we are looking at voice output communication aids which use digitised or recorded speech (Light, Drager and Nemser 2004; McDonald *et al.* 2008). Highly sophisticated aids are difficult to use, and take many years of training as well as support. There are, however, small communication aids that can be programmed with a single message that encourages the child to participate.

Computer software

There is a vast choice of software available which is accessible to children who can only use a single switch. It is important to remember though, that much of this is directed at 'learning' and may even be at levels above that of the child's developmental functioning, which leads to frustration for the child. Some software is available which involves popping balloons using a switch, or building a flower. These are fun for children and encourage independence, but also isolation, which we know this group of children are at risk for.

Accessing electronic assistive technologies

In order to use assistive technologies, there is a large range of alternative access systems which can assist children to use technology for play. Regardless of the switch type used there are a number of factors that must be considered so the child can use them successfully. Direct access has greater motor demand but less of a cognitive demand, and indirect access has less motor demand but greater cognitive demand (Arthanat *et al.* 2007; Copley and Ziviani 2004; Hoppestad 2007). The method of access needs to be chosen so that it is the most reliable for the child in order to try and guarantee their success, so that they can concentrate on playing, rather than the physical skills of accessing.

Direct access methods

Speed, efficiency and access are increased by direct access methods. Methods of direct access include using a joystick, a keyboard or a mouse. Because direct access is preferable, many pieces of adapted equipment have been developed in order to harness this accessibility. For example, touch screens for the computer, keyboards that have been made bigger or have a keyguard, so that children who might hit several keys at once can isolate their action. Adaptations to mouse access is also common (tracker ball and roller balls, which are essentially an upturned mouse with switches beside it).

Indirect access

The most common type of indirect access is via switching. This can be by a switch that someone touches (contact switch), or operates by another movement (non-contact switch). Examples of contact switches include a jellybean, string and infrared head pointer, while examples of non-contact switches include sip and puff, sound-activated or eye-blink switches.

Switch placement

The user must be in a comfortable, stable and functional position so that the movement that is used to operate the switch is voluntary and reliable. Switches can be operated by a body part that has the most reliable voluntary movement, such as hands or head (move from side to side), chin, mouth, feet or knees. For the child with a physical disability to be successful, the switch must be stable. The child must be motivated to use the switch, which means the activity must be fun. For example, the switch is used with appliances such as battery operated toys, kitchen appliances (try getting the child to operate a blender with the lid off via a switch – the mess is hilarious and very motivating!), radios, fans or even story books. Using these devices the supporting adult can then look at developing cause and effect, turn taking, building and choice making – all components that encourage the child to interact.

Case study: The power of play

'Tom' is six years old and has cerebral palsy. He attends a mainstream school, but has a full time helper. Tom's cerebral palsy affects all his limbs, he has poor tone through his trunk and high tone in his legs. His arms are high in tone but also dystonic, and he is unable to sit by himself. He has a great sense of humour, and laughs when those around him laugh. His speech therapist and teacher think that he has normal cognitive function, but because he has no speech, he is unable to let people know this. His occupational therapist and physiotherapist have found an adaptive seating system that allows him to use his hands, and he sits in this most of the day. The other times he has free body time on the mat, but he is unable to move himself. Often the staff take advantage of this by doing his physio exercises and stretching his legs. The other children ignore Tom on the mat, except for one girl, Emily, who tries to play with him in this position. She is shooed away by the helper, as she gets in the way of Tom's stretching. The staff set Tom up with his computer, single switch and educational software. He has a large Big Mac switch attached to the computer, and the staff are teaching him 'switch timing'. A pair of symbols appear on the screen and Tom is required to hit the switch when a matching pair appears. He practises this activity every day, but is successful 50 per cent of the time or less.

Tom was visited by a team of developmental therapists at the request of his family, health and educational professionals to investigate how to make his accessing of assistive technology more successful. The team consisted of a paediatrician, speech therapist, occupational therapist and psychologist, who did a thorough assessment of him. Using adapted equipment, they were able to ascertain that Tom had cortical visual impairment and could identify real objects, but had great difficulty with symbols. On a test of receptive language and development, he scored at a level of a much younger child. When given an activity at a cause and effect level, he was able to successfully hit his switch 100 per cent of the time. When given the symbol matching task, he was again unsuccessful, leading the team to believe that the activity was (a) unmotivating, (b) too difficult or (c) a combination of the two.

The team developed a programme with Tom, his family and the school and health staff, which was based around play and gaining control over his environment. Whilst the computer based games are an important learning tool, he needed to access activities that were at his cognitive, physical and sensory level and provided him with choices other than nonparticipation. A powered wheelchair was adapted, so that he could move the chair by hitting one switch and stop with a second one. At home, an AdVOCAte speech synthesiser was modified using the environmental control capacities, so that he could independently turn on and off the television, or change channels, causing great consternation to his eight-year-old brother. A programme was set up at school where Tom was able to use real activities by hitting his switch, such as painting, or painting on the computer screen.

At the three-month review Tom was able to access his switch with about 90 per cent accuracy. The staff were aware that if it was less than this, the activity was either not motivating or too difficult. His switch skills have become automatic, so that it is a real alternative to direct access. And he has started to work on matching pairs of objects, using an arrow directed by his switch, and he is now so successful that the school have tried matching pictures. He is more successful than previously. He now participates in story telling, by hitting his Big Mac at points when asked.

Finally, the school have changed their use of time with Tom and given him time where he can explore his own body through sensory play, such as sand, water and aromatherapy. He is now left on his own with Emily, and they end up giggling when on the floor together. Emily will pretend that he is her 'baby', 'shopkeeper' or 'husband' and Tom participates with Emily, although his speech is not comprehensible. They take turns to hit the switches in the sensory room, and Emily helps Tom play with fine motor activities such as playdough or turning pages in a book when he is seated in his specialised seat.

SUMMARY AND CONCLUSION

Play, as we define it, is a challenge to children with physical disabilities. There are many factors including their own bodies and sensory systems, the environment, non-interaction from people and equipment that doesn't suit their needs and can prevent them from participating in play. This can result in the child becoming deprived of play experiences, and even passive. One of the major influences on whether or not a child learns to play is often the people around them. When a child has a disability, the people who work with them often see them as someone whom things are done to, in order to 'fix' their problems. In so doing, we deny the child the ability and the richness of play opportunities that most other children take for granted. This can be a challenging area for families and professionals. However, if we think of the child as a spiritual being, and help them to develop their own sense of independence, mastery and control, the rewards are great.

RESOURCES

www.toysrus.com/category/index.jsp?categoryId=2257808
www.lekotek.org/resources/informationtoys/tentips.html

REFERENCES

Ahl, L. E., Johansson, E., Granat, T. and Carlberg, E. B. (2005) 'Functional therapy for children with cerebral palsy: An ecological approach.' *Developmental Medicine & Child Neurology 47*, 613–619.

Apache, R. R. G. (2005) 'Activity-based intervention in motor skill development.' *Perceptual & Motor Skills 100*, 1011–1020.

Appl, D. J., Fahl-Gooler, F. and McCollum, J. A. (1997) 'Inclusive parent-child play groups: How comfortable are parents of children with disabilities in the groups?' *Infant Toddler Intervention: The Transdisciplinary Journal 7*, 235–249.

Arthanat, S., Bauer, S. M., Lenker, J. A., Nochajski, S. M. and Wu, Y. W. B. (2007) 'Conceptualization and measurement of assistive technology usability.' *Disability and Rehabilitation: Assistive Technology 2*, 235–248.

Berry, B. E. and Ignash, S. (2003) 'Assistive technology: Providing independence for individuals with disabilities.' *Rehabilitation Nursing 28*, 6–14.

Chiarello, L. A., Huntington, A. and Bundy, A. (2006) 'A comparison of motor behaviors, interaction, and playfulness during mother-child and father-child play with children with motor delay.' *Physical and Occupational Therapy in Pediatrics 26*, 129–151.

Copley, J. and Ziviani, J. (2004) 'Barriers to the use of assistive technology for children with multiple disabilities.' *Occupational Therapy International 11*, 229–243.

Cox, D. L. (2003) 'Wheelchair needs for children and young people: A review.' *British Journal of Occupational Therapy 66*, 219–223.

Daniels, L. E., Sparling, J. W., Reilly, M. and Humphry, R. (1995) 'Use of assistive technology with young children with severe and profound disabilities.' *Infant Toddler Intervention: The Transdisciplinary Journal 5*, 91–112.

Drager, K. D., Light J. C., Speltz J. C., Fallon K. A. and Jeffries, L. Z. (2003) 'The performance of typically developing 2½ -year-olds on dynamic display AAC technologies with different system layouts and language organizations.' *Journal of Speech, Language and Hearing Research 46*, 298–312.

Eliasson, A. (2005) 'Improving the use of hands in daily activities: Aspects of the treatment of children with cerebral palsy.' *Physical and Occupational Therapy in Pediatrics 25*, 37–60.

Gibbs, M., Miles, H. and Lloyd J. (2005) 'Improving outcomes in children with disability.' *Paediatric Nursing 17*, 21–23.

Gupta, S. and Bhargava, S. (2008) 'Play based stimulation programme for infants with cerebral palsy and mental retardation.' *Asia Pacific Disability Rehabilitation Journal 19*, 114–121.

Hanna, S. E., Law, M. C., Rosenbaum, P. L., King, G. A., Walter, S. D., Pollock, N., Russell, D. J. (2003) 'Development of hand function among children with cerebral palsy: Growth curve analysis for ages 16 to 70 months.' *Developmental Medicine & Child Neurology 45*, 448–455.

Hanser, G. (2006) 'Promoting emergent writing for students with significant disabilities.' *OT Practice 11*, suppl: CE-1-CE-8.

Harkness, L and Bundy, A. C. (2001) 'The Test of Playfulness and children with physical disabilities.' *Occupational Therapy Journal of Research 21*, 73–89.

Harvey, A., Robin, J., Morris, M. E., Kerr, Graham H. and Baker, R. (2008) 'A systematic review of measures of activity limitation for children with cerebral palsy.' *Developmental Medicine & Child Neurology 50*, 190–198.

Hoare, B. J., Wasiak, J., Imms, C. and Carey, L. (2007) 'Constraint-induced movement therapy in the treatment of the upper limb in children with hemiplegic cerebral palsy.' *Cochrane Database of Systematic Reviews* 2007, 2 (CD004149).

Hoenig, H., Landerman, L. R., Shipp, K. M. and George, L. (2003) 'Activity restriction among wheelchair users.' *Journal of the American Geriatrics Society 51*, 1244–1251.

Hoppestad, B. S. (2007) 'Inadequacies in computer access using assistive technology devices in profoundly disabled individuals: An overview of the current literature.' *Disability and Rehabilitation: Assistive Technology 2*, 189–199.

Jutai, J. W., Fuhrer, M. J., Demers, L., Scherer, M. J. and DeRuyter, F. (2005) 'Toward a taxonomy of assistive technology device outcomes.' *American Journal of Physical Medicine & Rehabilitation 84*, 294–302.

Lacoste, M., Therrien, M., Cote, J.N., Shrier, I., Labelle, H. and Prince, F. (2006) 'Assessment of seated postural control in children: Comparison of a force platform versus a pressure mapping system.' *Archives of Physical Medicine & Rehabilitation 87*, 1623–1629.

Light, J. C., Drager, K. D. R. (2002) 'Improving the design of augmentative and alternative technologies for young children.' *Assistive Technology 14*, 17–32.

Light, J. and Drager, K. (2007) 'AAC technologies for young children with complex communication needs: State of the science and future research directions.' *Augmentative and Alternative Communication 23*, 204–216.

Light, J. C., Drager, K. D. P. and Nemser, J. G. (2004) 'Enhancing the appeal of AAC technologies for young children: Lessons from the toy manufacturers.' *Augmentative and Alternative Communication 20*, 137–149.

McDonald, R., Harris, E., Price, K. and Jolleff, N. (2008) 'Elation or frustration? Outcomes following the provision of equipment during the Communication Aids Project: Data from one CAP partner centre.' *Child: Care, Health and Development 34*, 223–229.

McDonald, R., Surtees, R. and Wirz, S. (2004) 'The International Classification of Functioning, Disability and Health provides a model for adaptive seating interventions for children with cerebral palsy.' *British Journal of Occupational Therapy 67*, 293–302.

McDonald, R. L. and Surtees, R. (2007) 'Longitudinal study evaluating a seating system using a sacral pad and kneeblock for children with cerebral palsy.' *Disability & Rehabilitation 29*, 1041–1047.

Meyers, C. and Vipond, J (2005) 'Play and social interactions between children with developmental disabilities and their siblings: A systematic literature review.' *Physical and Occupational Therapy in Pediatrics 25*, 81–103.

Missiuna, C., and Pollock, N. (1991) 'Play deprivation in children with physical disabilities: the role of the occupational therapist in preventing secondary disability.' *American Journal of Occupational Therapy 45*, 882–888.

Nilsson, L. and Nyberg, P. (1999) 'Single-switch control versus powered wheelchair for training cause-effect relationships: case studies.' *Technology and Disability 11*, 35–38.

Nilsson, L. M. and Nyberg, P. J. (2003) 'Driving to learn: A new concept for training children with profound cognitive disabilities in a powered wheelchair.' *American Journal of Occupational Therapy 57*, 229–233.

Nisbet, P. D. (2002) 'Assessment and training of children for powered mobility in the UK.' *Technology and Disability 14*, 173–182.

Odding, E., Roebroeck, M. E., Stam, H. J. (2006) 'The epidemiology of cerebral palsy: Incidence, impairments and risk factors.' *Disability and Rehabilitation 28*, 183–191.

Olds, D. L., Sadler, L. and Kitzman, H. (2007) 'Programs for parents of infants and toddlers: Recent evidence from randomized trials.' *Journal of Child Psychology & Psychiatry & Allied Disciplines 48*, 355–391.

Palisano, R. J., Snider, L. M. and Orlin, M. N. (2004) 'Recent advances in physical and occupational therapy for children with cerebral palsy.' *Seminars in Pediatric Neurology 11*, 66–77.

Pennington, L. and McConachie, H. (1999) 'Mother-child interaction revisited: Communication with non-speaking physically disabled children.' *International Journal of Language & Communication Disorders 34*, 391–416.

Rigby, P. and Gaik, S. (2007) 'Stability of playfulness across environmental settings: A pilot study.' *Physical and Occupational Therapy in Pediatrics 27*, 27–43.

Ruffino, A. G. and Mistrett, S. G. (2007) 'Toys... Everyone can play with: selecting universal design features.' *OT Practice 12*, 9–13.

Sandberg, A. D. and Lilliedahl, M. (2008) 'Patterns in early interaction between young preschool children with severe speech and physical impairments and their parents.' *Child Language Teaching & Therapy 24*, 9–30.

Sankar, C. and Mundkur, N. (2005) 'Cerebral palsy-definition, classification, etiology and early diagnosis.' *Indian Journal of Pediatrics 72*, 865–868.

Schaffer, R., Law, M., Polatajko, H. and Miller, J. (1989) 'A study of children with learning disabilities and sensorimotor problems or let's not throw the baby out with the bathwater.' *Physical and Occupational Therapy in Pediatrics 9*, 101–117.

Stavness, C. (2006) 'The effect of positioning for children with cerebral palsy on upper-extremity function: a review of the evidence.' *Physical and Occupational Therapy in Pediatrics 26*, 39–53.

Stineman, M. G., Ross, R. N., Maislin, G. and Gray, D. (2007) 'Population-based study of home accessibility features and the activities of daily living: Clinical and policy implications.' *Disability and Rehabilitation 29*, 1165–1175.

Tamm, M. and Skar, L. (2000) 'How I play: Roles and relations in the play situations of children with restricted mobility.' *Scandinavian Journal of Occupational Therapy 7*, 174–182.

Valvano, J. (2004) 'Activity-focused motor interventions for children with neurological conditions.' *Physical and Occupational Therapy in Pediatrics 24*, 79–107.

Verza, R., Carvalho, M. L., Battaglia, M. A. and Uccelli, M. M. (2006) 'An interdisciplinary approach to evaluating the need for assistive technology reduces equipment abandonment.' *Multiple Sclerosis 12*, 88–93.

Washington, K., Deitz, J. C., White, O. R. and Schwartz, I. S. (2002) 'The effects of a contoured foam seat on postural alignment and upper-extremity function in infants with neuromotor impairments.' *Physical Therapy 82*, 1064–1076.

Wiart, L., Darrah, J., Cook, A., Hollis, V. and May, L. (2003) 'Evaluation of powered mobility use in home and community environments.' *Physical and Occupational Therapy in Pediatrics 23*, 59–75.

CHAPTER 15

Play Focused Therapy: Different Settings, Different Approaches

Rodney Cooper

CHAPTER OBJECTIVES

This chapter briefly examines the therapeutic use of play. Four invited vignettes are presented to illustrate different play approaches used by therapists in very different settings. These include a play therapy session in a community hall; an ecological play and leisure intervention in a school setting; procedural play to help a child to gain mastery over an anxiety provoking medical procedure and a therapist's reflections on facilitating play in a culturally different environment – a remote Australian Aboriginal community.

THERAPEUTIC USE OF PLAY

Play-based therapy interventions broadly take two approaches – those that use play *in* therapy as a treatment modality and those that use play *as* therapy (Knox and Mailloux 1997). When play is used *in* therapy, the therapist introduces play to enable a child to develop new skills or to improve functioning in weaker developmental areas (Rodger and Ziviani 1999). When play is used *as* therapy, the outcome of intervention is the facilitation and development of play *for itself.* The therapist sets up the play environment to provide the child with choices and the 'just right' challenge that will encourage them to develop the play skills, playful attitude and self expression necessary to interact with the world through play (Ferland 1997; Saunders, Sayer and Goodale 1999).

The therapeutic focus on play *for itself* is well established in the play therapy tradition although less acknowledged in the paediatric practice literature. Play therapy, whether non-directive or directive, is underpinned by the belief that play is central to the child's way of making sense of their experiences of the world (Landreth 2002; Wilson and Ryan 2005). Play therapy is recognised as a powerful therapeutic medium especially when used with traumatised or abused children and although its effectiveness is supported by a large body of anecdotal literature and case studies, research studies have been few (Reade, Hunter and McMillan 1999). Play in therapy in clinical and educational settings on the other hand, is often viewed as a means to an end and may be utilised to engage the child and to practise play skills or promote cognitive, language and social development (Rodger and Ziviani 1999). Regardless of the approach employed, the goal of play-based therapy should be to provide a safe, non-threatening play environment for the child in which to facilitate playfulness, problem solving and self expression that will lead to increased play competence, mastery of emotions and the enjoyment of doing.

THE THERAPEUTIC PLAY RELATIONSHIP

The therapeutic play relationship largely depends on individual factors including how effectively a therapist is able to develop rapport and build a relationship of trust with a child and his or her carers. Play is optimised within the context of relationships and emotional security (Landreth 2002). The adult therapist brings his or her unique skills and individual perspectives to the therapeutic relationship including: how skilfully they employ play props; show enjoyment and an understanding of play; are 'transparent' and willing to take risks and believe in and respect the child (Cattanach 1992; Gil 1991; Wilson and Ryan 2005). When an adult therapist enters a child's play as a 'playmate' it is crucial that the element of player-control is not taken away from the child.

THERAPEUTIC PLAY SETTINGS

While focus is on the play activity itself or the process of facilitating, adapting and building a child's capacity to make play choices, what we often don't consider is the impact of the physical and social environment on the therapeutic use of play (Cattanach 1994). Not surprisingly, settings for therapy - hospitals, clinics, community centres, social services, schools, early childhood centres, playgrounds and the child's home – are often challenging environments in their own right for introducing play-based interventions. I have certainly spent much time playing with children on home verandahs, in preschool sandpits, on living room floors, and junk-filled utility rooms in schools, all far from ideal environments for nurturing play! Furthermore, as a male therapist I am also acutely aware of child protection issues and have come to appreciate this challenging but transparent way of working with children in open and public spaces within their normal environments. In the child's home environment, for example, I try to work closely with parents or carers and have often needed to improvise or be flexible enough to include siblings. Play groups for parents and very young children provide wonderful settings to introduce and model developmentally appropriate play and to strengthen parent–child attachment relationships through the mutual discovery of shared play interactions (see Chapter 10). Attachment theory research shows that successful parent–child play involves the same behaviours as other types of responsive care giving with attachment security related to maternal playfulness (Grille 2008; Hughes, Elicker and Veen 1995). Infants who have had adults as 'playmates' have also been found to develop more sophisticated cognitive and social play behaviours and emotional intelligence (Grille 2008).

PLAY ENVIRONMENTS

Each play environment affects a child in a different way. If the child does not feel safe, he or she will not play. Children play more readily in a familiar or nurturing environment, whereas an unfamiliar setting may elicit more exploratory or non-play behaviour, at least initially. In extreme cases, if a child perceives the environment as too stressful, their sympathetic nervous system may trigger physiological arousal, activating a survival 'fight or flight' reaction which prevents them from playing (Way 1999). In my own work with abused children, I have observed that the hypervigilant child's play attention and intrinsic motivation is largely absorbed by heightened physiological arousal and constant monitoring of his or her environment for potential threat.

THERAPEUTIC PLAY IN ACTION

Four stories of play in different settings are now presented. Each vignette describes settings which are quite challenging for the therapist wanting to introduce play as a therapeutic strategy. While the authors' therapy aims and theoretical approaches differ greatly, each vignette highlights individual play solutions.

The first vignette describes a play therapy session and, while modified, it is based on my work with abused children. 'Joe' a seven-year-old boy presented as an attachment disordered child whose insecurity and past trauma had caused him to shut down emotionally. During the initial sessions he played exclusively with Lego. His play themes in the early sessions were very 'nihilistic' with obsessive themes of death, violence and destruction – there were no 'winners' as his characters all ended up being killed, eaten by sharks or abandoned. My therapy aims were to increase engagement, build trust, increase his interactive play participation and to encourage expression of enjoyment and feelings through imaginative play. My approach was primarily non-directive.

'Lego therapy' *Rodney Cooper*

Seven-year-old 'Joe' had been placed voluntarily in the care of social services by his mother at age six after she became unable to care for him due to her hospitalisation. His mother had a history of poorly controlled mental health problems and frequent hospital readmissions. When referred, Joe was with his second foster carers in 12 months and had started a new school in a small rural community. Joe's early years were marked by repeated separations, multiple moves and domestic violence as well as physical and emotional abuse by a stepfather. He had continuing access with his mother when she was well enough, but her visits were sporadic and often cancelled.

A joint therapy management plan was agreed with social services, his mother, the foster carers and the school. This involved education and support provided to his foster carers (who were concerned about his lack of empathy, avoidance of affection and cruelty to pets) and appropriate behaviour management systems put in place at school and home. With his foster placement and school environment stabilised and regular case conferences ensuring communication, the focus shifted from managing him in his environment to addressing his emotional needs through individual therapy.

Setting

Because of distance, a room was booked in a community hall near his foster carers and I travelled fortnightly to see Joe. The setting was a large open space, so my approach was to bring a selection of toys in boxes or bags and a large mat, which determined the boundaries of the 'play therapy area'. This method of mobile play therapy is well described by Cattanach (1992).

Play therapy session

Joe appeared subdued. He entered the play area and quietly examined the toy selection. I asked 'What do you want to play today?' He selected the Lego box and tipped the Lego onto the mat – 'You know…the never ending story.' He selected his favourite Lego characters, gave some to me and suggested, 'Let's make bases like last time.' We both started making Lego constructions on the mat. After five minutes of parallel construction activity, I commented, 'I am building a very strong base, it's indestructible.' Joe's curiosity was piqued. He 'walked' his character over to my unfinished construction and examined it carefully. 'I don't think so.' He then plotted out loud how he could overcome the defences. I let him set the rules for this game and as it unfolded I responded with play actions and dialogues using the Lego characters. As this shared play action expanded he became more confident in directing and controlling the play themes. For example, his characters snuck up and stole the 'power crystals' without my characters 'seeing' them because they were 'invisible'. He then introduced a new Lego character, 'Alien'. He took great delight in Alien tricking me and no matter how many walls or men I employed to 'protect' my base he overcame them. This 'give and take' cooperative play was very fluid, with Joe fully engaged and showing increased enjoyment, animation and eye contact (he laughed uproariously whenever his characters tricked my characters). He now provided the narration while I suggested storyline variations, which he either rejected or adopted. Sometimes his Lego character would threaten mine, all the while watching for my response. 'I'm going to kill your guy.' I acknowledged that this made my character feel very anxious. Joe volunteered that his stepfather '…used to say this'. I asked him how he felt, 'scared.' I reflected on how this must have felt. Joe returned to his play announcing, 'I'm going to take your guy prisoner instead', which is what he did. He then reassured me that 'You can rescue him back by climbing this rope to the roof (dolls house), I'll show your rescue guys how to do it.' I asked 'What if *they* get trapped?' He replied 'You'll just have to take the risk (laughed)'. Of course it *was* a trap and all my characters ended up prisoners, much to his delight. He then suggested ways that they could escape. Eventually he decided that all the play characters could 'live in the house and share the loot', but his special character got to wear 'the magic hat which makes him invincible'. When I gave him the usual five minutes warning prior to the session finishing, he announced 'I don't need the magic hat anymore. I used up all its power...it doesn't work. Now I'm the really powerful guy.' He placed this character and the 'magic hat', which had been a key prop, into the Lego box and initiated packing up (the first time). As we both packed up I commented on the game and his relaxed appearance and obvious enjoyment. 'It was fun. I like making up games.' He related his plans for how the story would develop next session, 'You can bring some paints next time because I might feel like painting.' Outside, his foster mother commented that he looked happy and prompted him to tell me that he had got a merit award at school that week.

Reflections on Lego therapy

This brief description fails to capture the full intensity and complexity of the unfolding play narrative but does highlight some learning for me as a therapist. There are many subtle cues and insightful themes in Joe's 'never ending story', which probably parallel his own experiences and anxieties. He used Lego play to make sense of his feelings, to trust and to test boundaries and my reaction to his ideas and need to control the play. While there was some transference he also invited me into a shared, cooperative game which revolved around trust and mutual enjoyment. In turn, I was guided by him, reflected how I was feeling, occasionally challenged him and had to learn to speak the 'language' of shared Lego play. Lego is a wonderful medium for creative fantasy play especially with boys who are the acknowledged experts!

Play in the school environment

The complexity of the school environment can overwhelm the best intentioned of therapy interventions, especially if the potential that this environment offers for developing social play, pretend play and group games are not understood by the therapist. The second vignette describes a multifaceted approach introduced into social play settings in the school, home and community. In this vignette Anne Poulsen describes an ecological approach to assessment, planning and implementation of an intervention to increase social play in a 'stuck social system'. Anne is a paediatric occupational therapist, researcher with the Mater Children Hospital and academic at the University of Queensland, Brisbane, Australia.

An ecologically valid leisure intervention for a boy with developmental coordination disorder *Anne Poulsen PhD*

'Dan' was the ten-year-old youngest child of a single-parent family living in an urban community. His pastimes included playing computer games, collecting and painting miniature fantasy army characters, origami, reading and singing in the school choir. He spent large amounts of time engaged in these pursuits, coming home from school to an empty house until his mother and sisters arrived home. There was an eight-year gap between Dan and his two older sisters.

Dan was isolated both at home and at school. He had recently changed schools and was referred to me by his teacher who was concerned about his lack of friends and poor motor coordination. My playground observation of Dan revealed a quiet, solitary boy who spent his recess alone or engaged in onlooker behaviour on the periphery of the school oval where large groups of boys rushed around in packs playing touch football. Occasionally Dan would run up and down along the school fence acting out imaginary 'Kung Fu' fighting games, much to the amusement and derision of nearby children who would dart out and obstruct his progress. This one-sided teasing play further isolated Dan from his classmates.

My initial observations of Dan's play revealed a pre-adolescent boy who spent little time in either structured or unstructured social physical play activity. In late childhood, games with rules occur in multiple nested contexts, at home, in the neighbourhood and at school (Pellegrini 1995, 2005). Dan did not participate in chasing, ball games or rough and tumble play – popular activities for his age group. He also had no participation in structured social-physical activities such as team sports. These provide opportunities to experience regular interactions with peers while adult leaders model a code of conduct and provide a hierarchical group structure for working together. It appeared that Dan had no social play opportunities and although he was observed to engage in imaginary play, this took place in front of observers and was disparaged. For children of his age, pretend play more often takes place in the privacy of their own home or with small groups of trusted friends (Pellegrini 2005).

Extended observation and assessment

During my formal evaluation Dan completed the *Leisure Diagnostic Battery* (Witt and Ellis 1989) and a retrospective 12-month *Leisure Survey*

(Aaron *et al.* 1995). He described his current leisure interests, which were largely sedentary and solitary, expressed concerns about his friendship networks, his coordination difficulties and his anxiety about potential playground bullying. On the *Movement Assessment Battery for Children* (Henderson and Sugden 1992) Dan had severe problems on the balance and eye hand coordination tests, with parent and teacher reports confirming his motor difficulties. Dan had been diagnosed as having a developmental coordination disorder. The school psychologist reported that he had an intelligence quotient of 128 on the *Weschler Adult Intelligence Scales*. There were no underlying medical or neurological problems but his body mass index was high with Dan in the obese range.

I used the *Canadian Occupational Performance Measure* (COPM) (Law *et al.* 1998) to identify key problems and personal goals. Dan described a typical day. He listed two primary recess occupations that were personally important – finding someone to play with and being allowed to go into the school library on the alternate days it was opened. A self-identified goal during out-of-school hours was to have a friend over to play. He also placed high importance on a personal goal of participating in one of the school teams for rugby or cricket. At Dan's previous school he had tried out for these team sports but there were insufficient places available so instead he was allocated a place on the girls' netball team. Despite this setback, Dan signed up with a community rugby club but was ridiculed and publicly humiliated when he was dubbed the 'liability'. His coach also called him 'lazy' after he sat down during a game to look for four leaf clovers. Dan described fears about getting hurt and also not being able to run fast enough. A final goal was to learn the guitar so that he could participate in the guitar band at his new school.

Ecological interventions to facilitate social play

After discussions with Dan, his parents, teachers and school management personnel an intervention plan to facilitate social play opportunities was formulated. The school librarian instigated a broadened range of activities within the library setting. Board games and strategy games involving the miniature figurines that Dan loved were set up in the library. Dan became highly involved in these activities. In addition to satisfying some of his needs for pretend play, he developed a close friendship with Paul, who also collected the same figurines. An after-school invitation to play was eagerly accepted. Dan's mother commented that Dan had received few previous invitations to play at other children's houses and that her work commitments had prevented her from issuing invitations. Paul and Dan continued their fantasy and creative play during the after-school hours, spending time painting the miniature figurines and devising complex strategy game plays. This led to industrious activities designed to earn money to purchase more figurines to expand their collections. This type of occupation is well described by Erickson (1963) as typical of play in older childhood.

In addition, both boys enjoyed jumping on a trampoline and shooting basketball hoops. A plan was developed to join a community basketball club. Paul had previously received intervention for physical coordination difficulties and his motor abilities matched Dan's skill levels. Dan's mother offered to take the boys to basketball training sessions held at 6pm, a difficult time for Paul's mother, who had younger children.

As a consequence of previous adverse experiences, the parents of both boys were cautious about becoming involved in any competitive activity settings with potentially unsupportive coaches. An ecologically valid intervention was instigated where the best fit between child, activity and environmental characteristics was appraised. To do so, I accompanied Dan and his mother to a local club operating a junior basketball development programme and observed a training session. Informal conversations with parents and players helped obtain a sense of player enjoyment, as well as an idea about the competence levels required to join. Most importantly, the situational motivational climate created by the coach, but endorsed by parents and children, was assessed. Children were asked, 'Do you have fun?' and parents, 'Does your child enjoy coming to training and the games?' The coach was posed an open-ended question designed to tap whether he emphasised winning (an ego- or competitive motivational orientation) or learning skills (a mastery or task-oriented motivational climate). The prospective coach commented that he 'didn't have any star players but they all had a good time each week and all acquired core skills in a fun atmosphere'. Dan and his mate signed up and Dan's mother was able to assist with taking the boys to practices and games. Dan's father attended games on access weekends and offered his services as an assistant coach, thereby increasing Dan's social capital in this setting.

Back at school Dan made steady progress towards his personal goals. His new friend brought a basketball to school and a large group of boys joined Dan and his mate playing basketball on the school court during recess and 'snowball recruitment' to the community basketball club occurred. Dan's fitness levels improved and when rugby trials came around he was not only fit but quite a formidable player because of his larger size. In addition, his new school had a policy of including every player who tried out with teams ranging from A to F levels.

Dan's mother bought a lively Labrador puppy that spent hours with Dan and his mates, fetching and retrieving balls, and dragging family members out for neighbourhood walks. Dan received a guitar for his birthday and before signing up a guitar teacher, his mother asked for a free introductory lesson and Dan decided whether the guitar teacher suited him or not. Dan became involved in the school guitar band and has a wider circle of friends.

Reflections

On post-COPM evaluations Dan had higher scores for self-perceived competence and levels of satisfaction for all his personal goals. The ecological intervention increased Dan's social and community participation through age appropriate social-physical activities that included both structured and unstructured playful encounters. Rule-based play, imaginary play and peer interactions centred on collections of miniature figurines, combined with moderate to vigorous physically active play and facilitated engagement in formal, organised activities with peers. This had physical, social and mental health benefits for Dan.

Play in the clinical environment

The clinical environment of a hospital (see Chapter 9), can make for an inflexible and impersonal setting for play focused therapy. Championing the importance of play in this environment often means competing with a hierarchy of medical and other tertiary interventions. In the third vignette Ling Choon Lian, a play therapist working in a Singapore children's hospital, describes the use of medical play to empower a child fearful of an invasive medical procedure.

Play for a child to gain mastery over an anxiety provoking medical procedure Ling Choon Lian

Six-year-old 'Linn' was referred for an intermittent catheterisation procedure. Catheterisation is an invasive procedure which involves passing a small tube or catheter through the urethra into the bladder to drain out urine. Many children resist the procedure as it can be painful and traumatic for them.

During the initial catheterisation Linn was highly distressed. Despite the nurse's reassurance and her mother's comforting, Linn refused the procedure, and this resulted in her requiring physical restraint. A play specialist was called in to support Linn. During the first session she provided medical play to explain the purpose of catheterisation and to prepare Linn for the procedure.

I started supporting Linn during the catheterisation procedure after the use of distraction activities and a reward system had been established by my colleague. When Linn was engaged in a play activity like beading she was able to reduce the fear she experienced during the procedure. Though Linn's reduced anxiety level was noted by her mother and the nurses, her occasional crying and tensing of her legs delayed the procedure and interfered with her optimal care. Linn's distress was also not helping her mother who was learning to perform catheterisation on Linn.

One important factor for maximising hospital care for children is parental involvement. It was apparent that Linn's anxiety and her mother's confidence in performing catheterisation were inherently interrelated. Linn's mother felt a deep sense of helplessness when Linn became distressed. She reflected that her helplessness inhibited her ability to focus on the procedure and to reassure Linn, which indirectly heightened Linn's anxiety. It was therefore important that my play intervention focused on supporting parent–child interaction through medical play and expressive avenues.

Play intervention strategies

Helping Linn understand the catheterisation procedure and the reasons for undergoing it were a priority for encouraging her involvement in her own treatment. The initial play sessions gave Linn an experience of control and achievement by letting her take charge of the play activity. Though still anxious, Linn's ability to focus on play suggested that she was ready to be more involved. This observation helped to formulate play activity aimed to progressively support her in managing the most challenging part of the procedure. At the first signs of distress a game was initiated where Linn was encouraged to recall and draw pictures of the medical equipment used during catheterisation. After she drew each piece of medical equipment, she was invited to describe its function, the sensation and feelings it induced. This process enabled me to better understand her concerns and to reinforce her positive coping efforts. As she demonstrated her familiarity with the procedure she also checked that her mother was doing things correctly. When we approached the most distressing part, she began to cry and her breathing became shallow. She was actively led to focus on breathing slowly and deeply. In this way she regained control and felt competent to manage her emotion and body. As she accomplished each step, she crossed out the respective picture. This motivated her to complete the procedure so that she could proceed to her chosen play activity. Linn's autonomy became evident as she subsequently requested catheterisation to ease the pain of her distended bladder. As she became more self-directed, her distress diminished.

Reflections

Both developmental considerations and careful observation are vital to the setting of therapeutic goals and planning of a structured play intervention. Linn's chosen memory game not only stimulated her creative and cognitive competence, but enabled her to focus on a playful activity while learning to master her emotions and pain. Linn was able to maintain a sense of control as she coordinated her effort with that of her mother to get through the procedure. This enhanced a sense of trust between them and both became more aware of their respective roles during the procedure.

The initial medical play was to impart procedural and sensory information to prepare Linn for the procedure. However, after repeated catheterisation it was then necessary to provide Linn with post-procedural medical play opportunities. Providing Linn with a safe play environment to explore the medical equipment and to play out her experiences with dolls and other medical play props enabled her to maintain mastery. It also encouraged both mother and child to express their feelings. When I acted out the role of a doll in distress, Linn who was performing 'catheterisation' on the doll was able to experience her mother's perspective. I also modelled and reinforced ways of accepting and supporting the child's expression of pain and frustration, due to a repeated medical procedure, to Linn's mother through play.

At a follow-up interview post discharge, Linn's mother reported that they openly communicated, playfully negotiated and mutually encouraged each other to overcome the challenges of repeated catheterisation together.

Different cultural environments

Play exists in a context of culture and therefore mirrors cultural values and expectations, ethnic identity and gender roles (Dockett and Fleer 2002). Likewise, the cultural sanctions or cues that parents, extended family, friends and the broader community give to a child convey a message about the importance of play and permission to play (Dockett and Fleer 2002). Different cultural expectations and practices in homes or communities can greatly influence how play is therapeutically introduced especially when the therapist needs to bridge the potential barriers of different language and cultural or ethnic experiences and perceptions (see Chapter 11). The final vignette presents a glimpse into a very different world, in this case an isolated and impoverished remote Aboriginal community in outback Australia. Rachael Schmidt previously lived on a remote cattle station and worked with local Aboriginal communities as a travelling occupational therapist. Rachael is currently a lecturer at Deakin University, Geelong, Australia.

Playing with nothing – Reflections on playing with Australian Aboriginal children in a remote community Rachael Schmidt

To access this isolated community, I drive through the dry creek bed and up over the bank onto the 'river' flat into country that is dry and thinly shaded by sparse trees. The 'road' is grey dust on this hot morning but soon when the rains start this track will become sticky black clay, and no cars will come or go until the ground solidifies again.

This isolated community of 40 houses, formerly a mission, was typical of many remote Aboriginal communities in outback Australia with its characteristic government supplied cement brick housing – the design of which showed scant regard for specific environmental requirements. Over time the window glass had cracked or broken and few had fly screens to protect from the clouds of flies, or curtains to shade out the blazing sun or block winter winds.

Of interest to me were toys festooned on some of the house roofs. The toys varied in condition – rusty tricycles, bikes, battered skateboards, roller blades, broken tennis racquets and balls of all sizes displaying signs of long use and weathering. Why were the toys placed on the roof? I was both perplexed and curious as to why toys were not accessible to the children. As I was city raised, I was constantly learning about 'living in the bush' and often had questions I'd like to ask. Not for the first time I had wondered about the reasons for storing toys exclusively in this way, as I had learnt from others with greater experience that many Aboriginal communities practise a communal notion of ownership, where everything is shared (Smith 2004). Individual ownership was a Western cultural practice poorly understood and rarely practised within many of the remote Aboriginal communities which I visited in the 1980s and early 1990s.

So if toys are stored on roofs, what do the children play with? Often as I drove into this community, I would interrupt a couple of small kids and dogs playing in the middle of the dusty 'street'. Commonly, play activity was related to what was available at the time (Haagen 1994). Tin cans on long strings were dragged behind, while plastic bottles were pierced with a stick and pushed ahead. Long whippy sticks broken from tall eucalyptus saplings were often dragged in play to be abandoned and reclaimed by numerous children over a period of time, used over and over for practice whacking, reaching, poking or hitting. The target was whatever was available, sometimes discarded soft drink bottles but, best of all, tin cans that made a resounding twang with each successful strike. Thicker sticks were useful for batting practice and the 'ball' could be a bald tennis ball or any other discarded household item, which when pitched and struck became a cylindrical 'target'. All children would kick and dribble found items, thus mimicking street soccer or football.

Like all children, water was great for play, especially being a scarce reality in many Australian desert environments, so a leaking tap or puddle presented a magnet for vigorous play. Jumping, splashing, and running through the water sounded great fun if the degree of noise generated was indicative of enjoyment. Quiet water play was just as engrossing with children interacting together for hours building dams and releasing flows. I once observed hours of play involving one small child, a muddy puddle and a rusty pram frame. The play was simple but entertaining as the pram was whooshed through the puddle repeatedly.

I was employed fractionally for a number of employers as an occupational therapist, including the state and local regional health and rural community services. My involvement with this community was multi-layered, working with the Elders to facilitate hospital discharge and then with young mothers and their babies, as part of a remote early intervention team. The school therapy service was an addition after the previous therapist departed. This service covered a 100 km radius and while valued was poorly resourced – I only managed to visit each school on a five to six week rotation. To re-establish rapport with the children on each visit, I routinely enlisted their assistance to carry my therapy equipment to the school play area. There was always great interest in the contents of my car boot. The colourful footballs, basketballs, skipping ropes and hoola-hoops were scooped up with great enthusiasm while each child was keen to investigate the full toy inventory, to question the application and to experiment with the unfamiliar play things. Creating play with the introduced equipment was spontaneous with initial experimentation and then interacting, competing or collaborating depending on the toys. Unlike children who experience regular structured activities, these children did not need a goal post or basketball hoop to direct their ball play as they improvised with whatever was available.

Aboriginal children living remotely tended to be more interested in physical free-play and so I engaged them in movement and active play for 10–15 minutes before doing desktop learning activities. I found their attention was more focused after this active play and this had a positive impact on completing tasks related to their student role.

I never did find out why the toys were stored on the roof.

CONCLUSION

Therapeutic play intervention is as individual as play is for children. In my own experience, the setting frequently determines how a therapist is best able to introduce play into therapy or the curriculum. As therapists, we need to be clear about why we use play – is it to increase a child's developmental skills or is it for healing of the child's inner hurts, or both? This chapter attempted to illustrate some different therapeutic interpretations of play in very different settings. Each vignette gives a glimpse into the different therapists' purpose for using play, and the different approaches employed to facilitate children's play choices and interactions, playfulness and self expression. Across all the vignettes was the goal to develop and increase the child's play mastery.

REFERENCES

Aaron, D. J., Kriska, A. M., Dearwater, S. R., Cauley, J. A., Metz, K. F. and LaPorte, R. E. (1995) 'Reproducibility and validity of an epidemiologic questionnaire to assess past year physical activity in adolescents.' *American Journal of Epidemiology 142*, 191–201.
Cattanach, A. (1992) *Play Therapy with Abused Children*. London: Jessica Kingsley Publishers.

Cattanach, A. (1994). *Play Therapy: Where the Sky Meets the Underworld.* London: Jessica Kingsley Publishers.

Dockett, S. and Fleer, M. (2002) *Play and Pedagogy in Early Childhood: Bending the Rules.* Melbourne: Thomson Learning.

Erickson, E. H. (1963) *Childhood and Society.* New York: Norton.

Ferland, F. (1997) *Play, Children with Physical Disabilities, and Occupational Therapy: The Ludic Model,* trans. P. Aronoff and H. Scott. Ottawa: University of Ottawa Press.

Gil, E. (1991) *The Healing Power of Play: Working with Abused Children.* New York: Guilford Press.

Grille, R. (2008) *Heart to Heart Parenting.* Sydney: ABC Books.

Haagen, C. (1994) *Bush Toys: Aboriginal Children at Play.* Canberra: Australian Studies Press.

Henderson, S. E. and Sugden, D. A. (1992) *Movement Assessment Battery for Children.* Kent: Psychological Corporation.

Hughes, F. P., Elicker, J. and Veen, L. C. (1995) 'A program of play for infants and their caregivers.' *Young Children* (January) 52–58.

Knox, S. and Mailloux, Z. (1997) 'Play as Treatment and Treatment through Play.' In B. E. Chandler (ed.) *The Essence of Play: A Child's Occupation.* Bethesda, MD: American Occupational Therapy Association.

Landreth, G. (2002) *Play Therapy: The Art of the Relationship,* 2nd edn. New York: Brunner Routledge.

Law, M., Baptiste, S., Carswell, A., McColl, M. A., Polatajko, H. and Pollock, M. A. (eds) (1998) *Canadian Occupational Performance Measure,* 2nd edn. Ottawa: CAOT Publications ACE.

Pellegrini, A. D. (1995) 'A longitudinal study of boys' rough and tumble play and dominance during early adolescence.' *Journal of Applied Developmental Psychology 16,* 77–93.

Pellegrini, A. D. (2005) *Recess: Its Role in Education and Development.* Mahwah, NJ: Erlbaum.

Reade, S., Hunter, H. and McMillan, I. R. (1999) 'Just playing…is it time wasted?' *British Journal of Occupational Therapy 62,* 4, 157–162.

Rodger, S. and Ziviani, J. (1999) 'Play-based occupational therapy.' *International Journal of Disability, Development and Education 46,* 3, 337–365.

Saunders, I., Sayer, M. and Goodale, A. (1999) 'The relationship between playfulness and coping in preschool children: A pilot study.' *American Journal of Occupational Therapy 53,* 2, 221–226.

Smith, C. (2004) *Country, Kin and Culture: Survival of an Australian Aboriginal Community.* Kent Town, Australia: Wakefield Press.

Way, M. (1999) 'Parasympathetic and sympathetic influences in neuro-occupation pertaining to play.' *Occupational Therapy in Health Care 12,* 1, 71–86.

Wilson, K. and Ryan, V. (2005) *Play Therapy: A Non-Directive Approach for Children and Adolescents,* 2nd edn. London: Elsevier Science.

Witt, P. A., and Ellis, G. D. (1989) *Leisure Diagnostic Battery.* State College, PA: Venture Publishers.

Contributing Authors

Ted Brown *PhD, MSc, MPA, BScOT (Hons), OT(C), OTR, AccOT* is a senior lecturer and postgraduate coordinator in the Department of Occupational Therapy, Monash University, Australia. Ted has worked as a paediatric occupational therapist in Canada and Australia and has published over 75 articles in peer-reviewed journals.

Anita Bundy *ScD, OTR, FAOTA* is Professor and Chair of Occupational Therapy at the University of Sydney. She is internationally recognised for her work in play and playfulness. She is the author of two assessments of play: the *Test of Playfulness* and the *Test of Environmental Supportiveness*.

Rodney Cooper *PhD, BOccThy (Hons)* is a Tamworth-based rural mental health clinician with North West Slopes Division of General Practice and academic with the University Department of Rural Health, University of Newcastle, Australia. As a paediatric occupational therapist he has a broad interest in play therapy, child abuse and sustainable rural communities. He also has five children who give him plenty of opportunity to play!

Reinie Cordier *MOccTher, BOccTher, BSocSc Hons(Clin Psyc)* is a doctoral fellow at the University of Sydney. His PhD research compares the play of five to ten-year-old children with and without Attention Deficit Hyperactive Disorder.

Athena A. Drewes *PhD* is a licensed child psychologist and Registered Play Therapist and Supervisor. She is Director of Clinical Training at the Astor Home for Children, a multi-service, non-profit mental health agency in New York. She is Board Director of the Association for Play Therapy and Founder/Past President of NYAPT. She has written and lectured extensively in the US and abroad on play therapy.

Susan A. Esdaile *PhD, MAPS, AccOT, OTR* is an Honorary Professor in the Department of Occupational Therapy at Monash University and at the University of Sydney. She is a consultant, independent practitioner in health psychology, and an associate editor of *Occupational Therapy International*. She has conducted numerous parent-focused research studies and published widely.

Tiina Lautamo *PhLic, OT Reg.* is a lecturer at Savonia University of Applied Sciences in Kuopio, Finland. Her main research interest is the skill acquisition of children in activities of daily living, and especially in play. She has worked in the area of paediatric rehabilitation and is a mother of five children.

Rachael McDonald *PhD* is a senior lecturer in the Department of Occupational Therapy, School of Primary Health Care, Monash University, Australia. Rachel has worked with physically disabled children in England and Australia.

Judi Parson *PhD RN, BN, Grad Dip (Paediatrics), MHthSc (Nrg Ed)* is a registered nurse who has enjoyed an international career specialising in paediatrics. She undertook her doctoral research using descriptive phenomenology to investigate the integration of procedural play for children undergoing cystic fibrosis treatment from a nursing perspective.

Virginia Ryan *PhD* is a Chartered Child Psychologist with the British Psychological Society and a qualified Play Therapist and Supervisor with the British Association of Play Therapists. She is also a Certified Filial Therapist and Filial Therapy Instructor with the Family Enhancement and Play Therapy Center, USA. She previously directed the MA/Diploma in Non-directive Therapy program at the University of York, UK.

Karen Stagnitti *PhD, BOccThy, Grad Cert Higher Ed* is an Associate Professor in the School of Health and Social Development, Deakin University, Australia. Karen has 30 years experience working as an occupational therapist with families and children. She is the author of two play assessments and many national and international publications.

Jennifer Sturgess *PhD* grew up on a cattle and sheep property without electricity. She ascribes her creative problem solving skills to her childhood of playing in the bush with whatever was available! Jenny has worked as an occupational therapist, academic, researcher and more recently as an allied health manager for Queensland Health, Australia.

Subject Index

Author Index